THE PARADOX OF
WEALTH AND
POVERTY

THE PARADOX OF WEALTH AND POVERTY

Mapping the Ethical Dilemmas of Global Development

DANIEL LITTLE

University of Michigan–Dearborn

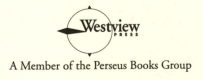

A Member of the Perseus Books Group

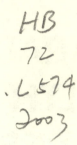

Copyright © 2003 by Westview Press, A Member of the Perseus Books Group

Westview Press books are available at special discounts for bulk purchases in the United States by corporations, institutions, and other organizations. For more information, please contact the Special Markets Department at the Perseus Books Group, 11 Cambridge Center, Cambridge MA 02142, or call (617) 252-5298, (800) 255-1514 or email j.mccrary@perseusbooks.com

Published in 2003 in the United States of America by Westview Press, 5500 Central Avenue, Boulder, Colorado 80301–2877, and in the United Kingdom by Westview Press, 12 Hid's Copse Road, Cumnor Hill, Oxford OX2 9JJ

Find us on the World Wide Web at www.westviewpress.com

A Cataloging-in-Publication data record for this book is available from the Library of Congress.
ISBN 0-8133-1642-1 (pb); 0-8133-6593-7 (hc)
The paper used in this publication meets the requirements of the American National Standard for Permanence of Paper for Printed Library Materials Z39.48–1984.

10   9   8   7   6   5   4   3   2   1

For Bernadette Lintz

Contents

Illustrations

Acknowledgments

SEVERAL INSTITUTIONS HAVE PROVIDED SUPPORT for this work over a number of years. I offer sincere thanks to the Social Science Research Council (SSRC)/MacArthur Foundation Program in International Peace and Security for its support at the beginning of my research on the issues that are treated in this book. The innovative Program in International Peace and Security was designed to lead scholars into a deeper interdisciplinary understanding of issues of peace and conflict in the world, and it had precisely this effect on my scholarly development. A two-year residency at the Center for International Affairs at Harvard University provided a fruitful context for learning about the empirical and theoretical complexities of development and poverty in the world today, as well as the moral issues that these facts force us to face. Colleagues at Colgate University and Bucknell University provided stimulating opportunities to try out many of these ideas. Responses received during formal presentations of some of this material at Yale University's Program in Agrarian Studies, the Harvard University Center for Population and Development Studies, the Center for International Studies at Princeton University, the Center for Ethics and World Society at Colgate University, the Muslim Social Science Association, and several sessions of the American Philosophical Association have provided valuable direction and criticism. The final stages of this book's composition took place at the University of Michigan–Dearborn, and I am thankful for the intellectual and material support I have received from the Inter-University Consortium for Social and Political Research at the University of Michigan during the crucial final period of research and writing. Several colleagues at the University of Michigan–Dearborn have offered very helpful criticism of various portions of the book, and I offer special thanks to Suzanne Bergeron, Paul Hughes, and Brian Green. I am grateful to John Harriss and Kok-Chor Tan, reviewers for Westview Press, for their constructive comments on the penultimate version of the book. David Featherman played a role on both ends of the process, having been president of the SSRC during the period of my Program in International Peace and Security fellowship and director of the Institute for Social Research in Ann Arbor, Michigan, during the latter stages of the manuscript. Finally, I express my deep appreciation to my friend and partner, Bernadette Lintz, for the support, encouragement, and intellectual stimulation she has consistently offered me.

Introduction

WE LIVE IN A TIME of human paradoxes. Scientific knowledge has reached a level of sophistication that permits understanding of the most arcane phenomena—and yet religious fundamentalism shakes many parts of the world. We witness the emergence of a civil, liberal constitutionalism in many regions of the world—and yet ethnic violence threatens the lives and dignity of millions of people. And we live in a time of rapid economic and technological advance—and yet several billions of people live in persistent, debilitating poverty.

This book focuses on one of these paradoxes, the paradox of wealth and poverty in the global economy. I will explore with an open mind the dimensions of moral complexity posed by this paradox and the policies that are under way today that will affect the level and intensity of human misery created by mass poverty in the near future. The processes of economic development—the development of new industries, the creation of new jobs and forms of employment, the extension of global trade, the transition from rural to urban life, the inconsistent satisfaction of basic human needs such as adequate nutrition, health care, clean water, and education—have vast human consequences. As citizens of a country and of the world, we have a role to play in determining that those consequences are the most beneficial possible to people across the globe. My topic is the ethics of development, and I will approach that topic through empirically informed philosophizing.

In the year 2000, the World Bank committed over $6.8 billion in concessionary loans targeted directly at facilitating economic development in the world's poorest countries. Official development assistance from all nations of the Organization for Economic Cooperation and Development (OECD) during that year represented another $54 billion (0.22 percent of total gross domestic product [GDP] of those nations), and nongovernmental organizations provided another $6.9 billion in grants to developing countries (Organization for Economic Cooperation and Development 2001: table 4).

These funds were expended on a range of projects and included: dams and water-control projects, loans for large national industries, funds for agricultural development and modernization, funds for health and education infrastructure, food security, microloans for small businesses and entrepreneurs, and many other initiatives.

In the same year, over a billion people lived in conditions of extreme poverty on less than a dollar a day, over 25 percent of the world's children showed signs of chronic malnutrition, only 42 percent of women in South Asia were literate (compared to 66 percent of men), tens of millions of infants and children suffered premature disease and mortality as a result of poverty, and hundreds of millions of families lacked the income needed to support a minimally decent human life. These figures do not represent a significant improvement over comparable data from 1985. Moreover, the inequalities of wealth and income between the First World and the Third World continue to grow. The ratio of the incomes of the top and bottom quintiles of income globally increased from 60:1 to 74:1 during the 1990s (United Nations Development Programme 1999: chapter 1). And development aid as a percentage of the GDP of the advanced industrialized nations has plummeted since the early 1980s.

Since 1945, the countries of the nonindustrialized world have made major efforts at stimulating modern economic growth. The variety of approaches is as great as the variety among these societies themselves—the Brazilian model (import substitution industrialization), the Korean model (export-led growth), the Chinese model (land reform, collectivization, and market reform), the Philippine model (aggrandizement of a small economic elite with near total disregard for the condition of the poor), or the Indonesian model (authoritarian development, substantial involvement of the military in economic affairs, and substantial use of state agencies to regulate and direct development). Economic development processes have resulted from a number of forces, including the domestic government's economic policy, the private activities of national and multinational corporations, the influence of industrialized-nation governments, and a variety of bilateral and multilateral development agencies.

The outcomes of these economic development strategies are at least as varied as the strategies themselves. Some parts of the less developed world have experienced respectable economic growth since the 1960s. South Asia's growth has been slightly lower than 2 percent per capita per year since 1965, and East

Asia has grown at a faster rate (3.5 percent). During this period, per capita GDP in India has grown at 1.8 percent; in the Philippines at an average rate of 1.9 percent; in Indonesia at a rate of 4.6 percent; and in China at a rate of 5.1 percent. Other parts of the world have been less successful. Portions of sub-Saharan Africa have witnessed falling per capita GDP since the early 1980s; the Caribbean economies have experienced almost zero growth (0.6 percent), and the Latin American economies have had slightly positive growth (1.6 percent) in per capita GDP (World Bank 1989). (These aggregated figures conceal substantial interregional diversity within countries.)

How has economic growth affected the poor in the developing world? Have the benefits of economic growth been broadly distributed over all income levels? Have incomes—and consequently welfare—risen for the poorest 20 to 40 percent of the population in developing societies?

Low income shares to the poorest income strata have direct effects on the well-being of the poor: malnutrition, disease, inadequate water, low educational levels, high infant and child mortality rates, and depressed longevity statistics. Illiteracy rates remain unacceptably high in countries such as India, Egypt, Sudan, and Nigeria. These countries likewise continue to show exceptionally high rates of infant mortality and child malnutrition. Yet these variables measure two of the most critical components of human well-being—education and health status. Some countries—for example, Sri Lanka—have made significant strides in raising the well-being of the poor, even in the absence of substantial economic growth. Other countries—such as Brazil and the Philippines—have witnessed stagnation in the incomes and well-being of the poor in the midst of respectable national economic growth.

Environments are suffering severe degradation throughout the world, and conditions of poverty and rapid economic development alike intensify pressure on the environment. Whether we measure the annual destruction of forests and grasslands, the volume of carbon dioxide production and the rate of change in this variable, the conversion of cropland into settlements, or the exhaustion of sources of fresh water, we find a profile of change that gives rise to serious concern about the quality of life and health that future generations will be able to enjoy. Extreme and moderate poverty creates one set of pressures on environments, as poor people seek out ways of satisfying their needs that have harmful environmental effects (firewood harvesting, overcultivation, destruction of forests). Intensive processes of economic growth probably pose ever greater risks for environmental quality through rising rates of fossil fuel usage (and the subsequent production of greenhouse gases), more intensive agriculture (and the pesticides and herbicides that this requires), and the exhaustion of nonrenewable natural resources.

The course of social and political development in much of the developing world is likewise a source of concern in terms of the future of humanity. Patterns of gender inequality and severe limitations on the opportunities and freedoms of women are found throughout the world. These patterns have deeply deleterious effects on women in those societies where the patterns of discrimination are the most prominent. And they have harmful effects as well on other aspects of economic development. The fate of democracy is an open question in much of the developing world. Will political institutions be created that give citizens a genuine and meaningful role in the formulation of law and policy? Or will elites and other powerful organizations continue to exercise their power within society to bring about the political outcomes that they favor? I will turn to these questions in Chapter 8.

Most urgently, in spite of over fifty years of respectable growth in many of the economies of the less developed world, problems of poverty are as severe as ever in many developing countries: The incomes flowing to the poorest 40 percent have climbed much more slowly than the GDP, social welfare indicators such as longevity and infant mortality have shown little improvement in the lower quintiles in many countries, and processes of modernization and structural transformation have had little effect on the poorest strata. These generalizations are not true everywhere; South Korea, Taiwan, and Sri Lanka represent exceptions (for different reasons). But this story is largely accurate for many more countries, among them India, the Philippines, Brazil, Nigeria, and Mexico. In a large number of developing countries, the benefits of economic growth have *not* reached the poorest 20 to 40 percent: Their share of income has fallen, and their absolute average income has risen only very slowly. Brazil's per capita income was a respectable $4,489 in the 1990s, but because of extreme inequalities in the nation's income distribution, the poorest 20 percent earned an average income of only $561. This sum is higher than the international poverty standard of $1 per day, but given that this group is itself stratified, we can infer that there are a large number of absolutely poor people in Brazil today. The same calculation applied to Egypt's income data results in an average income of $543—in spite of the fact that Egypt's average income is only one-quarter that of Brazil. The World Bank estimates that, out of a total population of 6 billion, some 2.8 billion people live on less than $2 a day and 1.2 billion people live on less than $1 a day in conditions of extreme poverty (World Bank 2001b: 3). Meanwhile, the gap between rich countries and poor countries has continued to widen; in the 1990s, the average income in the richest twenty countries was thirty-seven times that of the poorest twenty countries (World Bank 2001b: 3).

What are we to make of these facts? They suggest a series of questions. What economic processes are under way in the global economy today that lead to the increase of interregional inequalities of wealth and income? Why are problems of poverty so resistant to alleviation? How might richer nations and peoples effectively contribute to the alleviation of poverty?

Many such questions are empirical. The global economy is a complex system of causation and institutional interconnection, and it requires a substantial exercise in social science to come to recognize the workings of the processes involved. Economists, political scientists, and regional specialists have multiple theories and analyses that shed much light on these processes. However, the facts described here also demand that we ask a series of questions that are not primarily empirical but rather moral or normative. Is there an ethics of development? What does justice require in the face of continuing and massive human suffering? What does the duty of benevolence require? What is the moral importance of the multiple forms of human suffering represented by extreme poverty? How are we to compare the importance of several intrinsic goods and bads—for instance, human suffering and well-being versus environmental preservation? What conception of the ultimate goals of economic development ought to drive the design of policy? What obligations do governments and citizens of the developed world have to the people of the developing world?

In addition to substantial deprivation throughout the developing world (poverty), the global system provides striking instances of wide inequalities. Are inequalities inherently morally suspect? Are inequalities among nations or peoples intrinsically morally repugnant? At what point do they become so? What about inequalities within a country—for example, the inequalities of life prospects between a Mexican farmer and a Mexican banker or legislator? Is there a moral basis for any form of egalitarianism? Which, if any, of the inequalities that we find between and within countries today are morally problematic and in need of remediation?

The task I have set myself in this book is to attempt to take the measure of the ethical challenges that are presented by the facts of economic develop-

ment at the beginning of the twenty-first century and to provide a preliminary basis for answering those challenges. The choices we make as professionals, as citizens of a country, and as citizens of the world depend very
much on our understanding of both what human realities the world presents
and what moral duties these realities create for us as persons.

Seen from one point of view, this complex of issues is a relatively small part
of applied moral philosophy, of interest only to a rather specialized audience.
From another point of view, however, this area ultimately invokes virtually
all of the most difficult and important topics within normative social philosophy: the problem of planning for a process of social change, the justice
of the allocation of the benefits of social cooperation across individuals and
groups, the problem of intergenerational justice, the delineation of the legitimate claims that different groups and individuals have on each other and on
outsiders, and the definition of the good of human life and social arrangements. Thus, close study of the problems of economic development may have
a considerable contribution to make for social philosophers more generally.

Some Considered Judgments

This book addresses economic development in the poorest countries and the
attendant realities of poverty, inequality, and human suffering that continue
to be part of these processes. Why does economic development raise ethical
issues of any sort? In my view, ethical issues arise in those situations where
bad outcomes are affected by human agency, individual or collective, or
where the severity of consequences can be reduced through human agency.
Economic development falls in this category, since the outcomes are very
much affected by the choices made by individuals, groups, and governments.
So we, as agents and as beneficiaries of the global economy, are compelled to
ask, What are the imperatives of an ethics of development?

To answer this sort of question, we need to examine the human realities associated with the economic institutions, processes, and outcomes found in the
developing world today and consider the nature of the ethical issues these phenomena raise. What does justice require in the context of Third World poverty
and inequalities? What are the implications of the valid human rights possessed
by poor people? How should the goods of environmental preservation and
poverty alleviation be compared? Why is democracy important in development? There are debilitating realities in the global economy today that must

count as significant moral facts (in the sense that they have the potential of creating duties and obligations on us). So we need to assess these facts and try to determine what duties they create—for us, for governments, for corporations, and for other organizations. In particular, the outcomes and implementations of development strategies unavoidably raise problems of justice. This is because they have deeply significant distributive effects that may endure over many generations. Different groups do well or badly under different policy alternatives. Consequently, policymakers ought to be responsive to the demands of justice in their adoption of priorities and the instruments they choose in pursuit of the goods of development. Throughout the chapters that follow, I will explore specific moral issues that arise in the context of economic development and that appear to set challenges to us as citizens and decisionmakers: the role of democracy, the importance of gender justice, the role and implications of human rights, the goods associated with the environment, and so forth.

The book is thus an exercise in applied ethics—careful, morally informed thinking about a complex of practical problems in the world. Putting the point of applied ethics as simply as possible, the aim is to formulate relevant and credible principles, explore the complexities and nuances of the facts, and apply principles to cases to give rise to credible consequences for action. The ultimate objective is to answer the question, What ought we do?

To begin to probe the field of economic development policy from an ethical point of view, we need to have a basis for making judgments in this area. Let us begin with what John Rawls (1971) refers to as a set of considered judgments that appear relevant.

- People should be in the position of developing and realizing their human capabilities as fully as possible;
- People should be treated justly, fairly, and with equal consideration;
- People should have freedom to be autonomous and make choices concerning themselves;
- People should have rights that protect their freedoms;
- Democracy is a good thing;
- The natural environment ought to be sustained.

How far can convictions such as these take us in charting the normative waters of assessing alternative approaches to economic development policy? It is the central thesis of this book that we can go quite far on the basis of these simple ideas.

Moral issues arise in the area of economic development in several different ways. Moral reasoning always involves facts, principles, inferences, and remedies. In some cases, the difficulty lies in determining what the facts are; in some cases, it is difficult to determine what the relevant and binding moral principles are; in other cases, drawing the appropriate inferences from facts and principles presents the central difficulty; and finally, there are cases in which the greatest challenge is defining appropriate modes of remediation even when the facts, principles, and inferences are in order. Issues of gender justice probably fall in the final category, issues of equity probably fall in the "problematic principle" region, and issues of guaranteeing labor rights probably fall in the factual region.

The argument that is presented in this book is multifaceted in that it involves both empirical and philosophical considerations. The ultimate goals of the book are to provide a schematic acquaintance with some of the most important facts about global development at the turn of the twentieth century, to explore what appear to be the relevant moral principles and insights that should be invoked as we consider those facts, and to draw some conclusions about the sorts of values and goals that ought to guide economic development thinking in the early twenty-first century. Throughout the book, then, there will be a back-and-forth between empirical and historical reasoning, on the one hand, and normative reasoning, on the other. Chapter 1 opens the discussion by examining the fundamental question, What is human well-being? The next two chapters are more empirical and policy-oriented. Chapter 2 provides a schematic account of economic development, and Chapter 3 offers a discussion of the goals and strategies that are available for stimulating economic development. Chapters 4 and 5 return to a pair of central normative issues within economic development—the circumstances of justice that arise within the developing world and the role and importance of human rights within discussions of economic development. Chapter 6 offers a discussion of globalization and the obligations it creates for citizens and consumers everywhere. Chapter 7 examines some of the ways in which development and poverty alleviation intersect with another long-term human concern, the quality of the earth's environment. Chapter 8 raises questions on the role and importance of democracy within the process of economic development. And the concluding chapter offers a vision of a humane future within a globalizing world—the ideal of a global civil society.

1

Welfare, Well-Being, and Needs

ECONOMIC DEVELOPMENT IS AIMED AT improving the well-being of the people of the earth. But how do we understand the notion of human well-being? What is involved in improving a person's welfare? What is a human life, lived well? Such questions are foundational. Without compelling answers to this set of questions, we will have no convincing basis for advocating one form of economic development or another or assessing the obligations and rights that the various agents within the global economy have. Answers to these questions should serve to define the most fundamental priorities that ought to lead our thinking about economic development.

This chapter, then, focuses on these crucial questions: What is the nature of the good human life? What is it about human life that deserves our moral attention? What are the features of human existence that should guide the design and selection of public policies? Economic development is intended to increase the productivity and wealth of the many nations of the world. And the increase of the world's wealth in turn is expected to improve the life circumstances of the individual men and women who live within these nations. Economic development should result in improving the quality of life of the people affected; it should enhance the ability of all persons to achieve their full human potential; it should establish the conditions of free human expression and development. What is the most adequate way of characterizing the human good that we are aiming to advance through economic development policy?[1] How can we conceptualize the value of the human life lived well? Is it

1

possible to assess the effects of various policies on the human good? What, fundamentally, is "quality of life"?

Several important paradigms for thinking about the human good have competed in debates over economic development. There is a sophisticated theory of social welfare that identifies the human good in terms of individual utility and preference. There is an influential literature within development economics that gives chief emphasis to the concept of basic human needs. And finally, there is a larger perspective on the good human life that emerges from an important philosophical tradition and that emphasizes the free, flourishing human person as the key to our thinking about the human good. The ultimate good of economic development, on this approach, is that it establishes the conditions under which persons can freely and fully develop their human capabilities. These frameworks can be classified as "subjective" (focusing on a feature of human psychology or preference) or "objective" (focusing on external or material factors that are thought to contribute to the good human life).

It is important for us to address the issue of the nature of the human good because that issue defines an important part of the large question of concern in this book—what factors or principles shape the moral orientation of economic development policy and process? What is economic development *for*? The assumptions we make about human well-being will have a significant effect on the priorities that we attach to various choices within development policy. If we conclude that there are intrinsic goods in play in the process of economic development, then it is natural to formulate a principle along the following lines:

- Economic development policy ought to be constructed so as to maximize the intrinsic good of development (welfare, well-being, human perfection, the satisfaction of human rights, the satisfaction of basic needs, and so forth).

Such a principle would serve as only a part of a full theory of the ethics of economic development because it is likely that principles of justice, equality, fairness of process, or other intrinsically important moral issues need to be taken into account as well. But it would be an important step forward because it would imply judgments along the following line:

- Absent countervailing moral considerations, the fact that policy A creates a greater sum of intrinsic good than policy B is a compelling reason for choosing A over B.

In this scenario, then, A is morally preferable to B.

The Conception of the Person

How can we best investigate the conception of the good human life that ought to guide public policy (and economic development policy in particular)? How can we arrive at a principled resolution of the disagreements among theories of welfarism, basic needs, and human capabilities? Each of these theories corresponds to a conception of the human person—the assumptions that we make about what constitutes a good human life. The most convincing philosophical arguments that we can bring to bear on this set of issues will result from asking the more fundamental question: What is a human person? And which theories of the person are most compelling when fully articulated?

It has been observed that ethical theories almost always make presuppositions about the nature of the person, the nature of a good human life, and the nature and function of society.[2] Sometimes those presuppositions are explicit, and sometimes they are taken as unspoken assumptions. We can shed light on the adequacy of a given theory of the human good by focusing on these underlying assumptions and the fullness of the representation of the person in society that they offer. For example, an ethical theory that presupposes inherent racial inequalities would for that reason appropriately be challenged—even if the presuppositions are obscure in the explicit principles and findings of the theory. So let us examine the welfarist, basic needs, and capabilities theories in light of the theories of the person that they presuppose.

The Welfarist Model

A standard answer to the question—what is the human good?—underlies most economic reasoning. This response holds that economic policy should be designed to maximize social welfare and that social welfare is a sum of the achieved *utilities* of a group of individuals. Individuals are able to experience pleasure and pain, they are able to experience happiness and satisfaction, and they have preferences about states of the world. Individuals are better off with a greater balance of pleasure over pain, a higher level of happiness and satisfaction, and a greater satisfaction of their preferences. It is sometimes thought that the welfare theory comes close to being a direct logical or semantic implication of the very concept of "personal well-being," along these lines: Outcomes produce different levels of happiness in the individual. The individual knows what makes him or her happy. The individual prefers the outcome that makes him or her more happy. We can therefore infer that if the individual prefers O_1 to O_2, then he or she is better off when O_1 occurs; thus, bringing about O_1 instead of O_2 has the effect of improving his or her welfare or well-being. Consequently, satisfying more of the individual's preferences improves the individual's welfare and makes him or her happier (than would otherwise be the case).

The welfarist or utility-based approach faces a variety of substantive problems, but it is a simple theory. It proceeds on the assumptions that each individual's happiness or utility can be represented as a single quantity (a utility function); that it is possible to aggregate individual utilities into a measure of social welfare; and that the goal of economic policy is to maximize social welfare.[3] Utilities are sometimes interpreted in psychological terms, but the problem of establishing a basis for interpersonal comparison of subjective utilities has led economists and philosophers to understand the theory of utility in terms of the satisfaction of consumers' preferences (Elster and Roemer 1991). According to the social welfare approach, social policy ought to be directed toward maximizing the aggregate utility of society (or possibly the average utility of society).[4] The individual is regarded as a "vessel" that can be filled with more or less utility, and the goal of policy is to permit individuals to achieve a maximum quantity of utility, in the aggregate.

To assess competing policy choices, we need to be able to measure the effects of alternative choices on the overall welfare of the entire group. The theory of utility and preference as a conception of individual welfare can be applied fairly directly to the topic of social welfare (that is, the welfare of a group of individuals). If we can solve the problem of interpersonal comparisons of utility, then we can regard the welfare of the group as the sum (or average) of the utilities of individuals. If we regard this problem as unsolvable, then we can measure the group's welfare as the full set of individual utilities and preferences. On the first approach, the "best" policy is the one that creates the greatest total utility for the group. On the second approach, we also regard the welfare of the group as a composite of the welfare of the individuals, but because the individual utilities are not comparable, we must provide an accounting that keeps them distinct but still permits comparison of the effects of alternative policies.

This problem brings us to the crucial concept of a "Pareto improvement" of a policy on a group of persons. Intuitively, we can observe that the two outcomes O_1 and O_2 may have different effects on different members of the group. If O_1 is universally preferred to O_2, then we can also conclude that the group is better off with O_1. But what about the more common instance where some but not all prefer the first option and some but not all prefer the second option? Economists introduce the concepts of Pareto improvement and Pareto optimality to handle this typical problem of defining social welfare without interpersonal comparison. O_1 is said to be a Pareto improvement over O_2 just in case at least one person prefers O_1 and everyone else is indifferent between the two choices. A policy incorporating O_1 improves the welfare of the group, in this scenario, because it leaves at least one person better off and no one worse off. An outcome is a Pareto-optimal outcome just in case no remaining Pareto-improving choices can be made.

It is important to notice just how weak the concept of Pareto optimality is. It does not correspond to a more general notion of a social optimum—an outcome best for the group as a whole, all things considered or "the common good." This is true for several important reasons. First, the process of adjusting policy through a series of Pareto-improving steps is highly path-dependent; the outcome depends on which improvements were adopted early in the process. So it is entirely possible that there are outcomes that are manifestly better for the group as a whole but cannot be reached through Pareto-improving steps. But more fundamentally, the framework of Pareto optimality is deeply insensitive to issues involving equity in the distribution of resources. On intuitive grounds, a distribution of income that assigns Sally 10 units and Bill 1 unit is inferior to one that assigns Sally 9 and Bill 6. But there is no Pareto-improving pathway from the first outcome to the second, since Sally is less well off in the second scenario. (The second scenario would be preferred by a utilitarian because the total utility is greater in that scenario.)

A final issue that is relevant here concerns the concept of cost-benefit analysis. It is recognized that various actions or policies improve the welfare of some persons and harm the welfare of others. Consider the situation of Bill and Sally, and interpret the units as income. For vividness, suppose that the economic circumstances are that Sally owns two sewing machines and Bill owns none; each derives income from his or her labor and tools. The total income of this small society would increase significantly with a redistribution of the sewing machines, and Bill would in fact be able to compensate Sally for her lost income as a result of the redistribution. So Bill should be able to make an offer to Sally involving a transfer of the second sewing machine to him and a transfer of some quantity of income from him to Sally—say, 2 units. With the resulting distribution, we find Sally with 11 units of income and Bill with 4 units. Each has improved his or her welfare. We can now generalize the example as an exposition of the logic of cost-benefit analysis of competing policies P_1 and P_2. Suppose that neither is a Pareto improvement over the other. To perform a cost-benefit analysis of the policies, we need to estimate the incomes created by the policies for all members of the group and then ask whether the gains of the winners in one policy or the other suffice to permit them to compensate the losers. If so, then the policy could result from a free agreement between winners and losers, and it would be reasonable to judge that adoption of the favored policy leads to an improvement in the welfare of the group. This is the case in actual compensation. But cost-benefit analysis has been more controversial when applied to cases where compensation is not actually provided. Economists have taken a second and more questionable step in arguing that the possibility of hypothetical compensation is sufficient to establish that one policy is better than the other.[5]

This theory of the human good has a very significant advantage in the context of economic development policy. It provides a simple and powerful linkage between the theory of neoclassical economics and the specific challenges confronting economic development. If preferences and utilities constitute the human good and if free exchanges within a competitive market lead to efficient equilibria in the allocation of resources, then we can conclude that social welfare is maximized by efficient markets. We might also infer that progress toward improving the efficiency and universality of markets will have a positive effect on human welfare; more precisely, we might argue that the fact that a set of allocations of resources and incomes has come about through the workings of free-market exchanges demonstrates that the outcome is a welfare-enhancing one. However, if we find that this theory of the good is flawed or incomplete, then these inferences about the beneficent qualities of free markets—and associated recommendations for policy directions—will be undermined.

So let us consider the theory of the person represented by the welfarist framework. According to this theory, the person is understood as a rational decisionmaker who has a set of preferences about various outcomes and a set of beliefs about the properties of the world and who chooses actions on the basis of those preferences and beliefs. The individual is a utility consumer; in the simplest version, the individual acts so as to maximize satisfaction, pleasure, or happiness. And the good human life is conceived as the life that achieves the largest sum of utilities (or satisfies the greatest number of preferences). Putting the view in the language of preference, the individual is a rational preference-maximizer and charts a course through life based on reasoning about which actions will lead to the highest degree of preference satisfaction. Economic theory normally incorporates one additional feature: the idea of self-interest. Individuals are assumed to evaluate outcomes on the basis of the effect that various actions have on their own self-interests.[6]

Difficult philosophical issues arise in the endeavor to explicate the concept of preference. Are preferences entirely arbitrary and subjective? Or is there a principled relationship between an individual's fundamental values, plan of life, and conception of the good, on one hand, and his or her preferences (or a subset of them), on the other? Is there a principled basis on which others may criticize the individual's scheme of preferences? And finally, is there an objective basis for saying that some of a person's preferences are more important than others—or that one person's preferences are more important than another's?

Utilitarian philosophers adopt much of this set of assumptions about rationality, utility, and preference as a first-order description of human happiness and desire. But utilitarianism drops the assumption of egoism. Instead, it holds that it is possible for individuals to recognize the interests, preferences, and happiness of others and to choose to act so as to bring about the greatest overall balance of happiness over unhappiness among all affected by the action.[7] Further, it stipulates that moral action consists in choosing that action or policy that maximizes happiness. Utilitarianism thus assumes the possibility of other-regarding action, or altruism. But what other-regarding actions are oriented toward is something very similar to the simple "*Homo economicus*" model: the utility or degree of preference satisfaction of the individuals included in the calculation. Utilitarianism also views the individual as a vessel for utility or happiness. Outcomes have the effect of increasing or reducing the individual's happiness. And those actions and policies that create the greatest amount of utility should be chosen.

The welfarist model has the virtues of simplicity and plausibility. But it also confronts profound problems, both internal and external to the theory.[8]

The internal challenges include the problems of defining utility, defining a theory of preference, and interpreting the task of interpersonal comparisons of utility. What is involved in "measuring" my current state of happiness or utility? How is my happiness related to my preferences among choices? And how can we meaningfully compare my level of utility with yours in order to arrive at a sum representing both of us?[9]

A more profound set of criticisms derives from the theory of the person that utilitarianism presupposes. In its paradigm formulation, utilitarianism appears to assume that persons live for happiness or subjective satisfaction, that there are no morally significant differences among pleasures, and that individuals make choices solely in order to bring about the greatest balance of pleasure over pain. This is an impoverished theory of human agency. It reduces rationality to the task of weighing probable future utilities, it reduces planning to the task of preparing an optimal schedule of future utilities, and it reduces purpose to the goal of achieving the greatest sum of utilities.

What are some of the shortcomings of this theory of the person? To start with, it takes the notion of preference as fundamental. It does not allow for the possibility that there might be rational deliberation about one's preferences (Elster 1979). Rationality is therefore reduced to a choice of means for a given set of preferences. This approach significantly limits the scope of "practical rationality." As we will see, it is possible to put forward a more extensive conception of practical rationality according to which individuals are assumed to have the capacity to deliberate among various preferences as well as on the basis of a given set of preferences.[10]

Further, the welfarist approach to the human person is tone-deaf when it comes to issues of equity and distribution. If we imagine two possible worlds—Jones has 3 units of utility and Smith has 2 units of utility or Jones has 5 units and Smith has 1 unit—the welfarist model dictates that the second scenario is to be preferred because it results in higher total and average utility. In other words, the welfarist model is indifferent to the distribution of utilities across individuals; in its foundations, the theory is insensitive to the notion that it is important that *this* individual should have a decent human life.

Most fundamentally, however, the welfarist model is flawed because it implies a flatness in human life. It attributes to the individual no capacity to reflect on the nature of the goods that he or she will pursue, and it suggests that the individual follows a myopic path through life (choosing at each turn the branch that appears to maximize happiness)—an approach that is at odds with the notion of a deliberative relationship to one's life. It suggests a passivity in making life choices, which contrasts with richer alternatives that emphasize deliberation and freedom as essential elements of the good human life. And it provides no philosophical basis for saying what it is about the full human life, the flourishing individual, that is worthy of respect and admiration. I will turn to a more adequate and nuanced conception of the full human life later. Next, however, I will consider a conception of the human good that turns on an objective identification of human needs.

Needs and Primary Goods

Some theories of the human good attempt to identify objective features of human life as constituting the good. An important approach to the challenge of defining the human good focuses on the concept of need. It has been maintained that the goal of economic development ought to be the satisfaction of human needs, beginning with the most *basic needs.* An important distinction is made between wants (preferences) and needs; the latter include such things as access to nutrition, primary education, health care, and clean water, whereas the former include commodities such as luxury goods and other items that are "unnecessary" to human life.

What is a need? It is a feature of the human condition whose satisfaction is an essential component of human health, maturation, and development. Bruce Moon (1991: 5) characterizes basic needs along these lines: "The needs considered basic are those minimally required to sustain life at a decent material level. Conventionally, these are defined in terms of adequate food, water, health care, shelter, and minimum education." The basic needs approach offers a substantive criterion for assigning weights to the various categories of consumer preferences, and it holds that the more fundamental of these preferences (needs) should be satisfied first or receive higher priority in economic development.[11] The rationale for this approach is to attempt to identify the dimensions of absolute deprivation that are involved in deep poverty and then to construct public policy in such a way as to ameliorate these forms of deprivation. The approach also has the virtue of linking the definition of the goodness of the outcomes to an objective set of material factors (nutritional status, health status, education)—thereby avoiding the problem of the interpersonal comparison of subjective utilities. On this approach, we are not led into debates over the relative importance of various kinds of life goals and satisfactions that people adopt at the high end of the income scale. Instead, we can agree that the deprivations that correspond to extreme poverty are inherently bad things and that it is a good thing to ameliorate these deprivations. So the zone of disagreement about goals and objectives is narrowed, and choices among various development strategies are simplified.

John Rawls offers a somewhat different analysis of need in the construction of his theory of justice, in the form of a theory of "*primary goods.*" He defines primary goods as "things that every rational man is presumed to want. These goods normally have a use whatever a person's rational plan of life," and he includes "rights and liberties, powers and opportunities, income and wealth" in his list of primary goods (Rawls 1971: 62). His general perspective is that the pursuit of human goals requires access to resources and opportunities of various sorts: income, employment, education, and the like. Even if we do not have precise knowledge about the plans and goals that a given individual has defined for himself or herself, it is most likely that these resources will be needed for the fulfillment of these plans and goals. The theory of primary goods is intended to provide part of the foundation of a broader theory of equity in the distribution of resources and neutrality across persons in the principles that we adopt to govern the distribution of resources.

The theory of primary goods comes into Rawls's theory at two points. First, within the "original position," Rawls argues that individuals—even denied knowledge of their particular circumstances and conceptions of the good—will rationally prefer more rather than fewer primary goods (because of the instrumental role that these goods play in the achievement of most life plans). And second, he argues that the difference principle would be adopted within the framework of the original position: The distribution of primary goods across persons should be equal except insofar as inequalities of distribution lead to a greater quantity of primary goods for the person who is least well off. Like the theory of basic needs, Rawls's theory is designed to avoid the subjectivity of the utilitarian theory of welfare; Rawls aims to identify a noncontroversial set of objective factors that are universally relevant to human well-being.

Basic needs and primary goods have a close relationship to efforts to define and operationalize concepts of the "quality of life" or the "standard of living" of a given society.[12] Social and economic development ought to result in a rising standard of living for the population. Changes in economic institutions and opportunities ought to lead to an improvement of the quality of life of the people who are affected. But how can these concepts be defined? What does it mean to ask whether English workers experienced a rising standard of living from 1820 to 1880?[13] What does it mean to ask whether the quality of life in rural China has improved as a result of the reforms in agriculture in the 1980s?

Notice that there are two aspects to these questions: (1) at the level of defining the concepts of the standard of living or the quality of life for the typical individual within the society, and (2) at the level of identifying differences in degree of attainment of standard of living or quality of life across different groups within the population. We might say that the standard of living for an individual includes some or all of these elements: adequate nutrition, access to health care, access to clean water and sanitation, and access to comfortable housing. Would we also include less tangible factors such as job security, a satisfying social environment, and an attractive work and urban environment? Would we count the quality of political institutions (democratic, repressive) within our definition of the standard of living? How about the consistency and effectiveness of the system of law under which one lives? Social scientists typically limit their definitions of terms such as these to a more circumscribed list of social goods—in order to be in a better position to measure the results. But it is entirely fair to judge that one's standard of living and quality of life are affected by the more abstract factors as well.

Let us suppose that we have defined the standard of living to include these factors: nutrition, health, education, and housing. And suppose that we define quality of life more broadly to encompass the components of the standard of living as well as a set of factors corresponding to the quality of the lived environment, including the natural environment, the built environment (urban design, for example), and the quality of political and legal institutions. This gives us a basis for describing the standard of living for a specific person over an interval of time. We can then turn our attention to the question of the distribution of levels of the standard of living of a population over time, space, and social location. How would we measure the standard of living over time and place? Here, a variety of social science tools are available to us. We can carry out household studies that allow us to make inferences about each of the factors included in the definition; we can estimate house-

hold income and the other ways in which persons gain access to the components of the standard of living; and we can measure the results or symptoms
of the standard of living, in the form of life expectancy, height and weight for
given age groups, and educational attainment. We are then in a position to
consider what the results show concerning variation. Are there regional differences in the standard of living in a country? Are there gendered differences—for example, do women and girls show greater evidence of
malnutrition than boys and men in a given society? Are there class or social
differences—do farmers have shorter life expectancies than civil servants?

What role do income and employment play in determining a person's standard of living? The role is a large one in market economies, since individuals
satisfy the bulk of their needs by expending income on commodities and
services. So rising household incomes imply rising standards of living for the
persons who live in those households. However, income is not the sole determinant of the standard of living, for there are important nonincome sources
through which access to the components of the standard of living can be
achieved. If government provides access to free or subsidized health care, for
instance, then individuals will have a higher standard of living than they
would with the same income in a different social setting. Thus, to estimate
the standard of living of an individual, we need to estimate both income (including self-production) and the sources of need satisfaction that come from
other sources (including the state). Here again, there are substantial institutional factors that may lead to unexpected variations in the standard of living
of different persons—for example, within the household or across social
groups.

**The Link to the Human Development Index and the Physical Quality of Life
Index.** This discussion provides an important insight into a central issue
throughout this book, the definition of poverty. It is common to identify the
poor as those with exceptionally low income. But our discussion of needs
suggests that this definition is a blunt instrument. Given the possible diver-
gence between income and human well-being, we need to have other ways of
measuring the extent and depth of poverty in different countries. It is here
that a variety of quality of life indicators, based on the theory of human well-
being sketched in this chapter, prove their merits. For it is possible to measure
other variables besides income that have a more immediate relation to capacity realization. Malnutrition is directly and patently incompatible with full

realization of human capabilities; so, other things being equal, a society with a higher level of malnutrition than another is worse off in terms of the condition of the poor. Longevity is a general indicator of the quality of health services available to the population (and the poor, since inadequate health care for a large share of the population will translate into reduced life expectancy on average). Infant mortality statistics are generally taken to be another sensitive indicator of the health and nutrition status of the poor; downward fluctuations in the latter lead to significant increases in the former. Likewise, data about school enrollments at various levels—primary, secondary, postsecondary—provide important information about the extent to which a given society is succeeding in providing education to its poor, and lack of education is plainly intimately related to obstacles in the way of capability realization. Literacy statistics can serve the same purpose.

Measures of these nonincome variables provide a fairly sensitive indicator of the condition of the poor in a way that permits informative cross-cultural comparisons. Several important indexes of well-being have been constructed using such information. Central among these are the Physical Quality of Life Index (PQLI) and the Human Development Index (HDI).

The *Human Development Report*, published annually by the United Nations Development Programme (UNDP), offers development statistics for about 150 countries; these reports are designed to provide empirical information about the quality of life in developing countries. The methodology of these reports is very much influenced by the capabilities theory advanced by Amartya Sen, Martha Nussbaum, and others (United Nations Development Programme 2000). The Human Development Index measures quality of life based on three variables—educational attainment, life expectancy at birth, and GDP per capita. It is intended to capture three important dimensions of quality of life: income, health status, and educational opportunities and attainment (United Nations Development Programme 2000: 17). The *Human Development Reports* provide a valuable basis for monitoring the human progress or deprivation that results from various development efforts in different parts of the world.

Another effort to establish an index of human welfare that would permit comparison across national development experiences is the Physical Quality of Life Index (Morris 1979), devised prior to the HDI. This index identifies three variables that are arguably related to aspects of physical well-being (health, education, and longevity), and it collects data from many countries to permit comparison. Again, the goal of this construction is to allow us to arrive at judgments about the success or failure of various development strategies by assessing the effects of those strategies (after a reasonable period of time) on the outcomes for human well-being that they produce. And it emerges from both the HDI and the PQLI that there are significant differences across countries in the levels of well-being that have resulted—even at similar levels of national income.

How well does the theory of basic needs fare as a foundation for our reasoning about economic development? The basic needs approach has some significant advantages. First, it directs policy efforts toward the amelioration of a set of deprivations that are plainly the most serious affronts to a good human life—malnutrition, illiteracy, homelessness, preventable disease. Second, the basic needs approach surpasses the welfarist theory on the criterion of interpersonal equity. The approach provides a powerful basis for favoring greater equality, in that it privileges a distribution of resources that serves a broader number of people (by requiring that basic needs be satisfied before nonbasic wants are addressed). So the basic needs approach works well to anchor development policy to the goals of poverty alleviation and the improvement of social equity.

But the basic needs approach does not avoid the criticism of flatness in its conception of the good human life. It does not provide an affirmative conception of the person and all that is involved in a flourishing human life. The approach has succeeded in separating out an important aspect of the problem of economic development—the urgency of addressing the most severe forms of deprivation that are associated with extreme poverty. But it does not answer the most fundamental question and the question we are concerned with in this chapter: What is the nature of the good human life? So let me now take a brief excursion into an important tradition within moral philosophy in order to gain some traction on this important, foundational issue.

The Aristotelian Model

The preceding discussion raises substantial doubt about the adequacy of both the welfarist and the basic needs conceptions of the person. Most fundamentally, the welfarist conception fails to give adequate attention to the intentionality and planned structure of a human life. Aristotle's ethics provide the richest basis for theorizing about the good human life. The Aristotelian model

is a tradition that extends from Aristotle's *Nichomachean Ethics* through Georg
Hegel and Karl Marx to John Stuart Mill and John Rawls. Taking the tradition
as a coherent discussion, it provides a powerful and compelling vision of the
meaning and fullness of a human life. And this theory of the person can be
projected with great precision onto the theory of human well-being articulated in Amartya Sen's concept of capabilities. This approach therefore provides a coherent basis for much of development ethics.

Aristotle provides an extended theory of the individual as a practical
thinker. He asks persistently, What is happiness? And to answer the question,
he probes the nature of the human agent. He puts it forward that the human
agent is a deliberator: The person considers various goods, places them into a
hierarchy, and then constructs plans to bring these goods into being (Aristotle 1987). So the good human life involves reflection about one's fundamental
goals and purposes, formulation of plans through which to bring these goals
to achievement, and skillful activity using the powers that one has to accomplish the goals of the plan. This vision creates an important space for self-definition and self-realization—self-definition through the reflective choice of
goals and self-realization through practical activity aimed at bringing about
the achievement of these goals.

Hegel and Marx deepen the Aristotelian theory of the person by emphasizing the human significance of meaningful labor (Schacht 1970). Human beings realize themselves through labor; more fully, they do so by transforming
nature employing their skills and abilities, guided by a plan or design of their
own creation. Hegel and Marx emphasize the relationship between subjectivity and objectivity and the practicality of labor. The idea that the sculptor has
formed of the potential statue is subjective. But through his or her skilled use
of tools, the block of granite is transformed into something new—an objective thing in the world. The sculptor has thus transformed the block of stone
from a natural object to a fabricated object and has transformed his or her
thoughts into an actualized thing. (This vision is at the heart of Marx's theory
of alienation; modern industrial work breaks the connection between creative ideas, skill, and product [Marx, Engels, and Struik 1964].)

What Mill adds to this tradition is the important distinction between
"higher" and "lower" pleasures. He writes as a utilitarian philosopher, but he
takes great issue with the assumptions about the homogeneity of happiness
or pleasure that underlie the theories of Jeremy Bentham or Henry Sidgwick.

Mill argues that there are important differences among the pleasures that give us happiness (Mill et al. 1974). The pleasures that derive from the engagement of our more complex human capacities are the more satisfying. Given the choice, a person who is capable of both higher and lower pleasures will choose the higher pleasures. Thus, performing challenging music is more satisfying than watching *Seinfeld,* playing basketball at a skilled level is more satisfying than watching sports on television, and reading Aleksandr Pushkin is more satisfying than reading the back of the cereal box. Why is this so? It is because in each case, the preferred activity engages and challenges a complex set of our capabilities, and we take pleasure in the exercise of these capabilities. The full human life, then, is one in which individuals have amply developed their capability to exercise their talents in creative ways.

John Rawls builds on this tradition in *A Theory of Justice.* He emphasizes the importance for moral theory of a theory of the person, and the theory of the person that he advances is Aristotelian. Persons are reflective about their goals, they arrive at a plan of life that orchestrates their goals into a coherent plan, and they use their concrete human capabilities to bring their plans to fruition. Rawls emphasizes that each individual is free to arrive at a conception of the good—the ultimate values that he or she respects. The conception of the good may be religious or secular, individual or communitarian, aesthetic or spare, but it is fully within the moral scope of the individual to determine the particulars of the conception of the good.

Rawls stresses the importance of the individual's ability to reflect on the various goods that he or she values and to organize actions so as to bring these about. An individual possesses what we may call a *"plan of life"*—that is, an orchestrated conception of the states of affairs that are important to him or her and a conception of how he or she will attempt to realize those states of affairs over time. In its fully articulated form, this plan of life articulates all the goods that the individual wishes to realize (for example, friendship, creative accomplishment, family, or spiritual development). And it specifies (at some level of abstraction) the strategies through which the individual aims to accomplish these things.[14]

The other chief source of Rawls's theory of justice is Immanuel Kant's moral philosophy. Though it falls outside this Aristotelian tradition, Kant's philosophy offers several important insights that ought to be mentioned as we work toward an adequate conception of the person. His moral theory is organized around the idea of right action. He asks, What are the principles by which we ought to decide what to do? He argues for the categorical imperative: Treat persons as ends, not merely as means (Kant and Paton 1964). The underlying rationale for the principle is Kant's philosophical position that only persons have intrinsic worth.

We can extract an important moral principle from Kant's position. It is that

- Persons have intrinsic moral worth.

What is it to have moral worth? And what is it to be treated as an individual worthy of dignity? Kant's philosophy provides a powerful basis for maintaining that the dignity of the individual is expressed in the freedoms that he or she is able to exercise and the rights that the individual has to pursue his or her plans and goals in ways that seem best. The dignity of the individual, that is, must be expressed in terms of respect for the freedoms and rights of the individual.

These themes and insights represent philosophical moral thinking at its best. The tradition is a cumulative effort to provide an adequate "moral phenomenology" of human experience. And it provides a powerful basis for designing and evaluating social and political institutions. I will return to the conception of the person that emerges from this tradition in the final section of the chapter. First, however, I will look more closely at several of these ideas before attempting to synthesize a theory of the person.

Well-Being and Capabilities

There is a conception of the human good that is superior to both the welfare conception and the basic needs conception discussed above. This important alternative is the *"well-being"* approach, pioneered by Amartya Sen. According to this approach, the good of development can be understood in terms of the ability of typical persons to live full human lives. Sen conceptualizes the approach under a framework of capabilities and functionings (A. Sen 1983, 1984, 1987, 1993, 1999). This approach emphasizes the status of the person as a free agent who realizes his or her potential through choices. Human beings have a set of capabilities and talents that can be actualized through normal processes of development—education, play, nutrition, family life, and so on. These capabilities are present in all of us, but their fulfillment can be blocked by numerous obstacles. One's capacity for skilled and dexterous bodily movement can be blocked by malnutrition, the capacity for imaginative thinking can be blocked by poor or nonexistent primary education, and so on.

The central moral insight in this approach to policy is this: It is an inherently good thing that people are in a position to realize their human capabilities, and the establishment of the social, economic, and political opportunities and enablements that are necessary for the realization of these capabilities is the highest good to which social policy should be directed. Consequently, we are urged to take the fulfillment of each individual's human capabilities as the ultimate good of social arrangements and the ultimate goal of social policy. The fulfillment of human capabilities means the flourishing of the human person; it means that the person's most important needs have been met; and it means that the person is in the best situation possible to design and implement a plan of life that is most deeply satisfying—thereby contributing to the individual's "happiness." The well-being approach is thus more basic than either the social welfare approach or the basic needs approach. It explains the moral insights included in both but relates them back to a more basic theory of the human person.

Let us look more closely at several current efforts to express the perspective of human well-being that emerges from the Aristotelian tradition. Sen's writings have done much to clarify the human reality of economic development. His special contribution has been to establish the linkages between the philosophical theories and ideas in this tradition, on one side, and the practical exigencies of economic development planning, on the other. In his lectures on the standard of living, Sen distinguishes between a commodity-based definition of the standard of living and a "human functioning" view of well-being (Sen and Hawthorn 1987). His seminal insight is that we are centrally concerned with the human being in possession of a bundle of capabilities that can be either realized or impeded through the economic and social environment in which the person is located. Living well means having the opportunity to fully develop one's capabilities, to formulate a satisfying plan of life, and to have reasonable freedoms and opportunities to carry out one's life plan.

Sen's basic insight is that economic well-being is best defined in terms of the individual's capability to become a fully functioning human being. "In assessing the standard of living of a person, the objects of value can sensibly be taken to be aspects of the life that he or she succeeds in living. The various 'doings' and 'beings' a person achieves are thus potentially all relevant to the evaluation of that person's living standard" (Sen and Hawthorn 1987: 29). If we were fortunate enough to live in a world in which all persons, rich and poor, were fully capable of realizing their human capacities, then the issue of poverty and wealth would be of minimal concern. In our world, however, the limitations on personal development imposed by poverty are all too obvious: Clearly, malnutrition, illiteracy, poor health, boring and dangerous work conditions, and early mortality are serious obstacles standing in the way of full human development for the poor.

It is important to recognize that increasing the realization of capacities can be achieved through other means besides simply raising incomes; putting the point in another way, it is possible for the poor in one society to have higher income and lower capacity realization than the poor of another society, due to differences in the public provision of capacity-enhancing amenities. Societies in which there is extensive provisioning of education or health services, for example, will have a higher level of well-being in its poor population—even though the absolute income flowing to this stratum may be as low or lower than that of other societies. (This has been true in several important "anomalies" in the development experience of the world since 1945; in both Sri Lanka and Kerala, e.g., human well-being is substantially higher than would be predicted on the basis of the per capita income of those societies.)

Nussbaum's Formulation of Fundamental Capabilities

What are the most important and universal human capabilities? Martha Nussbaum attempts to provide a fairly specific answer to this question. She, like Sen, tries to define human well-being in an objective way, by identifying a set of core capabilities that are critical to full human functioning. The individual's level of well-being is assessed by the degree to which his or her circumstances permit the realization of these capabilities. The core of the theory is a principled account of a set of fundamental human capabilities that are held to be essential to a good human life. The Aristotelian origins of the approach are manifest. It is Nussbaum's contention that we can say a great deal about what is needed for a good human life, and this account is substantially independent of cultural variations (that is, human beings have the same capabilities for functioning in a wide variety of social and cultural settings). The capabilities involved in a good human life may be listed and justified, and the resulting list can serve as both a guide and a critical standard for development policy. Nussbaum devotes much care to the composition of this list. Her analysis enumerates the following capabilities:

- Being able to live to the end of a human life of normal length
- Being able to have good health, adequate nutrition, adequate shelter, opportunities for sexual satisfaction and choice in reproduction, and mobility
- Being able to avoid unnecessary and nonbeneficial pain and to have pleasurable experiences
- Being able to use the senses, imagine, think, and reason and to have the educational opportunities necessary to realize these capacities
- Being able to have attachments to things and persons outside ourselves
- Being able to form a conception of the good and to engage in critical reflection about the planning of one's own life
- Being able to live for and to others, to recognize and show concern for other human beings
- Being able to live with concern for and in relation to animals and the world of nature
- Being able to laugh, to play, and to enjoy recreational activities
- Being able to live one's own life and no one else's, enjoying freedom of association and freedom from unwarranted search and seizure[15]

Nussbaum characterizes the significance of this list in these terms: "My claim is that a life that lacks any one of these capabilities, no matter what else it has, will fall short of being a good human life" (Nussbaum and Glover 1995: 85). Further, she maintains that the list and its associated argumentation ought to be taken seriously by development theorists in the design of development strategies. Public policy must be guided by a conception of the human good that gives the policymaker strong direction in selecting goals and priorities for the development process. "The basic claim I wish to make . . . is that the central goal of public planning should be the capabilities of citizens to perform various important functions" (Nussbaum and Glover 1995: 87).[16]

Freedom as a Prerequisite of Human Capacity Realization

The centrality of freedom as an essential component of a flourishing human life has been emphasized. Social institutions that assure appropriate rights and a broad scope of freedom for individuals are therefore early rather than late requirements for a developing society that is aiming to establish the conditions of human flourishing for its population. What is freedom, and why is it important? Freedom involves, at its core, the ideas of autonomy and choice: An individual is free if he or she has the capacity to choose a plan of action and the practical ability to undertake actions that have a reasonable probability of bringing about these purposes. Freedom invokes the issue of choice, on the one hand, and constraint or coercion, on the other. A constraint is a condition that prevents the person from pursuing a goal that he or she has selected; coercion is a circumstance that compels the individual to pursue a goal that he or she had specifically not selected.

A series of questions that allow for a more refined understanding of the condition of freedom can be raised. The criterion offered here singles out a capacity and an ability—a capacity to formulate plans and a practical ability to pursue those plans. Consider various circumstances that can interfere with those capacities, however: limitations of attention or memory, physical disabilities, armed guards, thought police, and handcuffs. Are each of these factors conditions that interfere with freedom? Or is the concept of freedom limited to absence of coercion or external constraint on the pursuit of one's plans?

A second complexity derives from what we might call the "granularity" or continuity of freedom. Are there gradations of freedom? Is there a condition of life that could be called "absolutely free"? Can a person be free in one dimension and unfree in others—for example, free to formulate plans but constrained in the execution of these plans?

It is common to distinguish between negative freedoms ("freedom from . . .") and positive freedoms ("freedom to . . ."). The first concept includes protections of the individual against unjustified coercion—for example, freedom of speech and expression, freedom of association, and freedom of movement. The second concept takes note of the fact that the exercise of freedom often requires access to resources and other material conditions. So the positive conception of freedom advances the idea that persons are free when they are not subject to coercion *and* when they have access to the material conditions that would permit them to exercise this freedom. My freedom of speech can be limited in the negative sense if the police or a mob prevent me from speaking, but it is limited in the positive sense if the only ways of making public utterance require the purchase of media time and I lack the requisite funds. Advocates of the positive interpretation of freedom are not obliged to conclude that one is free only when the state provides the resources necessary to exercise freedom; rather, they can maintain that the condition of positive freedom requires only that the social and political institutions in which one lives be such that there are multiple and feasible ways of exercising one's freedoms.

It is plain that there are always limitations on an individual's ability to pursue his or her plans, and not all these limitations are morally reprehensible. A businessperson may have a plan to achieve 60 percent of the market share in a particular industry, but it is not an interference with the agent's freedom that competitors seek to deny him or her this result. So what kind of constraints count as interference with freedom?

As a first step, we can take note of a class of constraints that fall at the center of the overall notion of constraints on freedom. These are constraints on individual action enforced by coercive power. When the state uses its legislative or police powers to prevent assembly, the individuals so constrained have suffered in the exercise of their freedoms. All law constrains action, however, so an adequate conception of freedom depends on a theory of political justice or constitutionalism. Consequently, an adequate theory of freedom cannot be formulated in the absence of a political theory governing our thoughts about citizenship and the legitimate authority of the state.

A second limitation on freedom has to do with the formation of one's human capacities. If through childhood malnutrition a person has suffered neurological damage preventing him or her from formulating a plan, we would say that this person's freedom has been limited. So, pursuing this line of thought, we can assert that freedom requires that the individual be presented with life circumstances that permit the normal development of mental and physical capacities.

Can we say that freedom is a prerequisite to full human development? We can say more than that: Freedom is both a prerequisite and a consequence of full human development (A. Sen 1999). It is a prerequisite in that many of the capabilities important to human flourishing will only develop fully when individuals are free to experiment and try out their emerging capacities. For example, the capabilities to have friends, to write fiction, to work well within associations, or to collaborate on joint projects all require free play and exercise of the activities within which these forms of social agency take place. But likewise, the valuable exercise of capabilities achieved requires a zone of freedom within which the person can make creative use of his or her talents. And finally, the full realization of human capabilities gives us freedoms we did not previously have—the freedom to write an excellent novel, the freedom to effectively lead a social organization, or the freedom to design a stable bridge. These are new freedoms because they are new enablements for the person; the underlying capabilities have made it possible for the person to do and accomplish things he or she could not previously perform.

Human Dignity

Much of the harm of poverty is tangible and material: high rates of infant mortality, poor nutritional and health status, and so forth. However, the preceding emphasis on capabilities and functionings should alert us to the fact that poverty has an intangible side as well. For the underlying value, recall, is that of the fully developed human being—the person in realization of his or her capabilities and functionings qua human being. And among the diminishments imposed by poverty are enduring assaults to human dignity over the whole of a human life. The man who cannot afford minimally decent clothing will often be ashamed to present himself in public. The underemployed housemaid may be compelled to accept indignity and disrespect from her employers rather than risk losing her job. The tenant farmer with low income and little power will be obliged to kowtow to his landlord rather than face eviction. Each of these situations is one in which we find a human being in circumstances of indignity, and it would be hard to imagine the person being able to sustain a robust sense of self-worth and self-respect in such circumstances.[17]

Gender and Development

A central feature of human life is the fact of gender. And gender inequalities are prominent and debilitating in the developing world. Data on mortality, education, nutrition, health status, and access to income show substantial and significant differences between men and women in many developing countries. Women are often disadvantaged in their exercise of economic and political rights, they are disadvantaged within the household in the domestic economy, they are disadvantaged in terms of access to social necessities such as health care and education, and they are disadvantaged in many measures of well-being as the outcome of social processes. Likewise, traditional social practices in various developing countries often show a marked bias against women and girls. And these biases often have mortal consequences; demographic evidence suggests that through selective neglect, girls appear to show significantly greater mortality than boys in various countries (Drèze and Sen 1995; Coale 1991). These facts represent an important and pervasive source of injustice. This chapter will consider the issues of social justice and human welfare raised by these persistent patterns of gender discrimination.

The issue of the role of gender issues in development enters our story from another angle as well because women are in fact the agents of development as well as the subjects of development. Evidence suggests that patterns of discrimination against women also create a separate and significant impediment to effective economic development. Further, removing sources of social and economic discrimination against women can significantly improve a country's development performance. The role of women in agriculture is one such instance; women's labor and organizational skills are at the center of increasing productivity in many developing country farming systems. At the other end of the spectrum of generality, women's organizations—in support of female labor rights, child welfare, women's issues, health care, and democratization— have the potential for reorienting development policies in numerous countries in ways that are more favorable to a range of human development issues.

The data from many developing countries concerning the status of women are alarming. The United Nations compiles a periodic summary report on the status of the world's women (United Nations 2000). This publication offers data on the status of women in all regions and many countries, in many categories associated with measures of human well-being. Whether we consider basic measures of human development (education, nutrition, and health status), measures of political and economic rights (the right to hold property, the rights of political participation), or measures of cultural and social repression of women (enslavement, violence against women, and cultural and religious limitations of women's freedom of choice), we find that women in many developing countries are subject to severe disadvantage and restriction, resulting in massive differences in human welfare and in the realization of human rights for men and women. Studies of girls in rural South Asia show that female children have lower nutritional levels and lower levels of education than boys (Drèze and Sen 1995). Women in Brazil are disadvantaged in the labor force and in their right to hold and dispose of property. Women in Mexico are subject to traditional patriarchal limitations on their choices, resulting in significant stifling of the development of their human capabilities (Valdés 1995).

The multiple dimensions of gender inequality in the developing world tend to cluster together. At the most basic level, girls and women have more limited access to food in times of scarcity, and these disadvantages show up in inequalities of nutritional status in many countries (Behrman 1988, 1992; Haddad, Kanbur, and Bouis 1995; for a dissenting view, see Basu 1989). In addition, girls and women have more limited and less timely access to health care in many regions. Jean Drèze and Amartya Sen (1995) document these differences in the case of India and demonstrate the demographic consequences of differential access to even rudimentary health care in the form of the "missing women of Asia." If poor families are somewhat slower to bring a sick daughter to the clinic than a sick son, the consequence will be elevated mortality among daughters. India represents a particularly extreme case, where child mortality for girls is forty-two per thousand, compared to a rate of twenty-nine per thousand for boys (United Nations 2000: chart 3.5). And the effects of differential care are discernible in female-to-male population ratios. Girls and women are almost universally offered more limited educational opportunities in poor countries (Hadden and London 1996; Mak and Summers 1996)—with the consequences of lower literacy, lower development of cognitive capacity, and reduced ability to enter into independent economic roles. The UN report on the status of the world's women finds that two-thirds of the illiterate people in the world are female (United Nations 2000: 87). Women are commonly limited in their rights of participation in political processes—electoral politics, associations, parties, and local organizations. And women are commonly limited in the economic rights they are legally or socially permitted to exercise, such as the right to work outside the home and the right to hold property.

The cumulative effects of these forms of gender inequality are enormous. The girls and women who have been subject to discrimination have been stunted in their human development and in their true ability to realize their human capabilities. And they have been faced with life circumstances that severely restrict their human freedoms—the freedom to choose where to live, how to live, with whom to live; how to use their capabilities to pursue their life plans; and even what their life plans ought to include. So gender inequality amounts to a vast human ill, affecting hundreds of millions of human beings and affecting as well the character of the processes of social and political development that occur within these societies.

Principles of Gender Justice

I will now turn to the normative issues that gender inequalities raise. To make progress in this regard from a moral point of view, some of the moral principles that appear to be most salient must be considered. In the passages below, I will attempt to formulate several principles to capture the normative issues of gender justice.

The Priority of Human Development: Capabilities.   A touchstone of moral reasoning throughout this chapter has been the moral importance of human development. It is an inherently good thing that human beings fulfill their capabilities and freely pursue their plans of life. Persons represent specific collections of capabilities, and it is inherently good that they be in a position to realize their capabilities. A society therefore ought to be organized in such a way as to facilitate the full human development of all its citizens. Societies that fail to do so are faulty in a profound moral way: Those that discriminate in the realization of human capabilities across their citizens on grounds of sex, race, national origin, and so on have embodied an abiding injustice. A social system that blocks some individuals from doing so—through poverty, racism, or sexism—is one that creates great human harm and injustice. And the heart of that harm is the insult the system creates in the realization of the human talents, capacities, and plans of the individuals whose lives it stunts.

We can put the principle this way:
- Gender justice requires that a society secure the grounds for equal and full development of women's capabilities and functioning.

The Primacy of Human Freedom as a Component of the Good Society.   I have also emphasized the importance of freedom as a guiding value for economic development. Societies ought to be arranged in such a way as to most fully enable their citizens to exercise their freedoms in the pursuit of their life plans. Free human activity is an inherently good thing, and it is therefore good as well for social institutions to be designed to maximize human freedom. This statement implies that social reforms—processes designed to improve social, political, and economic arrangements within society—should be oriented toward the enhancement of human freedom.

The data described in the preceding pages serve to document a substantial impairment of the freedom of women and girls in many parts of the world.

Restrictions on a woman's right to seek employment, to hold property, or to participate in political processes represent a significant impairment of women's freedom. This conclusion is true in two senses. First, the life activities that are represented by work and employment are themselves important exercises of human freedom. As a line of thinkers from Aristotle and Hegel to Sen and Nussbaum have emphasized, individuals realize their humanity through the creative activity associated with work. Freedom is not "caprice" but rather the realized capability to exercise one's creative talents to accomplish one's goals, and work embodies this process. Likewise, participation in political activity—associations, organization, parties, and electoral processes—is an exercise of freedom. Through such processes, human beings are able to realize their social capabilities and to contribute to the definition of the public good, along lines articulated by Jean-Jacques Rousseau (1983; also see Colletti 1972). So work and politics are themselves concrete expressions of freedom.

More prosaically, freedom presupposes some degree of independence from the arbitrary will of others. And a very concrete form of dependency arises in circumstances where a person is wholly dependent on the support of others for his or her livelihood. Being deprived of access to employment is a very significant factor in creating dependency, and it therefore has high likelihood of interfering with freedom and choice. Likewise, because the state is so powerful in constraining and enabling in modern societies, it is critical for all constituencies to have a voice in the formulation of policy and law. If women are denied rights of political participation—or if their rights are limited by various informal mechanisms—they will be less able to represent their legitimate concerns and interests for action by the state.

We can put the point this way:
- Gender justice requires that a society create a sustainable context for the exercise of freedom for girls and women.

Normative Conclusions

What conclusions can we draw about the just treatment of women in developing societies? Can we elucidate more specific positions than those embodied in the general injunctions to "treat women fairly," "treat women equally," or "provide an equal basis for the realization of women's capabilities"? We can indeed be more specific, and we must be if our judgments are to be of use in guiding our thinking about justice in development.

First, social institutions should be arranged so that boys and girls and women and men have the same forms of access to the social resources needed to achieve a normal human life. These resources would include access to health care, access to education, and access to sources of nutrition and clean water.

Second, political institutions ought to embody equal and meaningful rights of participation for women and men. Women should have significant and secure roles within political parties, labor unions, and other associations and organizations; they should have full rights of democratic participation within both governmental and nongovernmental processes; and these rights should be secured against the several forms of intimidation that we have identified above. Gender equality requires political equality.

Third, the institutions of the family—whatever they are—ought not to unduly burden women and girls, whether through custom, religious practice, or patriarchalism. Women should be free to negotiate the terms of their participation within the household without coercion or violence against them.

Fourth, it is critically important that women have unfettered access to the formal sources of economic entitlement within the society: access to employment, access to credit, and eligibility for property ownership. These are the means through which persons are able to preserve their independence within society; they provide a basis for independent livelihood, they provide recourse against dependency and exploitation, and they fundamentally alter the terms of the woman's relationship to powerful men (father, brothers, husband).

Finally, the state has an affirmative responsibility to underwrite these requirements of gender justice. It is an important responsibility of the just state to guarantee the basic rights and liberties of all its citizens. And where there is a pervasive and evident pattern of limiting those rights within civil society and the institutions of society, it is the responsibility of the state to correct these patterns.

A Rich Conception of the Person

Here, then, is a conception of a person and a good human life that will serve as a model throughout the pages ahead. It derives from the Aristotelian tradition outlined above, and it serves as a concrete expression or vision of a flourishing human life.

A person possesses

- A set of capabilities—physical, mental, emotional—that can be realized through development and practice
- A set of rights and liberties
- A set of needs
- A conception of the good for himself or herself
- A set of preferences that derive from needs and the conception of the good
- A plan of life

Persons have needs because they are biological organisms. Their needs range from the most material—food, clothing, shelter—to the more refined—education, sociality, and a clean living environment. Persons have capabilities that are inherent in their biological and social attributes. Their capabilities are physical (a capability to dexterously use the hands or to run and jump). They are mental (a capability to reason and remember, to create, to organize activities). And their capabilities are emotional and social as well (a capability to form friendships; to adopt commitments; and to experience pleasure, humor, and sorrow). These capabilities, however, are only potential at birth; they need to be actualized through appropriate developmental processes. These processes include access to adequate nutrition, stimulation, loving care as an infant or child, appropriate educational experiences, and practice at forming friendships and associations. Persons have dignity, which entails that they have freedoms and rights that must be respected. This is centrally important because realization of individuals' capabilities requires that they be in a position to carry out their projects and plans (subject, of course, to the like freedoms of all others). Persons have deliberative agency in that they have the capability to reflect on their goals and purposes and to arrive at orchestrated plans through which they endeavor to accomplish their goals. The most fundamental personal deliberation has to do with defining a conception of the good for oneself—a conception of the most basic values and goods that one wishes to respect. Deliberation includes the capacity to consider the validity of one's preferences given such fundamental values; so preferences are not externally given or biologically or socially determined but rather are themselves subject to deliberation and choice. A person arrives at a plan of life that represents a best effort to formulate a coherent, long-term strategy for realizing one's goals and values through purposeful activity over the fullness of a lifetime. And finally, a person has a life in action: a series of deeds, choices, commitments, and acts of creation through which the individual gives external expression to his or her goals and values.

Here we have a rich answer to the question, What is the moral importance of human life? And it is an answer that provides extensive resources for addressing some of the foundational concerns that arise within the theory of economic development. This is so because if these are the defining or most important features of human life, then social institutions and outcomes should be sculpted so as to best satisfy the needs and functions that persons possess as they work to achieve their own version of human flourishing.

We also have in this formulation a powerful basis for judging the effectiveness of various development strategies and efforts. What are the effects of a given strategy on the fulfillment of the human capabilities of all segments of society? How rapidly are resources, opportunities, and incomes flowing to the poor to support the fulfillment of their human potential? How effectively have social and political institutions been shaped to secure human freedoms and rights? If the answers to these questions are discouraging—as they are in many parts of the world today and for the foreseeable future—then we need to ask whether there are other, more effective interventions that might be designed to more quickly create the foundations for full human flourishing across the whole of these societies.

The Poverty-First Dictum

A central assumption of this book is that human well-being is *the* fundamental good of economic development—an assumption linked to the idea that the central ill economic development should be designed to address is human poverty.[18] This approach clearly distinguishes between fundamental values and the means through which we attempt to achieve these values. It provides a powerful philosophical theory within the context of which to explain the importance of both growth and equity. And it serves to provide a principled basis for making the choices that policy formation always requires.

So I will offer a recurring argument for "putting the poor first" in economic development policy. This amounts to a statement of principle along these lines:

- Economic development policies, both domestic and international, should be structured in such a way as to give highest priority to improving the well-being of the poor in developing countries.

What is involved in putting the poor first in development? In designing a development plan, a range of choices must be made: whether to encourage export production, to promote cash crops or food crops, to favor heavy industry or consumer goods, and so forth. The choices that are made will depend on the criteria being used to evaluate consequences. Thus, if the goal is to increase GDP at the fastest possible rate, then one set of choices will be made; if the goal is a combination of growth and military security, another set of choices will be made. Putting the poor first involves making these choices with consideration of how various alternatives will affect the welfare of the poorest strata in society. Take, for example, a government deliberating between investment credits for an electronics assembly plant and for a sugar-processing plant. The electronics plant, let us suppose, will produce a greater amount of value added, generating a greater amount of foreign exchange, whereas the processing plant involves a substantially higher level of employment at a wage above than the current average for unskilled labor. On the face of it, these circumstances, conjoined with the poverty-first principle, entail that the government should select the sugar-processing plant, since this alternative creates a greater amount of additional income for the poor.

This proposal for a reorientation of development planning raises a number of important questions. What implications does this priority have for other measures of economic development? And what policy options are available to bring about the most immediate effects on the welfare of the poor? How would such a development plan differ from existing policies? And are there countries that currently pursue such a model of growth?

Why should we put such a high priority on the alleviation of poverty? Why is poverty such a singularly important problem, demanding our immediate and sharpest attention for remediation? Why should we place the problem of poverty ahead of other important values in the context of development and modernization, such as providing a clean and safe urban environment, preserving environmental resources, or raising the average standard of living for the whole population? One particularly compelling answer relates to the fundamental value of human well-being. The ultimate value that should drive our thinking about economic development is that of the human life lived well and fully, in circumstances that embody the freedoms of the individual and the rights and liberties of all citizens. And extreme poverty deeply interferes with the individual's capacity to live fully. It is possible to think of poverty as simply synonymous with low income, implying severe material deprivation, and none of us would choose to live in the material circumstances of the poor. But we can say more than this about the bad of poverty. There is a fundamental relationship between poverty and impaired human development. It is not merely that the poor are able to consume less than the nonpoor; it is also that they are less able to develop their full human potential. Poor or absent medical services lead to illness and premature mortality; poor education and illiteracy lead to stunted intellectual achievement; long and tedious work hours (when available) give rise to demoralized everyday experience; and the social stigma of shabby dress, poor housing, and low-status employment lead to an erosion of self-respect. So poverty is a unique bad in its concentrated and destructive effects on the realization of the full human capacities of the poor: It is not just that the poor have a lower standard of living but that they live less than fully human lives.[19]

Notes

1. The challenge of defining the human good for the purpose of guiding public policy has been addressed by many philosophers and social thinkers. Particularly valuable treatments include J. Griffin 1986, Dasgupta 1993, and Braybrooke 1987.

2. John Rawls pays attention to this feature of moral theory throughout his work. Strong expressions are found in *A Theory of Justice* (Rawls 1971) and several important articles on the theory of the good (Rawls 1999a, 1993b: 29–35). See also Parfit 1984, C. Taylor 1989, and Williams 1985 for important efforts to relate ethical theory to the theory of the person.

3. See Bonner 1986 and Mackay 1980 for good introductions to the theory of social welfare.

4. The conceptual foundations of utilitarianism have been subject to substantial critical attention since the 1980s. See Smart and Williams 1973, Scheffler 1982, Harsanyi 1977, and Hollis and Nell 1975 for important contributions.

5. See Hausman and McPherson 1996 for a careful and insightful discussion of the logic of cost-benefit analysis in the context of development planning.

6. Amartya Sen (1977: 336) criticizes the assumption of narrow rational self-interest in many places: "The purely economic man is indeed close to being a social moron." His general objection is that individuals do in fact take the interests of others into account in their deliberations, and he contends that it is rational to do so (A. Sen 1987). His central contributions in "Rational Fools" (1977) are his discussion of the role of commitments in practical rational deliberation and his point that commitments cannot be incorporated into a simple set of first-order preferences. See also E. Anderson 2000 for a good recent critique of the assumptions of narrow economic rationality.

7. Thomas Nagel puts forward powerful arguments for the rationality of altruism and the irrationality of egoism in *The Possibility of Altruism* (1970).

8. These conceptual and theoretical issues include interpersonal comparisons of utility, utility as preference satisfaction, risk and uncertainty, and strategic rationality.

9. Important sources on the theory of utilitarianism include Sen and Williams 1982, Mackie 1977, Scheffler 1982, and Harsanyi 1982.

10. See Jon Elster's writings (1979, 1983, 1989b) for recurring efforts to refine our understanding of deliberation about preferences.

11. There is a large literature on basic needs as the conceptual foundation of development economics; see Streeten et al. 1981, Moon 1991, and Braybrooke 1987 for several salient examples. See also Scanlon 1975 for an important philosophical discussion of the urgency of some preferences over others.

12. Amartya Sen has made important contributions to both questions. His lectures on the standard of living (Sen and Hawthorn 1987) offer an analysis of this concept in terms of the more basic notion of "capabilities and functionings," which I will discuss later.

13. For several recent contributions to the standard of living debate, see Lindert 1994, Crafts 1980, and Feinstein 1998.

14. John Rawls makes central use of this Aristotelian concept in *A Theory of Justice* (1971).

15. This list largely quotes Nussbaum's language (Nussbaum and Glover 1995: 83–85).

16. Nussbaum provides a similar but not identical list of capabilities in her more recent book, *Women and Human Development.* She refers to life; bodily health; bodily integrity; senses, imagination, and thought; emotions; practical reason; affiliation; other species; play; and control over one's environment (Nussbaum 2000: 78–80).

17. See James Scott's discussion of the social psychology of domination and subordination (Scott 1990).

18. At the level of policy statement, at least, the poverty-first approach is shared by the World Bank as well: "Reducing poverty is the fundamental objective of economic development" (World Bank 1990: 24). And in its 2000–2001 report, reflecting internationally agreed-upon goals of development, the World Bank report lists the goal of "reduc[ing] by half the proportion of people living in extreme income poverty between 1990 and 2015" (World Bank 2001b: 6).

19. Martha Nussbaum, Amartya Sen, and other contributors address a series of issues surrounding the definition of "quality of life" in Nussbaum and Sen 1993.

2

What Is Economic Development?

THE CENTRAL GOAL OF THIS book is to probe the normative issues that arise within the context of economic development. The volume is not a textbook in the economics of development. However, it is impossible to discuss development issues without a basic understanding of the nature of economic development—that is, the attributes of a developing economy; the goals that governments, agencies, and organizations usually have in trying to transform an economy; and the instruments of change through which this transformation can be stimulated.[1]

This chapter provides a schematic account of the main features of economic development in the world today. I will sketch the economic and social processes within a given society that constitute the system through which wealth and income are produced and distributed. I will also examine some of the outcomes in the developing world today—economic growth, technological change, urbanization, structural transformation, and globalization—as well as poverty, inequality, malnutrition, low literacy, low levels of democracy, and low life expectancy. And I will discuss the goals that are usually assumed to drive economic development planning and policymaking.

Discussions throughout the book will be focused on the world's poorest countries, which are sometimes referred to as the "less developed countries" (LDCs). The World Bank classifies national economies by income level, distinguishing between low-income, middle-income (lower and upper), and high-income economies (World Bank 2001b: 334–335). In using the terms *less developed country*, *Third World country*, or *extremely poor country*, it is important to avoid giving the impression of backwardness or unworthiness in the countries and cultures that we discuss. Economic development is a mixture of processes—economic, social, political, and cultural—whose dynamics are not well understood, and it is certainly possible to advance in one domain more fully than in another. There is no canonical pathway of development on all fronts that countries should aspire to—and consequently, there is no single dimension according to which countries can be classified as "less developed" or "more developed." Nonetheless, poverty and the various human limitations that come in its wake are critically important issues in the world today, and poverty is unmistakably associated with low per capita income. (It is also associated with high inequalities, weak governmental institutions, and regressive gender relations.) So it is entirely appropriate to single out the poorest countries for special consideration, and it is important to focus on the institutions and obstacles that affect the ability of these countries to succeed in raising the incomes and levels of well-being of their people.

It is also important to recognize that there is no homogeneous "developing world" whose experience we can summarize. It is certainly true that similar processes are at work in various parts of the world; this is what permits social scientific analysis of this cluster of problems in the first place. But there are also crucial differences between regions that lead to very different challenges and outcomes—for example, land and resource availability, demographic patterns, levels of education, political institutions, and levels of inequality. Moreover, this point about the diversity of circumstance is true at almost any given level of scale. We can no more talk about the uniform Indian experience of poverty than we can about the uniform global experience of poverty. Significant differences exist between states in India—for example, between Bihar and West Bengal or between Karnataka and Kerala,[2]—and this is just as true in Nigeria or Brazil. Useful analysis of the processes and outcomes, therefore, requires appropriate recognition of regional and subregional variation. The spatial patterning of development experience is profoundly important.

What are the key questions that we must ask to attain a better understanding of the realities of global economic development today and a better ability to design policy solutions? Fundamentally, we are interested in a small set of questions. What are the basic economic institutions within which individuals conduct their lives—property, labor, legal system, family, political system, and so on? What about the prior distribution of property and human assets that so directly affects outcomes for individuals? What are the economic processes at work that transform the current matrix of institutions and assets into future states of the economy? How does this matrix play out in terms of the well-being of the population? How does the institutional setting give rise to the observed pattern of human well-being distributed over class and region in the given economy? And what policy tools are available to increase the productivity of poor countries and improve the well-being of their people?

Goals of Economic Development

Why does economic development matter? Economic institutions and development are vitally important because we care about people and because the most basic life prospects of people are determined by the level and nature of the economies within which they live and work. If the economy is "poor," then many in the population will be poor. If the economy is stagnant, then the life prospects of the people will not change significantly over time. And if the economy is highly stratified, then some people's life prospects are dramatically worse than those of others.

Economic development is a process guided by agents for particular purposes. States, nongovernmental organizations (NGOs), and bilateral and multilateral agencies attempt to influence the direction and pace of economic development. So what can we say about the goals that give or ought to give direction to these processes?[3] Several possible goals emerge from the development literature: to increase the national income, to increase per capita income, to increase the productivity of the agriculture and manufacturing sectors, to reduce poverty, to reduce hunger, to support a process of industrial development and urbanization, and so forth. Different development strategies affect these goals in different ways; perhaps more important, different strategies have dramatically different consequences for the various strata of society in the less developed country. Put another way, different development strategies produce different sets of winners and losers. It is insufficient, therefore, to speak only of "modernization" or economic growth; it is also necessary to consider the effects on inequalities between various social groups that accompany a given development strategy.

Economists generally contend that the ultimate goal of economic development is to create a process of sustained economic growth, defined as sustained rise in per capita gross domestic product. This definition identifies the economic condition that is necessary for rising incomes and rising domestic welfare—in other words, *enduring growth in per capita income*.[4] The central characteristics of this process are easy to describe as well: modernization of industry and agriculture, technical and organizational innovations leading to increased labor productivity, and establishment of efficient economic institutions. This definition takes us in the direction of the variables of gross domestic product, population size, and trends in both over time. On this approach, the challenge of development economics is to identify the policy tools available to most effectively stimulate growth within the circumstances of low income and low capital accumulation that are found in the less developed world. Economic growth leads to increases in per capita income and wealth—so, on average, the members of society are materially better off each year.

Some development economists have qualified their exclusive emphasis on economic growth by directing attention to the issue of *equity within development*. Societies differ substantially in the degree of inequality that is created by the basic institutions of society—economic, social, and political arrangements that affect the individual's ability to pursue his or her life plan. Wealth and income inequalities are particularly salient in the context of economic development. Two societies may enjoy the same per capita levels of income but have vastly different human outcomes because of the extent of inequalities that each embodies. This observation has led some economists to argue for a strategy of "growth with equity."[5] According to this approach, planners and policymakers should choose policies in such a way as to satisfy two objectives: stimulation of growth in income per capita and enhancement of the equity of distribution of the benefits of economic life. Emphasis on equity involves a commitment to narrowing the range of social and economic inequalities in society. It also gives weight to the importance of working toward real equality of opportunity with respect to roles, positions, and resources within society.

However, a different approach to economic development begins with the notion of *human well-being*: the ability of the members of a society to live full, healthy, free, and rewarding lives.[6] In this perspective, economic growth is a means rather than an end. The goal of development is to enhance human well-being, and growth of per capita income is one important means of accomplishing this goal. Economic growth is important because access to income is one important factor in a person's ability to live a full life; low income is an abiding obstacle to the ability of the poor to pursue their life plans. Growth in per capita incomes is therefore an important goal for a developing society. On this approach, the planner should pay close attention to the factors and institutions that most directly influence human well-being throughout the society: reduction of poverty, expansion in the availability of jobs, stabilization of population growth, and support of the institutional basis for human capital (health systems, schools). Strategies should be selected that promise to enhance the overall well-being of the population over time, with special attention to the current and near-term future status of the poor.

This perspective on the human significance of poverty and development has begun to take hold within the development policy community, especially as a result of the writings of Amartya Sen. International conferences aimed at arriving at a shared set of development goals for the next fifty years have occurred since the mid-1990s, involving the OECD, the International Development Association (IDA), which is the World Bank's concessional lending affiliate, and the United Nations. This series of conferences culminated in the September 2000 Millennium Summit, in which the UN member states affirmed their commitment to a set of fundamental development goals for the next half century. These "millennium goals" include reducing extreme poverty, ensuring universal primary education, eliminating gender disparity in schooling, reducing infant and child mortality, reducing maternal mortality, combating HIV/AIDS and other diseases, implementing strategies for sustainable development, and developing global partnerships for development (World Bank 2001b: 6). These goals all pertain, directly or indirectly, to poverty and its human consequences.

What Is an Economy?

PRODUCTION AND THE CIRCULATION OF COMMODITIES

An economy can be described as an existing configuration of people, institutions, and technology through which goods and services are produced and distributed. Labor and tools, through specific social institutions, are applied to nature to produce goods—agricultural goods, manufactured goods, intangible services—that directly or indirectly relate to the satisfaction of human needs. Persons earn incomes that permit them to own or use some of these goods and services.[7] A nation's wealth can be measured as the sum of its natural resources, its human capital (labor skills, talents, and time), and its financial and real capital—factories, buildings, railroads, communications systems. It involves technology, knowledge, labor, and social relations and institutions (including the property system). An economy is a cyclical process, proceeding from a given set of economic inputs and giving rise to a given set of outputs—which become inputs in the next cycle of production. Goods are produced, goods are traded domestically and internationally, incomes are generated and assigned, savings are accumulated, and a national income is established. We can assess the effectiveness of an economy in a number of different dimensions. Production is more or less efficient. Agriculture is more or less capable of satisfying the food needs of the population. Technology is deployed at a given level. Institutions are more or less efficient at providing coordination and motivation for producers.

Figure 2.1 provides a diagram of this schematic description of an economy. Examination of the diagram shows that it is possible to increase the output, efficiency, or productivity of an economy in various ways. New technologies can be discovered and applied; more efficient systems of management can be designed; the labor force can be expanded; workers can be better educated (and therefore more productive); more land and other natural resources can be brought into production; and economic institutions can be enhanced for greater efficiency, incentive, or equity. Each of these avenues suggests a strategy or tactic of economic development, such as technological innovation, human capital development, exploitation of natural resources, enhancement of economic infrastructure (transportation, for example), or rapid accumulation of capital goods.

This schematic account highlights the most important components of an economy:

- Institutions (property system, wage system, land tenure, education and training, market system, banking and credit, government agencies, policies, decisionmaking processes)
- Technology (tools, machines, scientific knowledge, engineering knowledge)
- Capital (accumulated stocks of buildings, factories, mines, communications and transportation facilities)

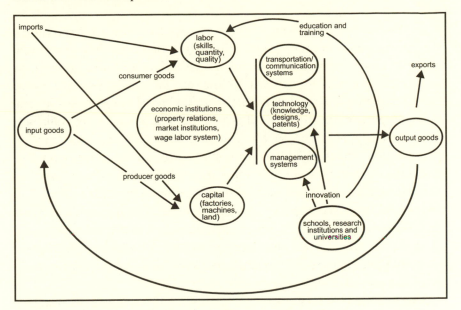

Figure 2.1   Schematic model of an economy

Economies in a process of sustained development display a trend toward what economists call "structural transformation"—a shift of the workforce from labor-intensive agriculture to manufacturing and industry. This change almost always goes along with a shift in the rural-urban balance of the population. As agriculture is modernized, it typically becomes less labor intensive. Therefore, fewer farm laborers are needed to accomplish agricultural tasks (as a result of mechanization, irrigation, and the application of pesticides, herbicides, and fertilizers). As farm jobs disappear, manufacturing expands (commonly in and around cities), leading to an expansion in the number of jobs available in manufacturing. And so, we should witness a transition in the labor force from agriculture to manufacturing and service sectors. This process should also reflect a transition from low-productivity labor to medium- and high-productivity labor, which in turn should result in rising incomes for workers in the high-productivity sectors and firms.

A final key component of a functioning economy is that of technique and technology: the mix of cultivation and manufacturing techniques and technologies through which workers transform raw materials and intermediate products into final products. All production uses some form of technology.

But one of the central elements of the process of economic modernization is the discovery and adoption of new technologies that result in an overall increase in productivity or efficiency (reflected in Figure 2.1 as "schools, research institutes and universities"). What are the social and institutional factors that stimulate rapid and effective technological innovation? It is clear that multiple relevant factors are at play in this regard. First is the availability of financial support for research and development. New ideas and their implementation cannot be achieved without the expenditure of resources. Second is the availability of effective research institutions, including universities and research centers. Third, because technological innovation is difficult or impossible if the overall level of education and skill in the population is low, an effective system of schooling is an important ingredient. Finally, an appropriate set of incentives for innovators is needed, in the form of intellectual property rights and the right to retain profits on more productive technologies when implemented.

Economic development has to do with improving economic performance. But what dimensions define the ways in which we would like to see economic improvement realized? Central measures of an economy include at least efficiency, productivity, equity of distribution, effective deployment of technology, and overall a high-level provision of material well-being for the whole population. We care about efficiency because inefficiency is equivalent to a waste of resources—resources that could otherwise be used to satisfy human needs. We care about productivity (and increasing productivity) because growth in productivity leads to an overall increase in the ability to satisfy the basic human needs of a given population. We care about equity because extreme inequality of wealth, income, and access to social goods implies that some citizens will have dramatically worse life prospects than others. We care about the deployment of technology because it promises to increase productivity and to reduce the deadening and dehumanizing aspects of work (in agriculture or manufacturing, for example). And finally, we care about material well-being because it is crucial for the ability of persons to flourish as human beings.

Thus, economic development can be characterized by various measures, including improvements in the health and education of the population, improvements in nutritional status, or modernization of the technologies of production. But a particularly central measure is the criterion of sustained growth in per capita income. An economy undergoing economic development creates a larger national income from one period to the next. This is the criterion of economic growth, and it is measured as a percentage of the base year national income. Another important growth measurement is the rate of population increase over time. If both national income and population are increasing at the same rate, then per capita income is constant. But if national income is rising more rapidly than population, then it may be possible to create the basis for a rising standard of living for the population. (This is only a possibility, however, because much depends on the pattern of income distribution that is present. Rising inequalities can concentrate the gains of growth in the top income deciles [Fields 1980].)

The goals of economic development policy can now be described at a high level of abstraction. The aim is to modify various inputs or features of the economy so as to improve the outputs and system properties in one or more ways: increasing productivity, increasing wealth, increasing equality/equity, increasing the well-being of the population, increasing the average education and health of the population, increasing environmental quality, and improving governmental institutions and the level of democracy. (I will discuss the goals of economic development more fully in the next chapter.) All of these goals are related in complex and sometimes contradictory ways. Consequently, plans that increase productivity might also increase inequality, plans that increase environmental quality might decrease growth potential, and so forth.

THE CREATION OF INCOMES

How do people earn their livings within a set of economic relations? Individuals have needs—among them, food, shelter, clothing, education, health care, transportation, and communication. These needs are represented in Figure 2.1 under the rubric of "consumer goods." But how do people meet their needs and gain access to consumer goods? The economic institutions of the given society (property relations and market institutions, for example) determine the answer to this question. Consider these means of access:

- Wages
- Profits, interest, rents
- Provisions by the state
- Self-production (e.g., peasant farming)

Figure 2.2 provides a simple representation of the flow of income through a model economy. The national income is distributed through existing economic institutions across categories of income flowing to individuals, corporations, and the state. Incomes are generated through the production and sale of goods and services. These incomes are distributed to the agents within the production process (workers, businesspersons, farmers, service providers, lenders, government) through a specific set of economic institutions (for example, wage labor, sharecropping, the credit system, the tax system).

Consider the human realities of the abstract system I am describing. An economy represents a set of social positions for the men and women who comprise it. These persons have a set of human needs—nutrition, education, health care, housing, clothing, and the like. And they require access to the opportunities that exist in society—opportunities for employment and education, for example. The various positions that exist within the economy in turn define the entitlements that persons have—wages, profits, access to food subsidies, rights of participation, and so on. Thus, the issue of fair opportunity of access to economic positions (jobs) and the means of gaining the skills needed for performance of these positions (education) is critical for the material well-being of individuals within the economy.

The material well-being of a person—the standard of living—is chiefly determined by the degree to which his or her entitlements through these various sources of income provide the basis for acquiring more than enough goods in all the crucial categories that permit the individual to flourish (A. Sen 1981). If wages are low, then the consumption bundle that this income will afford is very limited. If business taxes are low, then business owners may retain more business income in the form of profits, which will support larger consumption bundles and larger savings. There is thus a degree of conflict of interest among the agents within the economic system; the institutions of distribution may favor workers, lenders, business owners, or the state, depending on their design. An economy is not a zero-sum system, however, because it is possible for a redesign of existing economic institutions to result in an increase in the total national income while at the same time altering the balance of incomes flowing to the several categories of income earners.

Central in this schematic account are the institutions and social relations through which economic processes take place. This complex includes, first, the property system. The property system defines how individuals and corpo-

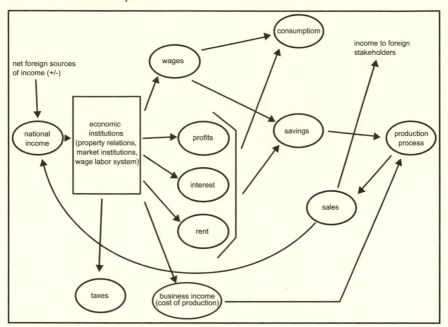

Figure 2.2 Flow of incomes through model economy

rations acquire and retain physical and nonphysical assets. What rights does the property owner possess? How is land owned? Is there a mix of private and public property (e.g., public ownership of utilities and roads)? Are there restrictions on the use and disposal of private property? What are the legal conditions of wage labor? Second, the institutions of the state—regulation, fiscal policy, property and contract law—set the context of economic activity. Third, there are the specific forms of labor in a given economy—farm labor, industrial labor, service labor; high-skilled versus unskilled labor; and so forth. Finally, there are the many ways in which self-seeking individuals can take advantage of existing institutional arrangements, leading to the possibility of corruption, both private and public.

Why do institutions matter? They matter because they affect efficiency and growth. A central discovery of the "new institutionalism" is that institutions have importance within economic development comparable to that of technological change (Brinton and Nee 1998; North 1990; Ostrom 1990). Bad institutions create perverse incentives for participants and interfere with both growth and efficiency. And economic growth is important because it increases the inherent capacity of a given society to satisfy the needs of its citizens. Institutions also matter because they affect the distributive outcomes that arise, and these in turn affect the justice of those outcomes and the well-being of all groups within the society. In addition, institutions matter because they set the terms of social cooperation, and they will be perceived as just or unjust in ways that affect the stability and productivity of society.

A substantial shortcoming of neoclassical approaches to development theory is the insufficient attention they pay to the institutional determinants of income distribution (L. Taylor 1990, 1983). Analysis of these institutional arrangements is mandatory if we are to have an informed basis for designing poverty-alleviating strategies of development. Local institutional arrangements—the property system, the institutions of credit, the characteristics of labor markets, and the circumstances of political power—decisively influence the distribution of the benefits of economic growth in existing rural economies. A chief determinant of the distribution and character of poverty in a given economy is the system of entitlements that the economy creates for its population: the means through which persons gain income through wages, interest and rent, sales of products, state-funded subsidies, and the like, as well as the distribution of ownership rights in productive assets. It is therefore essential to consider the institutional framework that determines the generation of income.

Institutional Factors in Defining the Circumstances of the Poor

Throughout this book, the condition of groups who are especially disadvantaged within developing societies is highlighted. We are particularly interested in poverty because poverty is the central condition through which human well-being is frustrated and blocked. Poverty is the core ill of economic development. To begin to understand the economic determinants of poverty, we must examine more closely the economic and social institutions through which people earn their livings. The particular institutional arrangements of a rural economy have profound effects on the character and distribution of poverty.

The most pervasive economic institution is the market: the institutional setting in which buyers and sellers, producers and workers meet and exchange products at market-determined prices. Goods are produced within any economy. Within a market economy, they are sold at a price that is set by the market mechanism resulting from competition among buyers and sellers. The market mechanism, ideally, applies to input prices as well as output prices; the central theorem of neoclassical economics is that the allocation of goods and services that results from competitive markets is optimal in technically definable ways. If political institutions interfere with market pricing—by setting minimum or maximum prices or by providing subsidies for producers or consumers—then these optimal outcomes are frustrated. For instance, if the state sets a lower-than-market price for grain in order to assure affordable food prices for consumers, there will be an insufficient supply of grain as producers shift production to more lucrative products. So markets have the advantage allocating resources, incomes, and commodities in a pattern that corresponds to the distribution of consumer demand and resource availability. However, markets distribute incomes on the basis of the productivity of the asset (labor, land, capital), and they distribute commodities on the basis of ability to pay. So it also follows that markets, when conjoined with sparse assets and low-productivity labor skills, often result in low incomes to disadvantaged groups in society. If we are to offset this outcome, specific steps must be taken to moderate the workings of the market.

A chief economic determinant of income is the ownership of property, including physical property, financial assets, and skills and knowledge. Ownership of property generates income as rent, interest, profit, wages, or subsistence. Landowners have choices through which they can generate incomes on their holdings: They can manage the property themselves and derive profits directly, or they can rent the land to others and derive income through the resulting rent. Owners of substantial financial resources are able to lend their capital for a rate of interest or invest capital in a profitable enterprise. The owner of a concentration of natural resources (e.g., petroleum or forests) can sell the resource directly or can sell licenses for access to the resource. And so it goes: Ownership of property conveys on the owner the ability to extract income from the use of the property.

Within a market economy, the income flowing to a "factor" of production, including labor, is related to the productivity of that factor. The low productivity of the labor of the poor is almost guaranteed by the low degree to which the poor have access to the services (education, health care) that would enhance the value of their single asset, labor capacity. Illiterate, innumerate workers are less productive than their better-educated counterparts, with the result that their incomes are lower as well. So a reasonably direct way of improving the welfare of the poor is to increase the productivity of their labor through education and training.

These points emphasize the centrality of ownership of assets in the distribution of income. Land is often very unequally distributed, access to credit is markedly uneven, ownership of capital is very narrowly concentrated, and access to education is distinctly unequal. The poor are poor, in large part, because they control few assets beyond their labor power. It is a familiar truth that productive activity requires proper tools; in economic terms, value added is a function of the amount of capital set into motion by a quantity of labor. The poor have scant access to capital goods; consequently, the products of their labor have relatively little value, and their incomes remain low. For this reason, many observers of poor countries have argued for the importance of land reform and other types of property reform (Herring 1983; Adelman 1978; Chenery et al. 1974).

The details of the land tenure system determine the relative shares of farm income that flow to tenant and landlord—thus profoundly affecting the ability of the tenant to survive hard times. The terms of labor hiring likewise have substantial effects on the well-being of workers: Where employers are required to meet minimal conditions of wage, security, health, and safety, workers who find employment will be better off. Economic institutions channel income into the hands of various groups; to the degree to which these institutions are skewed in the direction of the interests of the rich, the poor will suffer.

Another important group of institutions that are crucial in determining the quality of life of a population can be placed in the category of "public action"—programs and policies created and funded by the state (Drèze and Sen 1989). The economic condition of the poor depends a great deal on the character and quality of government programs for social welfare, such as food subsidy programs, rural health and education programs, and credit regulations and provision. The individual's well-being is influenced by the amenities and services that are provided to him or her by government. Is education free or subsidized? Is there a system of publicly financed health care? Does the state provide a social security net for unemployment, pensions, or disability? Are there state subsidies for food, transportation, or other necessities of life? The state is a substantial player in determining the well-being of the poor in developing societies (often by inaction rather than action). But equally important are the negative effects of state policy: antirural bias in agricultural policy, restrictive migration policies, antiagricultural bias in national credit programs, and the like.

For most people in developing societies, the main determinant of income is the structure of the institutions of employment that are in place in a given economy. Individuals who do not own significant physical assets are compelled to earn their incomes through their skills, knowledge, and time. They may sell their labor to an employer—farmer, manufacturer, or merchant. They may sell services directly to consumers—as barbers, house painters, martial arts instructors, or knife grinders. They may establish themselves as artisans, employing tools and skills to produce goods for consumers—as coffin makers, carpenters, or jewelers. Or they may become peddlers and merchants on a small scale, purchasing a stock of goods and selling these goods for a profit.

An important determinant of the standard of living, therefore, is the complex of regulations and practices that surround the system of wage labor. Are there regulations on health and safety in the workplace? Do workers have the right to join independent unions? Do they have the right to strike or boycott in support of their economic demands? Do workers have effective protection against violence and coercion as they pursue their economic demands? Answers to these questions determine the degree to which workers are able to secure their interests and needs—decent wages, safe working conditions, or some measure of job security.

The category of wage labor is itself a broad one, with much variation around the dimensions of skill level, wage level, predictability of employment, and quality of the working environment. Casual farm labor may involve extensive seasonality in the availability of work, as well as regular circuits of sojourning following the seasons of cultivation. The worker in a traditional urban factory may face harsh working conditions, long hours, and low wages.[8] Finally, combinations of activities are possible in many poor people's lives, for instance, handicraft production at home, seasonal agricultural labor, episodes of factory labor, and cultivation of a garden to meet some subsistence needs.

Here, then, we have a more segmented analysis of the microeconomy of poverty—the economic relations and categories that determine that particular groups will have low incomes. An important consequence follows from this analysis: Different groups of the poor may be very differently affected by different kinds of economic policies. This is true because the income and security of a given group depend on the stability of the economic relations within which it finds itself, so measures designed to improve one group's lot may actually harm another group. A classic case is the use of state-enforced grain prices to keep food prices low. Policies of this sort may have some immediate benefit for certain parts of the urban poor, but the policy has a depressing effect on farm incomes and output (since farmers, large and small, have less of an incentive to increase production). Moreover, a contraction of grain production will lead to a contraction in the demand for labor as well and a reduction in the incomes flowing to small farmers. (See Varshney 1995 for analysis of these sorts of effects in India's food price policies.)[9]

So far, I have looked at the institutional framework of income creation and distribution, noting that poverty is, in large part, the result of the individual's position within a set of entitlement-generating institutions. But there is also an important geographic dimension to poverty. Some regions are inherently poorer than others. Furthermore, there is an uneven distribution of resources across any national economy. Some regions have good cropland, whereas others have poor soil. Some regions contain extensive natural resources— coal, oil, or mineral deposits. Some are advantaged within the transportation system (ports, rail and road hubs, and so on), thereby making investment and economic activity more attractive to outsiders. And frequently, these patterns of unequal distribution of assets tend to coincide, so that poor farming areas are also poorly served by the transportation system, have low levels of social investment in health and education, and have low levels of nonagricultural economic activity. Disadvantaged and peripheral areas will tend to be poorer across the board than more advantaged areas.

As one important example, China's economy since 1949 has largely succeeded in reducing intraregional inequalities of wealth and income, through land reform and other social policies. But China has been much less successful in evening out interregional inequalities (Lyons 1991). Coastal cities and their hinterlands have gained substantially in past decades, whereas interior provinces have lagged behind. The most acutely disadvantaged provinces are in the southwest and northwest areas of the country (Perkins and Yusuf 1984).[10]

A clear result of this analysis of the diverse social positions of the poor has to do with the structure of stratification within a developing economy. We may think of the institutions and economic relations that define a given economy as a distributive system, channeling flows of income to various groups. It is also apparent that substantial inequality exists in most such systems in the developing world, with large streams of income flowing to some social groups and irregular trickles flowing to others. In analyzing patterns of inequality in particular countries and regions, it is important to ask, What are the distributive institutions through which these patterns emerge?

This analysis is important because a central determinant of the individual's quality of life is the sum of wages he or she is able to gain throughout the course of a year. And this in turn depends on the availability and character of the economic opportunities that confront the individual in the local environment. The poor have few assets to sell within a market economy. They are land-poor or landless and are dependent on the sale of unskilled labor for income. Beyond that, the institutional arrangements of poor countries—the property system, national political arrangements, and local power relationships—commonly leave the poor with little access to land and little political power through which to influence state policy. This analysis suggests that there are three broad avenues for boosting the income and well-being of the poor: improving their access to productive assets (chiefly land and education), increasing the demand for labor, and increasing the flow of state resources into amenities for the poor. This observation suggests several strategies for poverty reduction, among them employment-intensive strategies of development, asset redistribution programs (land reform, for example), economic programs that increase unskilled employment,[11] and what Drèze and Sen (1989) refer to as "public policy" spending—the provision of health and education services to the rural poor.

Concepts of Growth, Inequality, and Poverty

In this section, I will briefly review several central issues in the theory of economic development: the concept of national income and growth, the measures that can be used to analyze inequalities, and the several concepts that have been advanced in terms of which to conceptualize poverty.

National Income

One direct measure of the wealth of an economy is its gross national product (GNP) per capita; another is its gross domestic product per capita. The concept of gross national product can be defined as the sum of the value of finished goods and services produced by a society during a given year [excluding] intermediate goods. . . . Gross domestic product (GDP) is similar to GNP except that it excludes income earned by citizens of a country who are resident abroad but includes all production within the country including that that involves payments of income to people outside the country. (Gillis 1987: 39)

Gross domestic product is thus a measure of the value of all goods and services created in a given year or, in other words, the wealth produced annually. And because each dollar generated through the sale of a good or service becomes a dollar of income for someone (net of depreciation and indirect taxes; see Gillis 1987: 74), GDP also measures the national income.

Gross domestic product is important because it is a measure of the overall productive capacity of the society. Other things being equal, a society with a greater per capita GDP is more able to permit its citizens to achieve an adequate level of material well-being.

A prominent concern within development economics is the rate of growth in the GDP. To what extent is the given economy successfully expanding the nation's wealth and income through a variety of means (modernization of agriculture and manufacturing, improvement of infrastructure, effective savings and investment, and so forth)? An economy that shows constant levels of GDP over time is one that has little or no capacity to increase the overall standard of living of its people over time.

A related concern has to do with the relation between population and GDP and between population growth and growth of GDP. If we divide the nation's income by the population, we determine its income per capita. And if GDP is growing more rapidly than population, then this ratio will rise—reflecting a growing per capita income in the country. By contrast, if population is increasing at 3 percent and GDP is also rising at that rate, then the average income per capita remains constant. This means that the economy has little capacity to improve the material well-being of its citizens.[12] Figure 2.2 represents the components of gross domestic product in the model economy.

Inequalities of Income and Wealth

Important as absolute national income levels are, we must also consider the patterns of income distribution in various national economies. Here, we will find substantial variation across countries. In many poor nations, inequalities have grown significantly since the 1970s: Brazil, the countries of Central

Percent of income

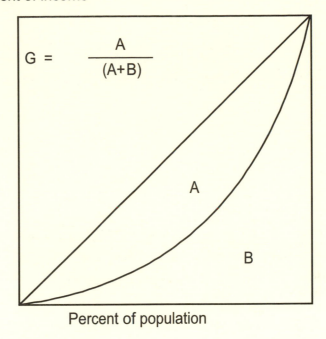

Percent of population

Figure 2.3   Lorenz curve of income

America, the Philippines, Thailand, and Nigeria, for example. In other developing nations, however, inequalities have remained constant or fallen, as in Korea, Indonesia, China, and Nicaragua. Inequalities are more pronounced in most countries in Latin America than in most countries in Asia.

Income inequalities can be measured in a variety of ways. Two common measures are the Gini coefficient (shown in Figure 2.3) and the shares of income flowing to each quintile of income earners. The dispersion of income is often depicted by a graph representing cumulative shares of income across cumulative shares of population (referred to as a Lorenz curve; see Figure 2.3). A society in which income is equally distributed across all persons will have a straight-line Lorenz curve at 45 degrees to the origin. The Lorenz curve for a particular income distribution permits us to read off how much of the national income is flowing to a given percentile of income earners. Corresponding to each Lorenz curve is a simple measure of inequality—the Gini coefficient. This construct measures the degree of inequality represented by a given Lorenz

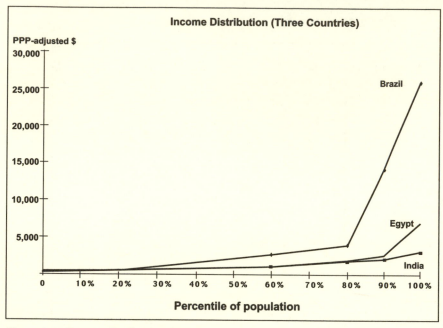

Figure 2.4   Income distribution data

curve as the ratio of the area enclosed by the curve and the 45-degree line to the area below the 45-degree line; thus, perfect equality corresponds to a Gini coefficient of 0, and perfect inequality corresponds to a coefficient of 1.[13] (The Gini coefficients and income shares to the poor—the bottom 20 percent of the population—are presented in Figure 2.5 for several developing countries.)

Another important measure of inequalities involves disaggregating the national income over quintiles of the population. This exercise lets us examine the proportion of national income that flows to the poorest 20 percent (or 40 percent) of the population; countries with more extreme inequalities display a lower percent of income flowing to the lower quintiles. Figure 2.4 provides a graph of the income shares for three countries (Egypt, India, and Brazil). The ratio of the income flowing to the top 20 percent of population in comparison to the bottom 40 percent of income gives a single measure of the degree of income inequality that permits comparison across countries.

Inequalities have generally worsened in many developing countries. The average ratio of the income of the top quintile to that of the poorest two quintiles rose from 4.14 to 4.45, 5.03, and 5.18 in four periods measured between 1956 and 1960 and 1971 and 1975.[14] These data suggest a downward trend in the share of national income flowing to the poorest 40 percent of population in these countries. As we have seen above, these inequalities derive, in large part, from the institutional arrangements through which income is generated and distributed, including the property and wage systems.

Poverty

How can we measure the degree and depth of poverty in various countries? There are two complementary approaches through which we can identify the poor.[15] First, we can identify poverty with low income. On this approach, we imagine the population as ranked in order of income levels (individual or family). We then choose a poverty budget: a level of income that is just sufficient to satisfy the minimal subsistence needs of an individual or a family. The poor are then defined as the portion of the income distribution of population that falls below this income level. These persons and families will find themselves unable to purchase enough goods—food, clothing, or shelter—to fully satisfy their human needs. They will tend to be malnourished, poorly clothed, and in poor health as a more or less immediate consequence of their low income. They constitute what we might refer to as the "absolutely poor." The current World Bank definition of the poverty line is an income lower than $1 per day (with moderate poverty defined as $2 per day). By the former criterion, the poor comprised 44 percent of India's population in 1997 (World Bank 2001b: table 4).

The other chief paradigm for defining poverty involves a substantive theory of human well-being in terms of health, longevity, freedom, and education—what A. K. Sen refers to as "human flourishing." Poverty is defined as the failure to achieve these forms of human flourishing. (See A. Sen 1999 and Nussbaum 2000 for the most important expressions of this approach to the definition of poverty.) Low income is a significant cause of the failure to achieve full human flourishing. But there are other causes as well, and there are other avenues of alleviating a country's poverty besides the strategy of "growing" the national income. The attractions of this approach to the definition of poverty are twofold. First, the approach leads us to focus on the genuine human values that are invoked by extensive poverty. Second, it encourages us to ask the critical question, What are the various types of policy reform through which the ills of poverty can be addressed?

Let us examine the "low-income" approach more closely. On the low-income approach, we have a simple definition of the poor: They are those persons or households whose incomes fall below the poverty line. We can then calculate the poverty rate for a given country; it is the percentage of persons or households who fall below the poverty line. This definition is undiscriminating, however. For one thing, it cannot distinguish between a case in which large numbers of individuals fall just below the poverty line and a case in which there is a wide dispersion of income below the poverty line. Thus, it does not provide a basis for measuring the depth of poverty.

Further, the low-income criterion of poverty fails to take into account non-income factors that influence the well-being of the poor. Public amenities provided for the population at large or for targeted subgroups are particularly important in this regard, but various types of informal assistance, subsistence farming, and other forms of in-kind receipts also affect the condition of the poor in a given society. It is entirely possible that the poor of Sri Lanka are better off than the poor of Brazil, even though they have the same income, because they have access to publicly funded goods and services that are not reflected in this accounting.

The low-income approach has one additional analytical flaw: It conflates radically heterogeneous groups. Some of the poor are poor because they are aged, some because they are physically handicapped or ill, some because they are unemployed, some because they have too little land to support subsistence needs, and so forth. It is important to supplement our analysis of poverty, therefore, by offering a functional analysis of the income structure of a given economy—an analysis that breaks down income earners into groups defined by source of income. Thus, we can distinguish landless workers, subsistence farmers, commercial farmers, itinerant merchants, landlords, owners of large businesses, owner-operators of small businesses, and so on. For whatever functional taxonomy of income earners that we provide, we can then consider the distribution of income within each group. Some of these groups will have a low average income, a low minimum income, and a low dispersion around the mean; that is, most members of these groups are poor.

These considerations show the importance of disaggregating national income over the population as a whole. But there is another form of disaggregation that is valuable as well—disaggregation over time for a given person or family. Two kinds of temporal variation affect the status of the poor: life-cycle variation in income-earning power and seasonal fluctuation in incomes. Consider the second point first. It may be that a very poor family in West Bengal subsists on an annual income of $200 per year, along with the products of a small piece of land. But this income and the produce have a strongly cyclical character over the course of the year as demand for labor fluctuates, leading to employment and wages in some seasons and unemployment and no wages in other seasons. And the period just before the harvest is likely to be a lean season as well: Food stocks have begun to run out, harvest-based employment has not yet begun, and grain prices are at their highest point of the year. During these periods, the very poor may become absolutely destitute, unable to buy food in sufficient quantities to provide one meal a day. Thus, poverty has its own cycle of ebbs and flows, and if we think only of the average level of well-being of the poor, we will have missed completely the extended periods of even greater hardship that have occurred throughout the year.

The other important kind of temporal fluctuation in poverty is life-cycle variation. A poor family is in its best circumstances when both parents are present and healthy and when the children are old enough to contribute their labor to the family's well-being as well. At the beginning and end of this period, by contrast, the earning capacity of the family is reduced. During pregnancy and infancy, the mother's capacity to labor is often diminished to some degree, and in the early years of childhood, the offspring are hungry mouths rather than sources of labor. At the other end of the cycle, aging, illness, and death once again reduce the income-earning capacity of the family. (Jean Drèze [1990] has written very movingly of the terrible situation of widows in rural India.) So when we think of the situation of the rural poor, it is important not to imagine a sort of homogeneous level of deprivation. Instead, there will inevitably be a range of experiences, from the disadvantaged but viable to the horrendously deprived at the bottom. And the various measures of well-being discussed earlier—infant mortality and health and nutrition status—are certain to be correlated with these variations.

The fluctuations of income over time point up the very great value of income stability as a factor underlying the well-being of the poor. A somewhat higher average annual income may involve long periods of unemployment and subsequent deprivation throughout significant parts of the year.

Both criteria—low income and low indicators of well-being—are important for our understanding of poverty in the developing world. Giving poverty a high priority within economic development means choosing strategies that (1) are particularly effective in improving the incomes and welfare attaching to members of poor functional groups, or (2) aid the transition process for members of poor groups moving to nonpoor groups (for example, landless workers in transit to urban industrial employment).

There is an extensive literature within development studies devoted to the relationship between inequalities and poverty in development. It is important to separate out inequalities and the direction of change of inequalities from the issue of poverty and the direction of change of poverty levels. The fact that there are differences in the distribution of income across economies means that two countries with the same per capita income may have substantially different amounts of income flowing to the poorest income groups. So if we are concerned with poverty, we need to pay close attention to the pattern of income distribution and to the amount and dispersion of income flowing to the poorest 20 to 40 percent of income earners. This observation suggests that we need to associate GDP data with a disaggregation of income across the population.

Figure 2.4 illustrates this set of facts. In this chart, the national incomes of India, Egypt, and Brazil are disaggregated over their populations. (These income data reflect dollars adjusted by purchasing power parity [PPP], based on 1987 data. The graph should be interpreted as representing a value for the average income flowing to the nth percentile of income earners.) There are substantial differences in the national income of these three economies, but as the chart demonstrates, the condition of the poor is strikingly similar in each case. Brazil's per capita income (PPP-adjusted) is $4,307, Egypt's is $1,357, and India's is $1,053. Brazil, then, is substantially better off than Egypt or India. However, Brazil's income distribution is much more skewed than that of either Egypt or India; the income distributions correspond to Gini coefficients of .358 for India, .419 for Egypt, and .591 for Brazil. The poorest quintiles of each of these countries receive approximately the same income. India and Egypt have about the same levels of income through the eightieth percentile, after which Egyptian income rises more rapidly than Indian income. In addition, the level of income of the Brazilian population begins to rise above those of Egypt and India after the poorest quintile, slowly at first and then very rapidly above the eightieth percentile. It is not unreasonable to interpret these data as showing that Brazil's relative affluence is chiefly concentrated on the upper quintiles of income earners, whereas the poor of Brazil are about as badly off as those of Egypt or India.

These points make it clear that economic growth by itself (improvement in per capita GDP) is not sufficient to produce improvement in the welfare of the poor. Instead, some growth strategies have harmful effects on the poor, and others have poverty-reduction effects.

Data and Outcomes

Economic development is an empirical phenomenon, and there are numerous sources of data with which we can study the process throughout the world. What are some of the sources of information that can help us arrive at well-informed judgments about these processes? Data about economic development are available at both ends of the spectrum of generality. Descriptive country data are provided in a number of reasonably rigorous sources. Particularly important are the annual reports published by the World Bank and the United Nations Development Programme—that is, the *World Development Report* and the *Human Development Report*. Each provides annual development data on more than 150 countries. Each also contains twenty to thirty statistical tables for these countries, representing several hundred variables grouped in different categories (among them "size of economy," "quality of life," "poverty," "distribution of income," "education," "energy," and "environment"). Both reports present the results of large-scale data collection and analysis efforts that are designed to permit comparison across country and across time.[17] There is some overlap between the two reports, but the UNDP document collects data that are pertinent to assessment of the status of human welfare indicators across all countries and regions. The UNDP approach is strongly informed by the "human well-being" approach championed by Sen, who also contributed to the design and methodology of these reports.

At the other end of the spectrum of generality are research studies of particular countries or particular development processes. The student who is interested in the economic development of India, for example, will find numerous studies that focus on such issues as agrarian relations (Desai 1979; Varshney 1995; Ramachandran 1990); environmental change (Agarwal and Narain 1989; Agarwal 1994); poverty reform (Kohli 1987); government policy (Hardgrave and Kochanek 1986; Kohli 1988); the green revolution (Byres and Crow 1983; B. Sen 1974); general economic conditions (Mellor 1976; Drèze and Sen 1995); or population dynamics (Mamdani 1973). Country-specific studies generally put forward claims about causation—how various structures or policies affect a given set of developmental processes. And they frequently provide a basis for making intranational comparisons that are masked at the national level. For example, there are very significant variations in measures of well-being across the states of India or the regions of China, and these differences are obscured by national-level statistics.

Finally, an important new source of information is available to students and researchers interested in economic development through the World Wide Web, in the form of data sources and position papers compiled by international agencies and nongovernmental agencies. The OECD website (www.oecd.org) provides access to major data resources maintained by that organization. Through this site, it is also possible to gain access to data and reports under the auspices of the OECD's Development Assistance Committee. Oxfam International provides information about its programs and the conditions of hunger and deprivation that it attempts to address on its website (www.oxfam.org). Similarly, the United Nations Development Programme maintains a valuable website (www.undp.org), as does the World Bank (www.worldbank.org), the British Overseas Development Institute (www.odi.org.uk), and the World Trade Organization (www.wto.org). The World Institute for Development Economics Research (WIDER) is an important international center for development research, and its website provides valuable research and data (www.wider.unu.edu). Several organizations maintain websites devoted to monitoring fair trade, labor practices, sweatshop practices, and fair trade agriculture (www.fairtrade.org.uk, www.fairlabor.org, www.fairtrade.net, www.workersrights.org). Human rights organizations have made good use of the Internet for disseminating their findings, including Human Rights Watch (www.hrw.org), Derechos Human Rights (www.derechos.org), and Amnesty International (www.amnesty.org). These are just a few useful sources; there are myriad others. The scholar, citizen, or consumer who wishes to be well informed about globalization has many powerful tools at hand, including search engines (such as www.google.com) that quickly locate relevant material on virtually any development topic.

Given the ready availability of data on economic development, it is unnecessary to provide extensive data tables in this chapter. But it may be useful to offer some examples of the sorts of information that can be assembled for describing and analyzing the situation of developing countries since the 1950s. Figure 2.5 presents economic and human development snapshots for eight countries in the late 1990s. The data categories include the major types of information needed in assessing and comparing the development experiences of various countries: basic economic data (national income, growth rates, foreign direct investment, indebtedness, measures of income inequalities); structural and causal factors (percent of workforce in agriculture, energy use); and human well-being measures (schooling, health status, infant mortality, and malnutrition). Based on this selection of data, we can pose questions about the state of development in single countries, and we can ask comparative questions across countries. (Notice, for example, that Indonesia's infant mortality rate is almost half of Nigeria's rate and that Indonesia's per capita income is almost four times that of Nigeria. Further, poverty rates in India and Indonesia are substantially greater than those in Brazil and Egypt.) Figure 2.6 provides data on these same variables for one country (Brazil) but over a forty-year period. This statistical presentation allows us to ask how conditions have changed over time. We can observe, for instance, that inequalities have apparently changed scarcely at all in Brazil; they started at a high level in the 1960s, and they continued in that range for the next forty years. Life expectancy for both men and women, however, has improved notably in Brazil over that same period. Carbon dioxide emissions—a variable that corresponds to industrial development but also represents a critical component of climate change—increased fivefold in Brazil from the 1960s to the 1990s. Also, we can see that official development assistance is inconsequential within Brazil's economy, and indebtedness is moderate (in comparison with more heavily indebted nations such as Indonesia or Sudan).

Several points emerge from this exercise. First, data are readily available through which we can form a reasonably detailed understanding of the conditions of economic development in many countries. Second, it is most important to be a critical user of such data sources—to pay attention to the criteria that are employed to define the measures of various categories, to assess the degree of accuracy that is likely to attach to the various measures, and to be alert to inconsistencies among measurements. (Why was there an eigh-

1995-99	Brazil	China	Costa Rica	Egypt	India	Indonesia	Nigeria	Sudan
Population, total (thousands)	163,658	1,229,651	3,462	60,406	962,907	200,445	117,632	27,771
GDP (constant 1995 US$ millions)	734,734	833,323	12,621	66,989	399,373	209,181	29,829	
GDP growth (annual %)	2.2	8.8	5.2	5.8	6.5	1.1	2.8	5.9
GDP per capita (constant 1995 US$)	4,489	677	3,646	1,108	414	1,045	254	
Labor force in agriculture (% of total)	25	48	21	34	67	44		
Life expectancy at birth, female (years)	71	71	79	68	64	67	50	56
Life expectancy at birth, male (years)	63	68	74	65	62	63	48	53
Life expectancy at birth, total (years)	67	70	77	66	63	65	49	55
Low-birthweight babies (% of births)	8		6	3	4	13		
Malnutrition prevalence, height for age (% of children under 5)	10.5	15.6	6.1	24.2	42.6	42.2		
Malnutrition prevalence, weight for age (% of children under 5)	5.7	12.4	5.1	12.9	45.43	4		
Physicians (per 1,000 people)	1.3	1.8	0.9	1.3		0.1		
CO2 emissions, industrial (kt)	288,203	3,555,728	5,274	111,081	1,014,806	251,830	88,902	3,813
CO2 emissions, industrial (metric tons per capita)	1.8	2.9	1.6	1.9	1.1	1.3	0.8	0.1
Foreign direct investment, net (BoP, current US$ millions)	18,784	38,337	486	738	2,628	2,124	1,336	259
Illiteracy rate, adult female (% of females ages 15 and above)	16	26	55	95	72	04	95	8
Illiteracy rate, adult male (% of males ages 15 and above)	16	10	53	53	49		31	33
School enrollment, primary, female (% gross)		120	103	94	90	111		46
School enrollment, primary, male (% gross)		120	104	107	110	115		55
School enrollment, secondary, female (% gross)		64	50	71	39	48		19
School enrollment, secondary, male (% gross)		72	46	82	59	55		22
Mortality rate, infant (per 1,000 live births)	35	32	13	51	72	44	82	72
poverty rate <$1/day PPP adjusted	5.1		9.6	3.1	44.2	26.3	70.2	
HDI	0.739	0.706	0.797	0.623	0.563	0.67	0.439	0.477
income ratio top 20%/bottom 40%	7.6	2.9	3.8	1.7	2.3	1.9	4.4	
%income to bottom 20%	2.5	5.9	4	9.8	8.1	8	4.4	
Gini coefficient	59.1		45.9	37.8	37.8	31.7	50.6	
official development assistance (% GNP)	0	0.3	0.3	2.4	0.4	1.3	0.5	2.3
debt (%GNP)	31	16	39	37	23	177	79	183

Figure 2.5   Summary of country data

Brazil	1960-64	1965-69	1970-74	1975-79	1980-84	1985-89	1990-94	1995-99
Population, total (thousands)	77,320	89,016	100,794	113,500	127,130	140,402	152,622	163,658
GDP (constant 1995 US $ millions)	143,046	179,918	291,052	427,118	499,472	597,788	627,432	734,734
GDP growth (annual % 5)		6.7	11	5.9	1.4	4.5	1.5	2.2
GDP per capita (constant 1995 US$)	1,849	2,016	2,876	3,758	3,934	4,256	4,110	4,489
Labor force in agriculture (% of total)					28.9	25.3	26.2	24.9
Life expectancy at birth, female (years)	57.3	59.5	61.7	63.9	66.16	8	69.6	70.9
Life expectancy at birth, male (years)	53.5	55.5	57.3	59.16	0	61.1	61.96	3
Life expectancy at birth, total (years)	55.4	57.5	59.4	61.4	62.9	64.5	65.7	66.9
Low-birthweight babies (% of births)						9.3		8
Malnutrition prevalence, height for age (% of children under 5)				32		15.4		10.5
Malnutrition prevalence, weight for age (% of children under 5)				18.47				5.7
Physicians (per 1,000 people)	0.4	0.4	0.5	0.6	0.8	1.3	1.4	1.3
CO2 emissions, industrial (kt)	54,886	72,975	113,434	172,892	181,156	208,140	230,912	288,203
CO2 emissions, industrial (metric tons per capita)	0.7	0.8	1.1	1.5	1.4	1.5	1.5	1.8
Foreign direct investment, net (BoP, current US$ millions)	-	-	-	1,671	1,873	1,166	1,035	18,784
Illiteracy rate, adult female (% of females ages 15 and above)			34	29	25	22	19	16
Illiteracy rate, adult male (% of males ages 15 and above)			27	24	22	20	18	16
School enrollment, primary, female (% gross)	93	108	119	87	97			
School enrollment, primary, male (% gross)	97	109	119	88	101			
School enrollment, secondary, female (% gross)	10	16	26	28	36			
School enrollment, secondary, male (% gross)	11	16	26	24	31			
Mortality rate, infant (per 1,000 live births)	112	102	93	81	67	57	43	35
poverty rate <$1/day PPP adjusted								5.1
HDI				0.639	0.672	0.687	0.708	0.739
income ratio top 20%/bottom 40%		6.2	9.5		7.7			7.6
%income to bottom 20%								2.5
Gini coefficient					60.5			59.1
official development assistance (% GNP)							-0.001	0.001
debt (% GNP)						49.1		30.6

Figure 2.6   Social indicators of development—Brazil

teenfold increase in foreign direct investment in Brazil in the late 1990s?) Third, it is possible to arrive at two sorts of comparisons on the basis of data of these sorts: comparisons across countries at a point in time and comparisons for a given country over a number of years. Both comparisons provide a valuable empirical basis for probing causation within economic development and for assessing the effectiveness of various policy "theories" that have been applied to development in the expectation of bringing about a range of desirable outcomes.

Notes

1. There is a large literature in the economics of development. Good textbooks on the subject include Gillis 1987, Todaro 1994, and Meier 1989. More specialized books on alternative strategies of development and the measurement of inequalities include Fields 1980, Seligson and Passé-Smith 1993, and K. Griffin 1988. Important recent theoretical essays on issues in economic development include Nussbaum 2000, A. Sen 1999, and Drèze and Sen 1995. An important handbook of development economics is Chenery and Srinivasan 1988, a volume that represents orthodox thinking on economic growth and development. Finally, valuable annual data sources on economic development are to be found in the *Human Development Report* (United Nations Development Programme 1990) and the World Bank's *World Development Report* (World Bank 1978).

2. Atul Kohli (1987) provides a fine analysis of the differences in policy and outcome in several Indian states. He attempts to demonstrate the centrality of party and policy in the experience of poverty reform in India. India provides a very important point of reference for development thinking, in that it illustrates a variety of strategies and outcomes that can help test our hypotheses and temper our generalizations about development.

3. It is also important to ask *whose* goals are in play—are they the goals of local political authorities, international lenders, U.S. foreign policymakers, or local people?

4. See Kuznets 1966 and Meier 1989 for various statements of this conception of economic growth. Chenery and Srinivasan 1988 is a rich sourcebook on development theory.

5. Particularly important in this tradition are Irma Adelman and Hollis Chenery.

6. The most persistent and effective voice in this tradition is that of Amartya Sen, who has placed the category of human flourishing at the center of his economic theorizing throughout his long and illustrious career. See particularly A. Sen 1984, 1993, and 1999, and Sen and Hawthorn 1987.

7. The school of "structuralist economics" has given particularly close attention to the importance of institutions, especially institutions of distribution, within modern economies (L. Taylor 1983, 1990).

8. For a detailed and current description of the coercive conditions of labor in China in the 1990s, see Chan 2001.

9. There is a large literature on food policy analysis in the developing world. See Streeten 1987; Sicular 1989; Timmer, Falcon, and Pearson 1983; Pinstrup-Andersen 1988; Pearson 1991; and Hollist and Tullis 1987.

10. Walther Aschmoneit has constructed a quality of life index based on the Chinese 1982 census that bears out this pattern (Delman, Ostergaard, and Christiansen 1990).

11. Keith Griffin (1988: 31) describes the requirements of a poverty-first strategy of development as involving the following elements: "(i) an initial redistribution of assets; (ii) creation of local institutions which permit people to participate in grass roots development; (iii) heavy investment in human capital; (iv) an employment intensive pattern of development, and (v) sustained rapid growth of per capita income."

12. A notable complication in measuring per capita income has to do with variations in purchasing power across national economies. If a significant part of the individual's consumption basket takes the form of locally traded goods, then a given dollar estimate of his or her wage will underestimate the size of the basket (and therefore the quality of life associated with that level of income). To correct for these international price differences, the United Nations undertook a program for adjusting estimates of per capita income to reflect differences in purchasing power in different settings (the International Comparison Program). This program permits a country-by-country estimate of "purchasing power parity" (PPP).

13. It is worth noting that the Gini coefficient represents less information than the full Lorenz curve; different Lorenz curves may possess the same Gini coefficient.

14. These estimates derive from data provided in *World Development Reports,* 1979–1991.

15. The literature on the definition of poverty is extensive. Useful sources include K. Griffin 1976; Fields 1980; Lipton 1983; Osmani 1982; Reutlinger and Selowsky 1976; and A. Sen 1980, 1981.

17. The World Bank also publishes a computer database on CD-ROM that gives the researcher easy access to much of the published development data included in the series of *World Development Reports* (World Bank 2001a).

3

Goals and Strategies for Economic Development

THIS CHAPTER WILL CONSIDER SOME of the goals that have been deemed central in defining the purposes of economic development. It will also examine the chief tools of intervention through which a given economy can be stimulated to economic growth. The discussion in the previous chapter focused on labor, technology, capital, environment, and institutional setting as key elements of the economic process. The challenge of economic development is conceptually simple: to discover innovations in one or more of these great factors that will result in increased productivity, efficiency, and equity in the economy; increased volume of products; and increased national income. How and where should we search out these potential innovations? And what guiding priorities should inform our choices among competing strategies?

Instruments of Economic Development Policy

In this section, I will discuss the tools and interventions that are available to economic development planners and how they can be aggregated into development strategies.

To stimulate economic growth, planners must accomplish a number of things. They need to find ways of stimulating investment in modern industry and agriculture. They need to encourage the expansion of the modern sectors of the economy. They must attempt to enhance increases in productivity throughout the economy. And they must help assure that the institutional prerequisites of an efficient economy are in place: smoothly functioning markets; efficient communications, transportation, and marketing infrastructures; and a low-overhead state that creates the conditions required for efficient economic growth without imposing the costs of corruption or unnecessary regulation that often interfere with economic transformation in developing societies.

Of particular concern is the infrastructure of the economy, including the efficiency and cost of transportation, the marketing system, and the system of communication. Here, the role of the state is generally reckoned to be large in any developing country, since these features of the economy have many of the properties of public goods. In an economy in which a fifth of the harvest may spoil during storage or the cost of transport from rural market to urban consumer is equal to the cost of growing the grain, development in these areas can have a major effect on output.

When human development and well-being are taken as central objectives within the development process, the planner needs to give attention to the services and resources that have the greatest promise of enhancing the well-being of the poor in a reasonable period of time. And many of these services fall within the category of public policy—state-funded programs aimed at improving the health, education, and nutrition of the poor.

Varieties of Economic Development Strategy

We can inventory the most important tools available to policymakers as they attempt to stimulate economic growth and transformation. Consider the following interventions and policies on the part of developing country governments in pursuit of economic development:

- Agricultural modernization—agricultural development, policies affecting grain prices and input prices, diffusion of technology and seeds, improvement of marketing systems
- Neoliberal reform—extending markets, "getting the prices right," reducing state intervention in the economy, ensuring property rights
- Improvement of human well-being through public policy—enhancing the infrastructures of health, education, and nutrition with special emphasis on the poor
- Establishment of a regulatory framework governing environment, health, safety, and conditions of labor
- Land and asset reform

- Encouragement of technological innovation and change—in agriculture, transport, communications, and industry
- State-guided investment in critical manufacturing sectors
- Encouragement of foreign direct investment
- Trade, tax, and tariff policies aimed at stimulating economic growth
- Industrial policy—export-led growth, import substitution, expansion of employment within the economy

This is a diverse collection of policy tools and approaches. Most of these approaches to economic development policy involve the exercise of state power in one way or another, through taxation, trade policy, institution building, regulation, or direct investment. But there are profound differences at the level of political values concerning the role that the state should play in development. Should the state be an important agent of economic activity? Should the state take a large responsibility for enhancing welfare? Or should the state restrict itself to establishing the legal and institutional framework of economic activity and permit private activity to determine the direction of development?

There is a diversity as well in the proximate goals toward which these policies are directed. Agricultural modernization takes its rationale from the fact that the majority of developing country populations are generally rural and agricultural, so modernization of agriculture is taken to be an important early step in improving the productivity of the economy as a whole. Agricultural modernization increases food security and rural incomes, and it also increases the potential pool of industrial labor—thereby enabling growth in the industrial sector. Neoliberal reform is inspired by the twin notions that the institutions of the market are the most powerful instruments of economic change and innovation available and that states tend to interfere with economic development through corruption, rent seeking, and excessive regulation. The strategy of land and asset reform proceeds from the theory that a high degree of inequality in access to land and other productive assets is an obstacle to both growth and equity and that justice and efficiency dictate that there should be a state-sanctioned process for redistributing assets.

Finally, there are varying levels of consistency among these approaches. Some can be exercised in combination, whereas others are in tension with each other. Neoliberal reform is generally unsympathetic to public policy welfare systems and to programs of asset redistribution. Advocates of the importance of public policy interventions in the economy generally acknowledge the power of the market, but they also emphasize the significance of market failures and the relative blindness of market-driven development to the conditions of the poor.

Existing Economic Development Strategies

Liberalization and Market-Driven Reforms

Neoliberalism comes very close to defining development orthodoxy today. The central assumption of development economists is that growth in per capita income is the fundamental goal of economic development and that efficient markets, privatization of economic life, and a severely restricted role for the state in welfare and economic regulation are the primary means of achieving this end.[1] On this approach, economic development is a largely technical process involving the improvement of market institutions, price reform, and free-market entrepreneurial activity. Growth and efficiency are the preeminent values. Free markets and privatization are emphasized. And it is generally held that distributive goals should not intrude; the state is regarded as a predatory, rent-seeking agency that almost inevitably interferes with efficient growth (Krueger 1991). A chief goal, therefore, is to minimize the role of the state—including subsidies and welfare systems. Market institutions should be permitted to select the most efficient techniques of production, products, and uses of resources.

"Liberalization" of national economies means reducing and eliminating trade barriers and tariffs. It means extending free markets within domestic economies and minimizing barriers to economic activity—for example, the abolition of price boards for agricultural commodities. And it means reforming domestic government policy in ways designed to enhance market processes—such as the reduction or elimination of food subsidies and the reduction of both social programs and regulations on economic activity. Finally, it often means reducing the role of the state altogether and reducing or eliminating existing social policies. International development agencies—including the World Bank—have placed great importance on liberalization and fiscal reform (and associated austerity programs) as central instruments of economic development.

The cluster of views that constituted the neoliberal agenda for development in the 1980s and early 1990s has been described as the "Washington consensus" (Williamson 1993). As summarized in the *World Development Report 2000/2001*, this consensus includes:

- Fiscal discipline
- Redirection of public expenditure toward education, health, and infrastructure investment
- Tax reform—broadening the tax base and cutting marginal tax rates Interest rates that are market determined and positive (but moderate) in real terms
- Competitive exchange rates
- Trade liberalization—replacement of quantitative restrictions with low and uniform tariffs
- Openness to foreign direct investment
- Privatization of state enterprises
- Deregulation—the abolition of regulations that impede entry or restrict competition (except for those justified on safety, environmental, and consumer protection grounds) and prudential oversight of financial institutions
- Legal security for property rights (World Bank 2001b: 63)

A direct element of liberalization is the determination of prices through competitive markets. Within a liberal regime, markets determine prices. The liberalization doctrine holds that prices reach equilibrium at the point at which "supply at price" equals "demand at price." Over the long term, economists reason that this system will optimize the use of society's resources. In circumstances where there is an undersupply of a good, the price for that good rises, permitting higher-than-average profits. New producers recognize the profit opportunity and begin producing the good. The supply rises, and the price falls. The slogan "Getting the prices right" serves as a reasonably accurate summary of the neoliberal approach to economic development (Timmer 1986). A central goal of neoliberal reform, then, is to establish the institutional context needed for market transactions throughout the economy.

Some goods have a particularly profound effect on the well-being of the poor. Access to food, energy, and transportation is particularly critical. When food prices fluctuate upward for an extended time while wages remain constant, the effect can be severe undernourishment for the poor. Likewise, when wages fluctuate downward in an environment of stable food prices, the poor will suffer nutritionally (A. Sen 1981). In other words, unconstrained market processes can lead to fluctuations in basic goods prices and wages that impose severe hardship on the poor, sometimes for extended periods. In these circumstances, it is crucial that there be state-supported mechanisms to ameliorate these hardships. Such mechanisms might include state-subsidized food supplements for the poor, state works programs for underemployed workers, and state-financed education programs that enhance the skills of underemployed workers.

Powerful criticisms of the liberalization agenda have been advanced since the 1980s. Most fundamental is that of Amartya Sen, based on his arguments advocating the economic and social importance of "public policies" designed to enhance the health, education, and well-being of citizens. Sen makes the point that such policies are both intrinsically good because they improve human well-being and instrumentally good because they have measurable effects on economic development and productivity. These policies require the expenditure of resources by the state in ways that are not directly related to market conditions. So the critique is that any view that limits the role of the state to securing the conditions of the economic marketplace (property rights, rule of law) is too narrow.

Another important line of criticism derives from an effort to assess the intermediate social consequences of austerity and liberalization measures (Przeworski 1992). Various analysts have documented the extension of inequalities in specific national contexts (Beer and Boswell 2001), and many observers have noted the worsening of human development measures (e.g., nutritional status of the poor and levels of infant and child mortality) in specific countries that have been subjected to extreme versions of the liberalization program and associated adjustment programs (Harrigan and Mosley 1991; Lindenberg and Devarajan 1993).

Distributive Consequences of Neoliberal Reform

Here, I will examine the effects of neoliberalism on the largest sector in many poor countries: agriculture. It is possible for rural development plans to successfully increase agricultural productivity and per capita rural incomes and yet simultaneously increase stratification and poverty at the bottom end. In this regard, we must consider the distributive tendencies contained in development schemes that work primarily through investments in private farming systems (market-driven development schemes). These schemes have a tendency to increase farm productivity and per capita income while at the same time increasing inequalities and creating a "surplus population" of rural poor.

Much of the literature on rural development suggests the following hypothesis: Rural development strategies that work through existing property relations have a built-in structural tendency to favor the interests of the rich over those of the poor—large landowners over small, owners over tenants, and managerial farmers over hired hands. Such schemes do not do very well at improving the welfare of the lowest stratum of rural society, and they help extend rather than narrow rural inequalities (Hayami and Ruttan 1985; Herdt 1987; Ireson 1987; Barker, Herdt, and Rose 1985; Scott 1985).

These conclusions rest on several converging lines of argument. First is a political point: Development strategies are the object of intense political activity within the developing country, and the extreme inequalities in political powers between large landowners and peasants guarantee that the former will have the preponderant voice in this political struggle. As a result, we should expect that development strategies biased toward the interests of the landowner will emerge.

Second, a structural tendency stemming from the character of stratified property holdings themselves leads to deepening inequalities between landowners and landless workers. Excluding tax revenues, incomes are generated through two basic sources—income on property (rent, profit, interest) and income on the sale of labor power. The effect of rural development is to increase the productivity of rural farming systems, ultimately increasing the yields on land. These increased yields are then converted into higher earnings for the owners of land and other capital resources. Wages grow only if the demand for labor rises, but to the extent that mechanization is part of the package of the technological changes that are introduced, the opposite is a more likely outcome. Thus, there is a tendency for the larger share of the gains made through innovation to flow to the owners of land and capital.

This tendency leads to greater inequalities between landowners and the landless. Another important feature of rural inequality is that between large and small owners (managerial farmers and landlords, on the one hand, and subsistence peasant farmers, on the other). How does rural development affect the microfarmer? There is much debate on this question in the literature, but several factors seem fairly clear. The very small farmer faces serious barriers to successful implementation of the technical innovations of the green revolution. First, his plot is very small—often too small to fully satisfy subsistence needs. He has little access to credit, since he has little collateral and little political influence. His current cultivation is frequently a food crop, whereas the available spectrum of innovations are oriented toward riskier market crops. And many—though not all—of the available innovations are indivisible, requiring a minimum acreage to be efficiently used. This is particularly true of mechanized innovations—tractors, harvesters, and the like. Finally, the small farmer is in the most precarious economic position: Because he is often heavily indebted, with few cash reserves, a bad harvest or a slump in the commodity market can lead to the loss of the land that he owns or rents. Moreover, as the potential return on land increases through development, there will be more pressure on the smallholder to relinquish his land. Thus, foreclosure, abrogation of tenancy, and intimidation likely result, pushing some small farmers into the wage labor sector. In sum, it would appear that, as a practical matter, larger farmers and landowners are in a substantially better position to implement green revolution technologies; to the extent that this is so, however, we would expect a widening gap between earnings on the two types of farms. And we should also expect a significant slippage in the number and size of small farms as peasants are proletarianized or marginalized by changing economic circumstances.

Progressive Economic Development

Are there rational alternatives to the neoliberal agenda for economic development? There are. I will sketch out a program of what might be called "progressive" economic development. (We might, without extreme exaggeration, refer to this as the "Delhi-Helsinki consensus," reflecting the fact that development thinking in India has tended to pay much more attention to distributive outcomes, poverty alleviation, and human well-being than the neoliberal approach does and offering homage to the vigorous research efforts in this area sponsored by the World Institute for Development Economics Research in Helsinki.) This model is not antagonistic to market forces or many of the goals of the liberalization agenda. But it holds that the neoliberal agenda gives too little weight to important instruments of development (in particular, the role of the state and public policy) and that it is too insensitive to what should be the driving goal of economic development: significant and rapid alleviation of poverty. Moreover, the neoliberal agenda pays too little attention to the regressive distributive effects that its policies often produce.[2]

The progressive economic development agenda may be defined as development with all or most of the following characteristics:

- It is designed to result in wide distribution of the benefits of growth across the broad population.
- It produces significant and sustained improvement in the incomes and assets of the poor and near-poor.
- It produces significant and sustained improvement in the quality of life of the population.
- It increases the availability of important life amenities for the whole population (health care, clean water, standards of health and safety in the workplace, education).
- It constrains the inequalities that develop between economic elites and the broad population.
- It constrains the emergence and persistence of rural-urban inequalities.
- It provides inducements toward greater democracy in politics.
- It gives weight to environmental concerns.

What would be required for a state to adopt a program of progressive economic development? It seems clear that, to be implemented, this family of strategies would entail a substantial use of state political resources. There is no reason to expect an unrestrained market economy to lead to greater equality over time, and markets have not generally done well in providing the infrastructures of public health and education. So these are areas in economic development where the state has an important role to play. Furthermore, it is evident that this exercise of state power is most likely to occur in societies in which the poor have an effective political voice. It is a truism that governments dominated by economic elites may be relied on to adopt policies that favor those elites. So what are the prospects for the emergence of progressive economic development strategies? I will return to these questions about the political context of development in the final chapter.

In the section just ahead, I will look more specifically at some economic development tools and strategies that would serve the goals of progressive economic development—propoor, prodemocracy, and proenvironment.

Employment- and Wage-Increasing Measures

Access to employment is a fundamental remedy to poverty. So I will begin by considering development strategies that emphasize employment-increasing measures. At any given time, a domestic economy can be tilted in a variety of directions: toward more heavy industrialization, more light industry, more agricultural development, more production for exports, more high-technology production, and so on. Some of these options have substantially greater impacts on the condition of the poor; in general, those products and production processes that create the greatest demand for unskilled labor have the most immediate and extensive impact on poverty. Irma Adelman explores this dynamic in numerous writings and comes to the conclusion that two strategies of development are most effective—agricultural development, increasing the demand for rural labor and decreasing food costs, and industrial development, oriented toward the production of labor-absorbing products for export (Adelman 1986). This line of thought suggests that developing states need to evaluate possible industrial strategies in terms of the net employment effects. In a perfect neoclassical world, it would be unnecessary to address this problem, since a labor-surplus economy would induce entrepreneurs to select labor-intensive products and techniques. However, many developing states have introduced a bias toward capital-intensive innovations through state-subsidized credit for industrial investment. And in circumstances where investment funds are undervalued, there will be a tendency for capital-intensive innovations to dominate, leading to a slack demand for labor.

We may also consider public works employment as a state-financed effort to increase the demand for labor, while at the same time increasing the stock of public assets (irrigation systems, roads, and so forth). There is disagreement over the net effect of such programs. John Mellor (1976) argues that public works programs have only a limited role to play in large economies such as that of India. Given the vast size of the Indian rural labor force, even major budget expenditures will have only a marginal effect on rural welfare (Mellor 1976: 101). He concludes that public works expenditures are most likely to have enduring effects in regions where other forms of agricultural development are proceeding as well (for instance, with the extension of irrigation and multiple cropping, the introduction of new seed varieties, and the use of chemical fertilizers). In these circumstances, the assets created by public works expenditures can have a positive effect on other improvements in agricultural productivity.

More recent observers of the Indian rural economy are more positive about public works programs. Atul Kohli (1987: 137) describes one such program in West Bengal that had a substantial effect on landless workers. And Drèze and Sen (1989: 113–115) emphasize the importance of public works programs as instruments of famine prevention, by providing emergency entitlements to endangered households.

Agricultural Modernization

The bulk of employment in most developing countries is still in agriculture, and the majority of the poor are rural. (This is true in spite of the fact that agriculture in most Asian economies is now less than 50 percent of GDP.) This fact implies, then, that agricultural modernization is an efficient way of addressing poverty in most poor countries—even though the overall agricultural growth rates are constrained by inelastic demand and the limits of nature. Development policies that are designed to increase the productivity of agricultural labor and to extend the demand for labor in the rural sector will induce a rising trend in agricultural incomes.

Developing states have generally neglected agriculture, for a variety of reasons. (Indeed, Nick Lardy [1989] argues that this is true of China.) First is the now familiar urban bias (Lipton 1976) and a related preference for industrial development over agricultural development. Second is an inference about the long-term process of economic development and the inevitability of structural transformation: If the long-term pattern indicates a dwindling of agriculture's share within modernizing economies, then there is some reason to think that investments in industry rather than agriculture will be more productive. And finally, there is an argument about the relative value of agricultural products versus manufactured products that suggests, once again, that the state should channel investment into the expansion of manufacturing.

Each of these arguments, however, seems wrong. A smaller agricultural sector may nonetheless be increasingly productive—thus justifying continuing investment in agriculture—and improving agricultural productivity is an important component of a national policy of enhancing food security. Moreover, progress in agricultural development may be a necessary macroeconomic condition for development in other sectors. And boosting the productivity of agriculture is the only plausible way to improve the incomes flowing to agricultural workers in the foreseeable future, since urban employment is unlikely to expand rapidly enough to absorb a sizable percentage of the rural workforce. The upshot, then, is this: The developing state needs to reverse the antiagriculture bias that is common in the developing world. It needs to make adequate investment funds available to the rural sector, through credit institutions that are broadly accessible. It needs to organize and fund a variety of agricultural infrastructure projects: agricultural research, roads and market facilities, extension services, and irrigation facilities. And it needs to pay adequate attention to the institutions of land tenure that are in place within the rural economy.

One central aspect of agricultural modernization is the *green revolution* that began in the 1960s. A simple definition of this movement includes these elements: increasing food output through cultivation of high-yield varieties, intensive use of chemical fertilizer and pesticides, irrigation, and mechanized cultivation. The green revolution has had dramatic results in terms of world agriculture and world crop production. Basic food grains such as rice and wheat witnessed double and triple yields, and improvements in food availability and price followed almost immediately. India tripled its grain production between 1961 and 1980. And in the meantime, international institutes have been developed to research and disseminate new seeds and techniques (e.g., the Maize Institute and the International Rice Research Institute).

Important criticisms of the green revolution focus on a number of concerns. For instance, the new techniques and seeds may have shifted the balance toward the economic interests of large farmers. These technologies also create greater risk for the farmer (through crop failure, for example). In addition, monoculture is risky and reduces the cropping portfolio of the small farmer. The new technologies require substantially greater inputs of pesticides and fertilizers as well—thereby increasing the farmer's need for credit—and they may have large and harmful environmental effects. Furthermore, critics point out, hybrid and genetically engineered seeds give legal powers to seed companies and thereby reduce the freedom of small farmers to use traditional seed stocks.[3]

Food Security and Hunger

Malnutrition and famine are among the most corrosive harms of poverty. People must have reliable access to food if they are to live healthy and fully developed lives. So a central goal of development must be to assure food security for the population. Described as "access by all people at all times to enough food for an active and healthy life" (World Bank 1995: 12), food security involves both the availability of food and the ability to gain access to food (through entitlements) (A. Sen 1981). Specialists sometimes mean two different things when discussing food security: (1) the capacity of a typical poor household to secure sufficient food over a twelve-month period through farmwork, day labor, government entitlements, and so on (Drèze and Sen 1989; A. Sen 1981; Reutlinger and Selowsky 1976), and (2) the capacity of a poor country to satisfy the food needs of its whole population through direct production, foreign trade, and food stocks (Brown 1985; Donaldson 1984). There is an obvious connection between the two definitions. However, it is also clear that a country may, in principle, have more than sufficient resources to satisfy the food needs of its population but fail to do so because of internal inequalities. Thus, achieving household food security in the less developed world requires both equity and growth.

An important goal of development, then, must be the design of effective private and public institutions through which people's food security needs are satisfied. In normal times, this means that individuals must have sufficient entitlements to purchase an adequate food basket to support the nutritional needs of the household. In times of food crisis, it often means that public food programs are needed to quickly provide affordable access to food (A. Sen 1981).

Ensuring food security is a challenging task, since many apparently plausible policy choices have significant negative economic consequences. Emphasizing food self-sufficiency leads a country or region to forego the advantages of trade (growing rice rather than higher-value tea, for example). Imposing price controls on grain limits the incomes flowing to farmers, including families who are themselves at or below the poverty line. Providing food subsidies likewise harms the incomes flowing to farmers, by reducing the market price for grain.

Investment in Human Capital Assets for the Poor

A fourth important progressive policy option for a developing state is to increase social spending on programs that enhance the human resources of the poor: education, job retraining, health care, public health measures, and nutritional status. [4] A related way of enhancing the productivity of the poor is to improve the quality of the infrastructure assets to which they have access, such as clean water, roads, market facilities, irrigation systems, electricity, and telephone service. The chief asset controlled by the poor is unskilled labor. Policies that work to increase the value and productivity of this asset through higher literacy rates and other technical competencies should raise the incomes that flow to the poor. Herein lies a major role for the developing state, for substantial state resources must flow into rural education and health programs—with the result of improving both the current welfare and the future productivity of the poor.

Each of these forms of public support involves the expenditure of state resources on public and private assets available to the poor: education, health care, public health programs, roads, market facilities, and food subsidies. The policies require the redirection of substantial state revenues toward the poor, first to improve the productivity of labor and then to improve the quality of life of the poor. But this in turn requires the expenditure of political power, which is likely to occur only in circumstances where the rural poor are capable of exercising political influence on their own behalf. Kohli (1987) and Lipton (1976) analyze the politics of poverty reform. Drèze and Sen (1991) provide a vigorous defense of public policy spending directed to the alleviation of hunger and poverty.

Agrarian Reform

A central argument here is that the distributive characteristics of rural development strategies are largely determined by the specifics of the institutional arrangements through which the strategies work, chiefly including the form of landownership and the distribution of political power. We may distinguish between two broad families of development strategies: those that funnel development through existing property relations and political power alignments and those that involve a redistribution of property and political power in favor of the dispossessed. In many parts of the less developed world, the existing property relations define an agrarian class structure based on highly stratified landownership, and existing political institutions that are very responsive to the political organizations of the elite are defined by this property system. Somewhat oversimplying, we may say that "laissez-faire" strategies of development aim at diffusing technology, new investment funds, expertise, and the like through existing private property arrangements and then letting the distributive chips fall where they may. "Poverty-first" strategies, by contrast, attempt to alter these fundamental institutional arrangements in such a way as to confer more power, autonomy, and welfare on the least well off strata of rural society.

What, then, is agrarian reform? It is a process through which property relations and political powers are redistributed to favor the interests of the rural poor. Ronald Herring (1983: 11) puts the point this way: "Agrarian reforms worthy of the name transform rural society through alterations in the property structure and production relations, redistributing power and privilege."

As we saw in the previous chapter, a fundamental determinant of the distribution of income within an economy is the set of property relations through which production occurs. Property relations in the less developed world are typically highly stratified, with a small class owning the majority of wealth (chiefly land). Ownership of wealth confers both high income and substantial political power, so large wealth holders are able to absorb innovations and influence the political planning process in a way that is advantageous to their interests. In most developing economies, there is significant stratification of landholding, with consequent stratification of income. In an agrarian economy, landownership is a primary source of income. So without land reform, it is difficult to see how the lower strata of rural society will be able to improve on their distributive share of income generated by the rural economy. From this, we may infer that development that proceeds through existing economic and political institutions will tend to reproduce and perhaps intensify inequalities between classes. This analysis suggests that if we are interested in a process of development that reduces the structure of inequalities, it must be grounded in a set of institutional reforms that redistribute property rights and political powers. Put another way, development strategies that aim at reversing inequalities will plausibly embody a program of agrarian reform.

A Comparison of Development Strategies

I will take a step toward greater abstraction by examining some of the long-term consequences of several clusters of economic development policies. Specifically, I will look at the economic consequences of three "ideal-typical" development strategies: a neoliberal strategy (NL) that emphasizes markets and growth; a poverty-first strategy (PF) designed to create the conditions of economic growth within a policy framework attuned to the condition of the poor and to the extent of inequalities; and a "welfare-first" strategy (WF) that pays little attention to economic growth but devotes substantial resources toward immediate improvement in the well-being of the poor.

This section presents a very simple model that can be used to focus our thinking about the trade-offs that exist between growth, equality, and poverty. Consider the time profiles of three pure strategies: the growth-first strategy, the poverty-first strategy, and the strategy focused on immediate welfare improvement.[5]

- NL (neoliberal growth): Choose those policies and institutional reforms that lead to the most rapid growth—unfettered markets, profit-maximizing firms, minimal redistribution of income and wealth
- PF (poverty-first growth): Choose those policies and institutional reforms that lead to the most rapid growth in the incomes flowing to the poorest two quintiles
- WF (immediate welfare improvement): Direct as much social wealth as possible into programs that immediately improve the welfare of the poor (education, health, food subsidies, housing subsidies)

These strategies are stylized and reflect a set of assumptions about the dynamics of growth and distribution. (Distribution is measured by the percentage of GDP flowing to the poorest 40 percent of the population.) Here, I will examine a simple simulation of the medium- and long-term dynamics of the three strategies. I have assumed that the NL strategy has a consistently higher rate of growth (5 percent); that PF begins with a growth rate 1 percent lower

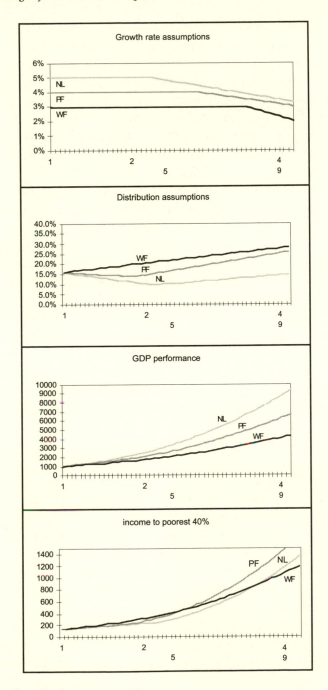

Figure 3.1   Three development strategies

than that of NL (4 percent); and that WF begins 2 percent lower than NL (3 percent). I have further assumed that each growth rate begins to fall in later decades (reflecting the notion that exponential growth is not permanently sustainable). Then, I have assumed that both NL and PF show a Kuznets-U pattern of distribution over time, with inequalities increasing and then declining, but that PF declines less and recovers sooner. Figure 3.1 illustrates these assumptions. On the basis of these assumptions, I have computed GDP and income to the poor for each strategy over a 50-year period; the results are provided in panels C and D of Figure 3.1.

Several points emerge clearly from inspection of these graphs. First, the neoliberal strategy succeeds in accomplishing its central goal: It produces a substantially higher GDP at the end of the 50-year period—a 33 percent advantage over the poverty-first strategy and a 110 percent advantage over the welfare-first strategy. From the point of view of the welfare of the poor over the bulk of the period of development, however, the NL strategy does less well. The aggregate advantage created by NL does not translate into superior outcomes for the poor—even over the long term (75 to 100 years). After 50 years, the PF strategy produces a 24 percent advantage for incomes to the poor as compared to the NL strategy. And if we extend the simulation out to 100 years—freezing inequalities and growth rates at the level achieved by 50 years—the advantage to the poor remains at 7 percent.[6] Eventually, the higher growth rate of the neoliberal strategy will allow the poor to surpass their counterparts in the poverty-first world, but that will take over 100 years. For the first 25 years, the incomes to the poor are higher on both the PF and the WF strategies—even though the NL's GDP is substantially ahead of both alternatives. The critical period, though, is the medium term. In this period, the poverty-first strategy passes the immediate-welfare strategy, and it retains the advantage over the maximize-growth strategy as well. The immediate-welfare strategy loses ground in the medium term because it has made too little productive investment in the national economy and has directed too much of the available surplus toward immediate welfare improvement. Incomes to the poor then stagnate (along with GDP) and improve only slowly from this point on.

This example has significant implications for development policy if we give credence to the crucial importance of poverty alleviation within development. Strategy WF leads to an immediate improvement in income to the poor. Strategy PF provides the basis for a sustained and substantial improvement of the incomes flowing to the poor, over the full period of the simulation. Strategy NL produces a higher rate of growth in GDP throughout the period but gives rise to a slower rate of improvement in the condition of the poor.

This exercise offers several important lessons. First, these idealized strategies show that development policy forces us to choose among various things: average income versus income to the poor, rate of growth versus rate of improvement in welfare of the poor, and improvement in the present versus well-being in the future. Second and equally important, however, the exercise shows that if we pay attention only to efficiency and growth, the interests of the poor in the short term and the medium term will not be well served. Third, this example makes it clear that privileging the interests of the poor does not entail neglecting economic growth. It is plain that sustained economic growth is the only long-term solution to the problem of poverty. National economic plans that work primarily toward channeling existing income into welfare assurance plans have short-term benefits but promise long-term stagnation. (This may have been what happened in Sri Lanka in the 1970s and 1980s.) Only if a national economy is able to produce substantially greater per capita income and wealth will it be possible to create and sustain improvement in the condition of the poor. This example makes it clear that, other things being equal, economic growth is desirable from a poverty alleviation point of view. Growth makes possible a sustained improvement in the income and welfare of the poorest strata of the developing economy. But whether that improvement occurs depends on the particular characteristics of the growth process and the institutions and institutional innovations through which incomes are distributed. If growth is stimulated by capital-intensive investment for world markets, there will be only a sluggish increase in the demand for labor, which means that the pool of modern sector labor will expand only slowly and modern sector wages will rise only slowly. To give priority to poverty alleviation, then, entails ranking strategies by their impact on the income and welfare of the poor, irrespective of overall growth rates.

These lessons also suggest that economic development planning should be time-sensitive. In a distributive environment in which there is extensive poverty and deprivation, policy should sacrifice some economic growth in exchange for more rapid improvement in the welfare of the poor. As the situation of the poor begins to improve substantially, the mix of policy tools should then be adjusted to accommodate a higher-growth strategy. And in fact there is a mixed strategy that could be pursued. It would certainly be possible to shift the balance of strategy priorities over time, favoring the poor in the early stages and growth in later stages (as the absolute welfare of the poor improves substantially). This would be a time-sensitive approach: Choose the poverty-first strategy while there is widespread, abject, debilitating poverty, then begin to shift to the growth-first strategy as the poor pass the level of abject poverty, in order to maximize the well-being of the least well off in future generations.

What Obstacles Stand in the Way
of Progressive Economic Development?

The arguments above suggest that progressive economic development is feasible. Moreover, from a neutral observer's standpoint, it seems clear that such a strategy has greater social welfare consequences than the growth-first strategy. So why is it so difficult to introduce this type of strategy into domestic and international development planning? The short answer is that development policy is unavoidably contentious in terms of politics because it imposes costs and benefits on different groups in different ways. There are winners and losers in any given choice of development policy; thus, we should expect that groups will mobilize their political resources toward the government decisionmaking bodies to secure the most advantageous policy mix for themselves. The benefits of a progressive economic development strategy are reverse-stratified: The least well off receive the greatest benefits, whereas the best off receive the least benefits. We now need to ask which groups are likely to have the greatest political resources to deploy in defense of their preferred policy. And here the answer, if not wholly unambiguous, is fairly clear: The more advantaged a group is in economic terms, the greater its political resources are likely to be in a typical developing society. This means that the advocates of a progressive strategy are at a substantial disadvantage within the domestic political system, for the primary beneficiaries of such a strategy are the least powerful groups in society.[7]

Political aspects of development create obstacles to the implementation of strategies of progressive economic development in a variety of ways. Regime stability, security interests, and the domestic political interests of the ruling party all play important roles in development policy formation in the developing world.

If we are to have a basis for understanding the forces that underlie national choices in the area of economic development policy, it is necessary to provide an analysis of political power at the local and national level. Given that different strategies affect local interests differently and given that the strategy chosen will result from a complex political process involving various affected parties, it is crucial to know what players will be most able to influence the goals and implementation of the development plan.

Thus, it is necessary to locate the process of economic development within the broader context of class politics and political power in the developing country. As one salient example, consider the political prospects for a program of land reform within a national politics dominated by the rural elite. Land reform runs contrary to the most fundamental interests of the rural elite, and this elite generally has substantial or even decisive political power. Land reform can only be the outcome of a political process—either through the exercise of state power or through collective action on the part of land-poor peasants. If it is the former, however, the interests of the individuals, coalitions, and organizations involved will play a determining role in the way in which institutional changes are adopted, and the various players have greatly unequal powers.[8] Consequently, an analysis of political power at the local and national levels is required.[9] In this context, it is worth recalling the situation of land reform in the Philippines in the late 1980s. There, a popularly elected president who was also a major landowner put forward a moderate proposal for limited land reform and expected it to be adopted and implemented by a legislature dominated by a landholding elite. Predictably, the proposal had little success.

This rough calculation leads to a conclusion: We should expect that there will be a bias in national development strategy toward the interests of the more advantaged. And this conclusion is even stronger when we turn our attention to the feasibility of entitlement and asset reform. The political obstacles to agrarian reform are obvious, both in theory and in history, for agrarian reform is directly contrary to the economic interests of the politically powerful. Thus, agrarian reform appears to presuppose a dramatic increase in the political power and influence of the rural poor; in fact, successful large-scale land reforms have only occurred in politically exceptional circumstances (postwar Taiwan and Korea, postrevolution China). The outcome of a process of rural reform through existing political arrangements will be sharply tilted toward the economic interests of the rural elite, and as long as this elite retains decisive political power, the goals of land reform will be difficult to achieve. Thus, Herring (1983: 50) writes, "Land to the tiller is a direct attack on private property and seems to presuppose an organized and militant peasantry, a revolutionary situation, or some extraordinary concentration of power, perhaps from outside the indigenous political system (as in Japan and Taiwan)." This line of reasoning suggests that a successful policy of asset reform requires very exceptional circumstances; in any nation in which the dominant political and economic elite is the landowning class, land reform would seem quite improbable.[10]

Notes

1. This set of doctrines falls under the category of "the Washington consensus" (Williamson 1993).

2. See Ramachandran and Swaminathan 2002 for a coherent set of essays on various aspects of contemporary economic development and globalization that proceed from the perspective that I have called "progressive economic development."

3. There is a broad literature on the social effects of the green revolution in poor countries. For some representative views, see Blyn 1983; Byres 1972; Byres and Crow 1983; K. Griffin 1974; Otsuka, Cordova, and David 1992; and Pearse 1980.

4. For an extensive discussion of the role and variety of food subsidy programs, see Pinstrup-Andersen 1988.

5. The model discussed here adopts time-specific assumptions about economic growth and distribution and runs these assumptions forward over a 50-year period.

6. Empirical data confirm the plausibility of this finding. Between 1971 and 1975, Brazil had an income ratio of 9.51, with the poorest 40 percent of the population receiving about 8 percent of the national income. Brazil's growth rate in 1986 was about 4.3 percent. If we assume that this rate of growth was uniformly distributed across all income earners (a highly unrealistic assumption), then the average income for the poorest 40 percent would have risen from $91 to $95, whereas that of the richest 20 percent would have grown from $855 to $892. If we use $125 as the poverty level, it would take about 40 years of growth at this rate to bring the average income of the poorest 40 percent up to the poverty level. On the more realistic assumption that the benefits of growth flow disproportionately to higher income groups, this disparity becomes even more pronounced.

7. Ronald Herring (1983, 1984, 1991, 1999) has directed a great deal of attention to this question throughout his career.

8. "Although land reforms are universally argued for in terms of social justice and economic efficiency, the political reality in South Asian societies is that such reforms are promulgated by ruling elites largely composed of, or structurally or electorally dependent on, agrarian elites" (Herring 1983: 3).

9. In what is otherwise a stout denial of the claim that the green revolution has exacerbated inequalities, Jujiro Hayami and Vernon Ruttan (1985: 360) write, "It is a common observation that, in a society characterized by extreme bias in economic and political resources, it is difficult to bring about institutional reforms that are biased against those who possess substantial economic and political resources. A disproportional share of institutional credit and subsidized inputs will, in such situations, be directed into the hands of the larger farmers. . . . It is extremely difficult to implement institutional changes that are neutral or biased toward the poor in a society characterized by extreme inequality in economic resources and political power."

10. A somewhat different analysis is needed for a large and complex nation such as India. In this case, a much broader range of political powers and interests is at work, with a substantial urban sector whose interests may sometimes join with those of the rural poor against the rural elite.

4

Justice

PEOPLE OUGHT TO BE TREATED justly. But what does this assertion imply for the ethics of economic development? Does this considered judgment provide guidance for us as we explore the ethical issues raised in economic development policy and process? What does the requirement of justice involve? What are the circumstances of justice in economic development? And what conditions invoke our judgments of injustice?

At its broadest, the concept of justice easily encompasses virtually every aspect of public life—for example, inequalities, opportunities, democracy, liberty, and individual rights. At its narrowest, it may be thought to encompass little more than the idea of procedural correctness: that individuals should be treated neutrally and impersonally by the rules, laws, and procedures that govern them, whatever those are. In this chapter, I will explore a fairly compact conception of economic justice, focused on fair returns to participants within the economic process. Essentially, the approach explores ideas of fairness within the context of a set of market institutions. This approach does not invite a full and general theory of justice, but at the same time, it provides more traction than a narrow theory of procedural justice. I have selected this level of analysis in order to keep the treatment close enough to the ground to permit application to real problems of justice within developing societies. And it will become clear that establishing the conditions required by this conception of justice would represent a very genuine step forward for the poor and powerless in most societies.

For these purposes, I will explore some examples of circumstances that raise issues of justice in developing societies. Thinking about the examples will allow us to elicit our moral intuitions about fairness, justice, and equality and the ways in which these factors play out in the institutions of a given society. Consider the following scenarios:

- Miners are required to purchase the necessities of life from the company store.
- Workers are prohibited from forming labor organizations and bargaining as a group.
- An African state requires peasant farmers to sell their peanuts at state-determined prices.
- The Chinese state imposes a tax on the purchase of cooking salt, thereby extracting substantial revenue from the poorest strata of society.
- An Asian state prohibits labor organizations from establishing unions in apparel shops.
- State subsidies for clean water, sanitation, and basic health care flow disproportionately to urban population; rural people are less well served (urban bias).
- Guest workers have limited labor rights relative to citizen workers.
- Women have limited control of resources within the peasant household in East Africa.
- Farmers in Gansu, China, have much lower standards of living than those in coastal regions because of the resource and land depletion in their province.

These examples force us to think about the institutional origins of the circumstances and inequalities that are represented here. What are the sources of injustice in these cases (without presupposing that all these examples do in fact represent instances of injustice)? In some instances, individuals are treated differently without reason (women, guest workers, rural people). In other cases, individuals are denied the exercise of reasonable rights and freedoms within the sphere of their economic activities (labor organizations, purchase and sale of commodities). And in yet other instances, individuals are disadvantaged by structural inequalities between regions or groups (soil productivity, mineral resources, access to transportation). The implications of institutions that discriminate against some citizens in favor of others are particularly profound because of the depth of influence that institutions have on the life prospects and present and future well-being available to all people.

We have relatively clear intuitions about injustice in basic social and economic institutions. Persons are treated unjustly when they are exploited, when they are coerced, when they are illegitimately deprived of goods or privileges to which they have a valid claim, when they are objects of discrimination, or when they are deprived unfairly of access to resources to which they should have access. On the positive side, a just system of institutions should be impersonal (that is, no individual should benefit for purely personal reasons). It should assign "fair" benefits to all parties—that is, all parties should enjoy the benefits of their contributions to cooperative projects. It should also treat all persons with equal consideration and dignity. Finally, it should be sensitive to the creation of inequalities of wealth and income, given the centrality of factors such as income, wealth, and access to health care in leading a full human life and pursuing a life plan.

It is important to keep in mind two levels of reasoning about justice—reasoning about fairness within existing institutions and reasoning about alternative sets of institutions. At the local level, we need to ask what principles allow us to judge that various persons are being treated justly within existing economic and social arrangements and outcomes. And at the higher level, we can question whether these institutions themselves are just in comparison to other hypothetically possible institutions.

Is justice a feature of the social outcomes under review, or is it a feature of the process that has led to these outcomes? I will take the view that the justice of a given set of social arrangements and distributions—outcomes—depends on the process through which the arrangements and distributions came about. Social processes involve the actions and choices of many agents within a set of institutions defining the terms of their transactions. If we are confident in the fairness of these institutions, then we can have a prima facie level of confidence in the justice of the outcomes. But this approach requires that we be able to offer an account of "fair institutions," a topic I will turn to shortly.

Justice has much to do with inequalities and the question of whether a given set of inequalities among persons is justified or fair. What forms of equality are morally compulsory? Conversely, what forms of inequality are morally suspect or morally acceptable? Within any society, there are often inequalities of assets and incomes, inequalities of opportunity, and inequalities of ability to realize talents and capacities. What is the moral status of such inequalities? Once having distinguished these different forms of inequality, we then must consider whether there are moral reasons, based on considerations of justice, for concluding that some such inequalities are unjust. Is there a general moral basis for the value of equality? Or is the value of equality derivative rather than intrinsic—a result that follows from other more fundamental moral requirements (e.g., to minimize the poverty of the least well off)? Are inequalities inherently undesirable?

Central to many of these judgments about injustice and justice is the concept of fairness. People should be treated fairly by the basic institutions within which they live. We can easily identify some of the many ways in which institutions can be manipulated by the powerful to impose unfair disadvantages on others. Can we say anything more specific about this intuition of fairness, however? Perhaps the key insight contained in John Rawls's theory of justice ("justice as fairness") is his analysis of the fairness of basic institutions in terms of the idea of rational acceptability. According to this conception, a person is treated fairly by a set of institutions if she would have accepted those institutions prior to engaging in social interaction (Rawls 1971, 1985, 1993b, 2001). I will turn now to a more detailed treatment of some of these ideas.

Economic Justice

The issue of economic justice can be addressed from two points of view: Are the institutions fair and neutral? And are the outcomes fair? The perspective I will adopt here is the institutional one; I will work on the assumption that fair institutions will, by definition, lead to outcomes that are just. Box 4.1 illustrates this assumption.

This conception emphasizes several independent factors that capture the requirements of fairness: equality of opportunity, noncoercive economic transactions, and a fair prior distribution of productive assets. If the conditions on the left of the box are satisfied, then we have reason to be confident that participants are being treated fairly and that the outcomes will be just. The approach is incomplete in that it does not offer a basis for evaluating differences of outcomes that result from interpersonal differences, inequalities of skills and tal-

Background conditions	Results
Fair institutions (equal treatment, institutions that would be universally accepted)	
Fair equality of opportunity (non-discrimination in employment and access to social positions)	
Fair prior distribution of productive assets	➡ Just distribution of incomes and assets
Fair opportunity to develop one's human talents (fair access to education and health)	Secular tendency toward a reduction of inequalities
Free bargaining by all agents concerning the terms of use of labor and capital	

Box 4.1   Conditions for distributive justice

ents, or physical disabilities. But it is a significant start that provides substantial leverage in evaluating the justice of outcomes in developing countries. This approach highlights the insight that there are important preconditions for just economic transactions: lack of coercion, just initial distribution of assets, fair equality of opportunity, and fair access to education and health care, in particular. And it provides a prima facie basis for supposing that the institutions of a market are an important component of economic justice. If the conditions on the left of the box are not satisfied, then we need to ask what is required by way of restorative or compensatory justice. For example, do failures of prior asset distribution imply the need for entitlement reform, land reform, or taxation policies aimed at reducing inequalities in assets?

On this approach, a theory of economic justice must give particular attention to several issues:

· Wide and fair provision of the requisites for human development (Chapter 1)
· Equality of opportunity
· Neutral treatment of all persons and groups by basic institutions

- Market institutions that are not dominated by economic, social, racial, or political elites
- Freedom from coercion in determining economic activity (labor, contracts, residence)

Two other features are important to a just society and will be discussed in later chapters:

- Security in basic rights and freedoms; no extrastate coercion (Chapter 5)
- State policies that are fairly and democratically adopted (Chapter 8)

The institutions that govern economic activity include the legal context of private agreements, the specific configuration of the property system, and the regulatory context that the state presents to economic agents. They include as well the mechanisms, formal and informal, through which individuals gain access to important social resources: education, health, housing, and employment. Systemically unfair treatment for some agents can emerge through any or all of these institutions. I will examine several of the dimensions of fairness that are especially central in defining a just economic process.

Fair Return to Productive Contribution

Individuals make productive contributions to the economy, and they have a right to expect a fair return in the form of income (wages, profits, interest, and so forth). But what constitutes a fair return? Individuals contribute to a process of economic cooperation, making use of their individual talents, efforts, time, and assets. The economic and social institutions that are in place define a set of roles and positions for economic agents, and they determine the incomes and life prospects of the individuals who fill those positions. An economy is a system of extensive cooperation, coordination, and competition among types of agents, among them workers, farmers, business owners, bankers, merchants, miners, and government employees. The inputs to economic activity include labor, land, and capital; more specifically, they include many kinds of specialized labor, factories, machines and tools, mines, trucks, railroads, ships, electric power systems, farmland, forest, and grazing land. Most of these assets are owned by someone—workers own their labor capacity; capitalists own land, factories, and machines; governments own ports and electric power networks, and so on. Productive activity takes place. Workers are hired in factories, manufacturing occurs, mines yield quantities of coal and iron, farm products are harvested. The value of the output of economic activity is (normally) greater than the value of the inputs to the process, and the value of the output is divided among the agents in the form of income streams—wages, rent, interest, and profit. These rewards are determined by (1) the institutions within which transactions take place, (2) the assets owned or controlled by each agent, and (3) the agent's productive contribution to the process. A low-productivity economy results in small shares, whereas a high-productivity economy produces a larger sum to be distributed.

What constitutes a fair system for distributing the benefits of economic cooperation within a society? How should the income and wealth that is created through economic activity be assigned to the various participants in the economic process? Given that the productive contributions of each of the agents are necessary for successful economic activity, how should the benefits of this joint process be distributed? A central intuition defining our understanding of economic justice arises from the idea of a *fair assignment of benefits that result from joint efforts*. Virtually all economic activity involves cooperation among agents who contribute to the output of the process. What principles should guide our judgment as to whether a given agent receives a fair or just return on his or her contribution? And what principles ought to guide our judgments about the fairness of the institutions and the justice of the prior distribution of assets? These questions point to the central problem of economic justice. What income should each party receive in compensation for his or her contribution to the process of production?

Consider this approach to economic justice:

- Just distribution results from a free and noncoercive bargaining among the factors of production (1) within fair institutions, (2) subject to fair equality of opportunity, and (3) within the context of a just prior distribution of assets.

According to this approach, each agent of production is treated fairly when his or her income is the result of the free bargaining process within fair background circumstances. This principle requires qualification, however. First, we need to make explicit the requirements of equality of opportunity for all participants. Second, we need to take account of the effects of the antecedent distribution of assets across persons.

In particular, the distributive shares that result from this model depend on the *prior distribution of assets and labor*. When labor is abundant (that is, when there is a surplus of available labor), producers will choose labor-intensive techniques of production, economizing on more costly production factors. When the cost of labor rises, producers will search out different production techniques that replace labor with less costly mechanization. Labor is commonly abundant in the circumstances of developing economies, as farmers and peasants are displaced in rural areas and as the population increases rapidly. This situation implies that production will be adjusted in such a way as to take advantage of "cheap labor"—with the result that the marginal product of labor will be low, and wages will remain low as well.

Moreover, the outcome of the idealized bargaining process described here is sensitive to the *institutional arrangements* within which bargaining takes place. Do workers bargain as individuals or as members of unions? Does government provide financial incentives to favor one technique of production over another? Do mine owners have the right to limit production in order to push up the price of their product?

Fair Institutions

I will focus next on the requirement of fair institutions. What do we mean when we say that social and economic institutions ought to be fair? Among the many things that institutions do is allocate scarce resources and opportunities across a number of persons. And individuals care about the outcomes of this distribution; they generally prefer more of the good to less, and they want their interests to be treated with due consideration during the process. The most fundamental element defining the fairness of a rule or procedure is captured by the idea that those who are affected by the rule would have accepted it as a basis for allocating some good prior to the moment of division. Steven Brams offers an account of distributive justice that generalizes on the notion of fair division and rational acceptability of process (Brams and Taylor 1996). More generally, we can identify several important features of institutions that rational agents would demand as a condition of fairness.

First, there is an important connection between the conditions of fairness, freedom of choice, and the absence of coercion. An individual is exploited, we may say, if he receives less than a fair share of the results of economic activity, relative to his level of contribution to the creation of the output. Coercion usually plays a central role in exploitation.[1] The notion of exploitation, then, depends on the idea that certain agents are able to exercise coercive power over others and to use that power to confiscate some part of the income stream that the latter deserves. People will seek out ways to avoid being exploited; so, in order to continue exploitation, it is usually necessary to find ways of compelling them to continue to engage in the exploitative activity. Serfs were exploited within feudalism in a particularly visible way: They were compelled by force to provide part of their labor time to the lord without compensation. Coal miners may be exploited by the mine company if there is no other source of employment in their valley and if the mine operator controls both the wage and the prices in the company store. But owners of property can be exploited as well. Consider, for example, a situation in which a government requires a factory owner to continue to produce a commodity at a state-set price that just covers the cost of production. Here, the factory owner is exploited in that a coercive institution compels economic activity but limits the agent's return on that activity through coercive means. Intuitively, the factory owner has made a contribution to the total social value of the output but has not derived an income that permits him or her to enjoy some part of the social product. What these examples have in common is coerced participation in an economic process. It is reasonable to suppose, then, that freedom of choice is an important aspect of distributive justice. And it is a natural step from this insight to the further notion that *outcomes that result from uncoerced agreements among agents are fair.*

What is wrong with the so-called company store? It is the fact that the individual is denied the ability to choose from alternative providers of the necessities of life, which means in turn that the privileged provider is able to exploit the consumer through higher prices. What is wrong with the so-called price board through which Senegalese peanut farmers are compelled by the state to sell their produce? It is the element of state coercion that prevents the farmers from selling their products in competitive markets; this system creates the possibility or likelihood that the state will exploit the farmers through imposition of low prices. What is wrong with the harsh conditions of labor that Anita Chan (2001) documents in various parts of coastal China in the 1990s? It is that immigrant workers are often forcibly confined to the factories where they work and are therefore prevented from finding better working conditions elsewhere. In each instance, it is the ability of an agent in society to coerce others that permits exploitation, rent seeking, and predatory pricing. Turning the point the other way around, institutions that permit individuals to seek out the commodities, prices, or sales that best serve their interests among a number of competing offers are institutions that bear the mark of fairness.[2]

Second, institutions ought to be impersonal; they should treat all citizens equally. This is the condition of procedural fairness—that institutions should treat like cases alike. But this principle also entails a condition of interpersonal neutrality of institutions: Institutions should not be designed to benefit specific persons or groups over other persons and groups. The principle also implies that institutions should not favor one set of interests over another— urban/rural, wealthy/poor, elite/nonelite, Chinese/Muslim, and so on.

Third, a condition of equality of opportunity must exist concerning access to positions and resources (entry into schools, eligibility for government positions, eligibility for employment). Narrowly, this principle entails that the opportunities and resources created by institutions need to be open to all and that selection for limited opportunities must be based on valid selection criteria. (That is, institutions must not discriminate against individuals on the basis of irrelevant criteria.) More substantively, it can be argued that fair equality of opportunity requires more than nondiscrimination at the point of entry into positions. On this approach, individuals must have fair access to the resources that will be needed to prepare them to fairly compete for positions within society; thus, they need to have had a fair opportunity to achieve reasonable development with regard to nutrition, health, and education.[3]

Fourth, it is compelling to suppose that fair institutions need to satisfy a requirement concerning their contribution to social welfare. Institutions must be designed in such a way as to enhance the welfare of the population as a whole. (In other words, institutions that treat everyone impersonally but wretchedly are unfair to everyone.)

We can provide a motivation for each of these requirements of fairness on institutional design by asking the question, Would a citizen rationally accept these constraints prior to agreeing to living under the institutions that are created within the constraints if she could make such a choice prior to entry? (This is the hypothetical question that underlies Rawls's construction of the original position; see Rawls 2001: section 6.) The requirements of freedom, impersonality, equality of opportunity, and social welfare all have a powerful appeal from the point of view of prior choice. No prospective citizen would want to accept the idea that some individuals might have status- or person-defined advantages, each would want to insist on conditions of equality of opportunity and maximum freedom, each would want to assure that institutions have been adjusted to improve efficiency, and so forth. So we can judge from the more global perspective that these conditions would be endorsed by rational citizens considering membership in a given society and that they consequently define conditions of fairness that institutions need to satisfy. This in turn gives us reason to assert that such conditions constitute part of the requirements of institutional fairness.

The most important economic institutions include property arrangements; the market system; the system of employment; government regulations and taxation; and institutions governing access to health care, nutrition, and education. The workings of these institutions create the most significant determinant of the life prospects of individuals within society. So I will look more closely at these areas in the following passages.

Fair Equality of Opportunity

Justice requires fair equality of opportunity concerning access to positions in society—for example, jobs, entrance to schools and universities, positions in government, or access to credit (Elster 1992). This is so because positions in society confer benefits, both tangible and intangible, on the men and women who gain access to them, and it would be unfair to exclude some individuals from these positions for unjustified reasons. There are many ideas to be unpacked in this moral intuition, however. What is the range of positions that are covered by the principle of equality of opportunity? What counts as a "justified reason" for excluding a person from a position? And how deeply does the principle extend—does it simply prohibit formal discrimination in employment, schooling, and so forth, or does it further require providing each citizen with the preparation that he or she would need to compete fairly for a position (education, access to health care, adequate nutrition)?

The fundamental question is: Why does equality of opportunity in society have so much moral importance? The most compelling answer to this question derives from the conception of the person that was discussed in the first chapter. It was argued there that we should conceive of the person as an individual with inherent moral importance, an individual with a set of capacities and qualities that will be developed and actualized through complicated social processes (education, for example), and an individual who develops a "plan of life" that organizes her activities around a set of fundamental goods that she has chosen to follow. To realize her capabilities and to have a reasonable chance of carrying out her plan of life, the individual needs to have access to social resources, income, and meaningful work. So equality of opportunity is fundamental to the realization of each individual's human potential, realization of the individual's human potential is a morally good thing, and there is no convincing reason to favor one person's good over another's. Therefore, a principle of fair equality of opportunity appears to follow from the principle of the inherent moral value of the individual and the nature of the processes through which people pursue their conceptions of the good.

Is there some basis for determining what sorts of positions are subject to fair equality of opportunity? Jobs clearly fall within the scope of the principle, as does schooling. But what about religious schools? What about jobs such as "pastor" that require a particular religious affiliation? What about marriage? Is there a principled distinction between public and private choice—choice that must be neutral and impersonal versus choice that can involve personal preference and arbitrariness?

Equality of opportunity is typically invoked at the point of recruitment and selection for positions in society. Some candidates are excluded and others are selected on the basis of reasons advanced by the agencies that make the choices. Some such reasons are manifestly improper—"Bill is selected for this position because he is Hindu"—and others are manifestly appropriate—"Jane is selected for this position because she is the best engineer among the candidates." A first effort at formulating a criterion of fair equality of opportunity could be expressed in these terms: Selection for positions in society should involve the impersonal application of criteria of predicted performance that are rationally related to future performance in the position. The idea could be more fully developed as follows:

- Access to positions and opportunities ought to be neutral and person-independent.
- Access ought to be based on selection criteria that are rationally seen to be relevant to the needs of the position—"merit."

Negative criteria can be formulated as well:

- Selection for positions in society must not involve preference for persons having irrelevant characteristics—for example, family history, religion, ethnic group, or regional origin—in the absence of compelling moral reasons to the contrary.
- Access to positions should not be dependent on the individual's race, religion, social status, family background, or gender—in the absence of compelling moral reasons to the contrary.

Defining equality of opportunity in this way sets a prima facie standard for the processes through which individuals are selected for positions in society. It is worth emphasizing, however, that the principle is not unconditional. There may be compelling reasons for making exceptions to the principle in particular circumstances. For example, a history of racial or ethnic discrimination within a given social context may justify some degree of preference for members of the affected group, based on a theory of restorative justice. Like virtually all moral and legal principles, the requirement of equality of opportunity is qualified by the clause, "in the absence of other compelling moral reasons." What the principle rules out is unjustified preferences. So debate about affirmative action in the United States cannot be resolved by appeal to a simple principle of equality of opportunity. Rather, it is necessary to take into account the multiple factors that affect the justice of past racial discrimination, present institutions and opportunities, and future social outcomes.

This component of equality of opportunity may be referred to as the "nondiscrimination requirement." There is a more demanding interpretation of equality of opportunity, however, that may be referred to as the "level playing field interpretation." On this account, every person should have a reasonable chance of developing the talents that he or she has so as to be able to effectively compete for positions in society. In particular, all members of society should have comparable access to educational opportunities. This aspect of the requirement of equality of opportunity is much more strenuous than the nondiscrimination requirement, in that it would lead us to identify de facto educational disadvantages for some groups in society as an affront against equality of opportunity. And it would be logical to infer that justice demands that these disadvantages be erased.

- Equality of opportunity requires that individuals have reasonable access to the means necessary to develop their talents.

I will return to this point in the next section.

Fair Access to the Prerequisites of Human Development

Thus far, the discussion of fair equality of opportunity has focused primarily on the moral issue of discrimination at the point of selection for positions in society, which is an important moral feature of fairness. Equality of opportunity focuses on negative limitations on opportunity. Equality is violated when certain individuals or groups are systematically denied access to opportunities of interest—entry into schools and universities, entry into jobs, entry into social clubs in which economically significant opportunities exist, and so forth.

But intuitions of real equality of opportunity run deeper. Consider these facts:

- Schooling is often available only to the affluent/powerful/middle class/urban dwellers.
- Nutritional status is often lower for rural people than for urban people.
- Overall health status is often lower for poor people as compared to rich people.

These inequalities plainly affect the ability of individuals in different groups to compete fairly for positions in society. And they occur without regard to individual merit, effort, or personal qualities. A broader understanding of equality of opportunity begins with the recognition that individuals can only take advantage of social opportunities when they have had a chance to develop their human capacities to a reasonable degree, and this requires fair access to social goods such as education, health care, and nutrition. Again, we may refer to this as the level playing field interpretation of equality of opportunity. It is understood that individuals need to have developed many of their human capabilities in order to compete successfully for positions in society: They must be literate, for example; they must have normal levels of strength and agility; they must be able to communicate clearly; and so forth. And the resources required for these attainments must be available over an extended period of time—through extended education, extended nutrition, extended health, and the like. It is very obvious that the social inequalities in virtually every society impose disadvantages on some children relative to others in the degree of access they have to these essential social resources. Yet moral reasoning takes us to a principle of equality along these lines:

- Every child should have reasonable access to the resources necessary to develop his or her talents.

Or, to put it even more strongly:

- Every child should have approximately equal life prospects.

That is, society should be arranged in such a way that each child has an approximately equal opportunity first to realize his or her human capabilities through education, nutrition, and health and then to compete fairly for positions in society on the basis of these human capabilities.

It is apparent that the level playing field interpretation is substantially more demanding than the nondiscrimination interpretation. This means that there is ample room for moral and political debate about where to set the standard that we wish to apply.

Institutions

I will turn now to a more specific consideration of some of the central economic institutions that define the life prospects of people in developing societies. What do the conditions of fairness require of these institutions?

Labor

The distributive outcomes for the majority of the population in most developing societies depend, directly or indirectly, on the institutions governing labor. The great majority of the people in poor countries lack significant assets, so their incomes derive from their ability to work for a wage. Why is labor especially important? The answer to this question stems from the fact that labor is a human universal. Every individual has labor to offer. Each human being has a collection of productive assets: intelligence, strength, skill, knowledge, and creativity. These are productive assets, essential to economic activity. Persons who own no other assets must negotiate the expenditure of their human capacities in exchange for an income. What determines the terms of the use of these human capacities? Labor capacity has been organized in many ways throughout history, including a number of coercive mechanisms such as corvée labor, slave labor, and compulsory factory labor. The scheme of economic justice under consideration in this chapter depends on the premise of free labor and a market in wage labor. I assume a competition among enterprises and the real ability of the worker to choose among employers. The wage is set as a result of competition among workers and firms.

A number of institutional questions need to be raised concerning labor. Can workers join together and form unions? Is there collective bargaining, including a right to strike and boycott? Can workers move freely to seek jobs, either regionally or sectorally? Do workers have the right and the opportunity to acquire new economically valuable skills?

In virtually all parts of the developing world, a significant imbalance exists in the bargaining positions of labor and property. Landless workers, unskilled workers, farmhands, factory workers—the mass of workers in developing countries generally confront the power of the state and the power of property in forms that reduce their ability to negotiate advantageous contracts with their employers. Power can be expressed in the use of force to intimidate worker or peasant organizations, the use of economic means to restrict cooperatives and unions, the use of legislation to restrict labor rights and mobility, and so on. More abstractly, the power to organize the productive process gives the owners of property the ability to de-skill that process, thereby reducing the bargaining position of labor (Braverman 1975; Sabel 1982).

The following scenarios provide examples of the structural disadvantages confronted by labor in developing countries.

- Large landowners are able to exert pressure on small peasant proprietors, leading to replacement of small cultivators by plantation agriculture.
- Factory employment in developing country industries often depends on coercion against unskilled workers. We can infer that if workers had genuine freedom to negotiate the wage, the balance between profits and wages would shift toward the worker.
- Developing countries generally have an absolute oversupply of unskilled labor, so wage rates remain low. Desperation wages keep the workers' standard of living low.
- When wages begin to rise, the owner can threaten to relocate production near other global sources of low-wage labor.
- Government institutions are generally in the control of the powerful agents in society—the propertied, the military, and the government elite. Legislation and policy therefore generally tip against the interests of the poor.

Several principles are important in considering the status of labor within a market economy. First, there is an important suite of labor rights that must be respected by the economic institutions and firms that constitute the economy. (These rights will be explored more fully in the next chapter.) If these rights are not respected, then working people will not be able to effectively represent their interests and needs within the economic system, and they are likely to receive less than a fair share of the economic product. Second, it is plain that the earning power of workers depends critically on their potential productivity, which in turn depends on the degree of development of their human capabilities. To the extent that workers have been enabled to extend their talents through education and other developmental opportunities, they will be able to contribute strongly to the new wealth created by the economy and to bargain effectively for a reasonable share of the incomes that result. So institutions that secure the rights of workers and the full development of the talents of workers through effective education are crucial to a just economy.

I will consider the rights of labor more extensively in the next chapter. Here, it suffices to postulate that the elements of coercion and exploitation identified above as antithetical to justice are especially pertinent in considering the circumstances of justice within which the working poor earn their incomes. Workers are particularly vulnerable to exploitative practices, since the urgency of hunger and the needs of their families compel them to aggressively seek out work. Employers have an interest in keeping wages low, they have a stake in preventing the formation of labor unions, and they often face competitive pressures that work against the maintenance of healthy and safe workplaces. So it is particularly important for the state to establish both a set of fair regulations codifying the rights of working people and a set of regulations requiring minimum standards of health and safety in the workplace.

Are Markets Fair?

Another vital issue involves the fairness of the marketplace as a central determinant of economic outcomes. A market is a system of economic activity in which all goods are sold at prices determined by supply and demand and wages are set within competitive labor markets regulated by supply and demand. Under conditions of market competition, the prices of inputs and outputs are determined by competitive bidding among buyers and sellers. The price of the good reaches equilibrium at the point at which markets clear, and

	% of population	per capita wealth	per capita income
unemployed	10%	$ -	$ 500
landless workers	20%	$ -	$ 900
small farmers	20%	$ 1,000	$ 1,200
traditional industry workers	20%	$ 500	$ 1,700
modern industry workers	10%	$ 1,000	$ 2,500
managerial farmers	7%	$ 10,000	$ 4,500
modern industry managers	3%	5,000	$ 6,500
professionals (doctors, lawyers, accountants, professors)	7%	$ 10,000	$ 12,000
owners of wealth—money, land, factories, businesses	3%	200,000	$ 20,000

Figure 4.1   Hypothetical distribution of income and wealth

the quantity of product at the given price is equal to the quantity of demand at that price. Likewise, wages are set as employers determine the quantity and quality of labor that they require for production purposes and then offer a wage to attract workers. If the wage is too low, the firm will fail to attract sufficient workers, and the employer will be obliged to increase the wage.

Consider an economy that is organized around well-functioning markets in commodities, capital, and labor. This situation entails that prices, wages, and profits adjust in response to demand for various goods and that investments and labor are shifted throughout the economy in response to demand. Suppose that this economy embodies at least the nondiscrimination criterion of equality of opportunity—positions are open to talent, and there is an open and impersonal competition for positions, jobs, and opportunities. And suppose that income and wealth are the result of the prior distribution of assets and a free competition for jobs and opportunities. Finally, suppose that Figure 4.1 represents the distribution of wealth and income that results from normal economic activity in this society. Is this a fair distribution of income and wealth? And how could we begin to answer the question of fairness in this instance?

The distribution of income represented here corresponds to a Gini coefficient of .55—comparable to that of Mexico and Kenya and significantly lower than that of Brazil. The distribution of wealth is significantly more unequal than that of income, with a Gini coefficient of .89. So the hypothetical example falls within the group of high-inequality societies but not at the extreme end of the group. Nonetheless, there are very significant inequalities represented here. Landless workers earn only 36 percent as much as modern industry workers and less than 10 percent of the incomes of professionals. Owners of wealth earn more than ten times the average income of the poorest 80 percent of society. And inequalities of income at the bottom end of the income scale have exaggerated effects on quality of life; the difference between the life circumstances of a landless worker and a traditional industry worker in this example is likely to be great. In other words, this figure represents very significant inequalities in life prospects, and those inequalities can be predicted to have major effects on the quality of life achieved by members of the various groups. Are these differences fair?

I would begin discussion of this example by observing that it is virtually impossible to imagine that this society embodies the level playing field version of equality of opportunity. Rural people are likely to have more limited access to education and health care than urban people, they are likely to have restricted information about the availability of careers outside the rural sector, and they are unlikely to have the social skills needed to compete for high-paying jobs. To put the point differently, it is likely that the children of landless workers and small farmers will themselves become landless workers and small farmers, not professionals and owners of wealth. And this low probability of significant social mobility is itself an indicator of limited equality of opportunity. (We can ask the fruitful question, What institutional changes would be needed to give the children of landless workers a likelihood of becoming professionals that is comparable to that of the children of more affluent groups? The answer would probably involve substantial state investment in education, nutrition, and health resources for the poor.)

It is important to observe that we can infer that the prior distribution of assets plays a critical role in the distribution of income (as well as wealth) in the example. A managerial farmer must have a minimum level of wealth in order to occupy that position; he or she must be able to purchase or rent land, acquire tools and equipment, and finance the costs of farming over a season. So a landless worker with all the talents needed to be a successful managerial farmer will nonetheless be excluded from this opportunity by the fact that he or she lacks wealth. Likewise, possession of a degree of family wealth is an important asset for acquiring the specialized higher education involved in becoming a professional; once again, the child of the landless worker is unlikely to be in the educational track that leads to a professional career. Differential distribution of inherited wealth is thus a major determinant of income, even within the context of a fair market system without exploitation or discrimination. (Another fruitful question arises: What institutional changes would be needed to offset the substantial unequal life prospects created for children by the wealth of their parents and families?)

But let us continue with the hypothetical example and retain the assumption that fair conditions of equality of opportunity have been established. Assume, then, that the inequalities of income that are evident here have been created by open and fair market processes. Imagine that individuals have prepared their talents through education, that they have had fair opportunities to do so, that they have constructed life plans that lead them to compete for specific careers, and that they succeed or fail based on their qualifications relative to other applicants. All of that notwithstanding, is the resulting inequality fair? Are markets fair, even when they work correctly, competitively, and neutrally? Is the scheme of income and wealth represented in Figure 4.1 a fair outcome? Are all parties treated fairly in this scheme?

I will examine some of the questions that the market approach fails to answer in a moment, but it is worth emphasizing the moral qualities embodied in the notion of a market economy as stipulated in this example. Individuals are treated impersonally, coercion is absent, and distributive outcomes are determined by the free choices of large numbers of actors. Institutions that establish the conditions of a free market are well designed to eliminate some obvious and common sources of unfairness and injustice: privilege for certain individuals by virtue of their status, coercion of some agents through the use of force, discrimination against some agents on the basis of their religion or race (Buchanan 1985).

The example diverges from the requirements of economic justice spelled out above at the point where prior assets (physical assets and human capital assets) become relevant in the eventual distribution of income. We have already inferred that differences in the wealth of families have most likely had a direct effect on the distributive outcomes. Families who own significant real wealth are able to provide substantial advantages to their children; children who grow up

{just prior distribution of assets and income}

→ | free competition within market institutions |→

{just posterior distribution of assets and income}

Box 4.2   Markets and prior distributions of assets

in families of privilege have a greater likelihood of good health and advanced education. And differences that affect a person in adulthood but depend on features of his or her natal family circumstances cannot be judged fair.

It follows from the perspective on economic justice articulated earlier that, on the assumptions embodied here, the outcome is largely fair if judged by one important set of characteristics but unfair if judged in terms of inequalities of inherited assets. The outcome postulated in this instance is the result of a fair competition among individuals, and we have stipulated impersonality in the institutions and equality of opportunity in their workings. In these respects, the outcomes are substantially fairer than many circumstances that exist in developing countries. However, the degree of inequalities that emerge from the example derive from a mix of justified and unjustified factors—differences of luck, talent, and discipline, on the one hand, and differences in educational opportunities, health, and inherited wealth, on the other. The latter set of factors identify this case as one that embodies significant distributive injustice.

Is the market responsible for these enduring patterns of injustice? The answer is both no and yes. It is not responsible in the sense that we have reasonable grounds for supposing that markets transform just circumstances onto just outcomes. As indicated in Box 4.2, we have reason to believe that the market is capable of mapping just prior distributions onto just posterior distributions.

So the market is not itself the source of injustice in this case. However, we can also judge that the market does not have an inherent tendency to correct the background injustices associated with unjust prior distributions.

Property Rights

The property system in a given country is another complex of institutions that are crucial to both efficiency and justice. Every society embodies a system of property rights, and these rights are central to both economic activity and economic justice. Equally important, every society represents an existing pattern of asset distribution across persons and groups. And these differences wield great influence on the overall outcomes for individuals within the society.

Economic activity involves the use of land, machines, factory space, roads, power lines, raw materials, and other physical assets. A system of property rights defines the owner's scope of authority over the use of an asset, his entitlement to the income generated through the use of the asset, and his right to retain or dispose of the asset. There are many feasible systems of property, among them private ownership by individuals, corporate ownership by legal entities (corporations), community ownership (commons), or state ownership (collectivized industry). So there are significant differences, with different outcomes, among feasible institutional embodiments of property systems. Further, the several rights that define property ownership can be unbundled, so that a system involves some but not all the rights of ownership. For example, a system of property rights governing the use of land might give the "owner" the right to determine the use of the land and the right to collect the revenues deriving from use of the land but not the right to transfer ownership (through sale or gift) to another person. The right of alienation might be withheld for another agent—for instance, the village, the state, or another stakeholder. The legal institutions and practices of a given regime determine the bundle of rights that go along with "ownership" and implicitly determine the flow of revenue that is associated with property rights as well.

It is certainly true that complex economic activity requires a system of property rights. It is also true that there are very substantial differences among the range of institutional systems that could serve to define rights of use, access, and income deriving from property. Finally, it is true that there are substantial differences in the social outcomes that result from economic activity conducted under one set of rules or the other—differences in effectiveness, in productivity, in the distribution of income and political power, and the like. Is there such a thing as a "best" property system? It is credible to argue that there is no uniquely best system; rather, various institutional alternatives have a range of desirable and undesirable characteristics, and a society must choose one system or another.

The theory of private property stipulates that a given range of assets are subject to individual ownership. (A corporation counts as an individual in this context.) The owner has a bundle of rights that permit her to use the property, derive income from the exercise of the property, and alienate the property through gift or sale. The state guarantees the individual's property rights; it prevents others from using or appropriating the asset without permission from the owner, and it refrains from confiscating the property without legal justification. The owner's rights of use are not absolute, since the use of a given asset may impose harms on others. So the state establishes a regulatory context governing the use of property: speed limits, environmental regulations, zoning requirements on construction, and so forth. It is through this exercise of regulation that the public's interests are balanced with the interests and rights of the property owner.

The theory of social ownership stipulates that a given range of assets are subject to ownership by a collective entity—the community, the lineage, the village, the county, or the state. Examples of social ownership include the medieval village commons, in which villagers had equal rights to lead their sheep to graze; the lineage association temple; worker-owned cooperatives; county manufacturing facilities; and state-owned farms and factories. The same questions of use, income, and alienation come up in the context of collective ownership as with private ownership. Who has the authority to determine the use of the asset? Who can determine the assignment of incomes generated through the use of the asset? And who has the right to alienate the asset? Because social ownership implies that a group of people jointly own the asset, the topic of politics immediately comes to the fore. Groups do not act with the same unity of will that individuals do, so it is necessary to have some process of collective decisionmaking in place to make choices about the use of collective assets. This may take the form of electoral politics: The elected government of a given political unit has the responsibility for managing the collective property of the unit. Or it may take the form of unit-level democracy: The workers or farmers own the factory or farm collectively, and they make decisions (including appointment of managers, setting of wages, organizing the work process) according to a public political process. Finally, the collective property may be managed by the national government, with or without democratic process (as was true of state-owned enterprises in the former Soviet Union).

Plainly, it is possible for a single polity to embody elements of both private and social ownership. There is nothing incoherent about a system in which the state owns and manages the national airline, workers own enterprises in several sectors, and private persons and corporations own land and factories in most sectors. Likewise, it is possible for a regime that is primarily founded on collective ownership of the chief economic assets to also embody small private ownership in gardens and trucks. It is clear that enterprises have different economic characteristics under private and social ownership.

A central problem in terms of the justice of outcomes is the fact that a property system—and the distribution of property rights that exists at a given time—can be received by one generation from previous generations. In such a case, the society does not choose its property system (though it may modify it), and it does not choose the nature and degree of distribution of assets within that system of rights. It is possible to amend a property system through the use of the power of the state; for example, a state can undertake a program of land reform in which both the institutions and current distribution of landownership are changed. But such changes inevitably interfere with the previous expectations of some agents within the society, and it is an open question whether that interference is itself an unjust intervention.

The general perspective of this chapter assumes that just distributive outcomes reflect both assets and talents. But since the particular configuration of the property system is subject to control by the state, it is possible for the political process to alter both the distribution and the institutions of property. The state can adopt policies designed to achieve some degree of redistribution of assets across the population (toward greater equality of assets, for example). And it can undertake reforms that change the institutional setting of the property system (for example, privatization of state industries). Consider a range of policies that affect the property system:

- Inheritance taxes
- Nationalization of industry (partial or total)

- Redistribution of land ("land to the tillers")
- Redefinition of property rights in land (e.g., the family production system reform in China in the 1980s)
- Privatization of state industries (as in the United Kingdom, Poland, Russia, China)

What principles should guide the state in its policies toward the property system? Do any considerations of justice entail that the state should engage in certain kinds of property reform? Without attempting to provide a full answer to these questions, I would note that several points are particularly compelling. First, as I emphasized in Chapter 1, the ideal of the person as a bundle of capabilities is fundamental for development. Social arrangements ought to be designed to provide an environment in which all persons can most fully realize their human capabilities. We can cite many examples of poor countries in which these conditions are not present and in which it is deficiencies in the property system that is to blame. So property reforms—land reform, tenancy reform, redistribution of large wealth—may be essential in some countries if they are to succeed in constructing an environment for human flourishing. Second, I emphasized above the importance of equality of opportunity. Extremes of inequality in the possession of assets represent a serious obstacle to equality of opportunity, since opportunities follow assets and the human goods that assets can purchase (education, health services). Once again, the moral urgency of equality of opportunity may dictate the need for some degree of property reform in certain developing countries. Third, it is sometimes argued that there is a range of inequalities of wealth and income that may exceed the limits imposed by the moral equality and dignity of persons. And finally, there is a significant literature that shows that extreme maldistribution of assets can have negative effects on growth and modernization; thus, property reform may itself be an appropriate instrument for enhancing the development prospects of a country. I will now examine the question of property inequalities more closely.

Fair Access to Assets

Our simple theory of distributive justice implies that property owners should derive incomes from the use of their assets and that these incomes should result from a fair and noncoercive process of negotiation with other agents. Several things are true in this regard, however: (1) that there are highly unequal distributions of property ownership in most developing countries; (2) that those distributions are the result of historical processes that often violate principles of fairness; and (3) that those inequalities have substantial effects on the distribution of power, well-being, and opportunity in such societies. Are there principles of justice that would constrain the extent of inequalities in property ownership? And does the violation of such principles lay the basis for the state to launch a program of property reform when they are violated?

One difficulty that arises in confronting the justice of inequalities of property is the fact that we quickly find ourselves on a slippery slope, with the considered judgments at the two extremes apparently pointing in opposite directions. To begin on the high side of the slope, we can consider an example where absentee landlords enjoy a near monopoly in landownership. Imagine an agrarian system in which individuals making up a tiny minority own all the land, hire landless workers to farm the land at low and insecure wages, earn great incomes from the resulting farming activity, and acquire the power and privilege that permits them to function as a permanent elite within the local society. In this case, we are inclined to judge that this inequality is too extreme and too profoundly important to the life prospects of the mass population to be just. This judgment implies that justice requires some degree of property reform and land redistribution.

At the other extreme, imagine a situation in which a small segment of rural society (10 percent) has no land (landless workers); 60 percent of the people are smallholders who own plots of land that exceed the subsistence threshold (prosperous peasants); 20 percent own managerial farms that employ labor (modern farmers); and 10 percent are large landowners who derive rents from their holdings (landlords). Suppose, finally, that there is substantial intergenerational mobility among the groups. This situation has a moderate degree of inequality. Here, we may be inclined to judge that this distribution is fair (assuming that it came about through a just process).

The theory of private property strongly suggests the possibility of inequalities in property ownership. This is because the theory postulates extensive rights of usage and income for the property owner—suggesting the possibility or likelihood that some property owners will be able to acquire more property over time, whereas others will lose some of their property. And it postulates a substantial degree of institutional guarantee over the rights that the owner has in the asset—thereby eliminating the possibility of a frequent redistribution of property. So if there are morally compelling reasons for thinking that an economy ought to be organized around private rights in property, then some degree of inequality appears to be the morally and institutionally predictable consequence.

Can we draw a principled distinction between the "high-inequality" and "moderate-inequality" cases? The problem is that each case can be adjusted by small degrees in the direction of the other. We are considering the possibility that the former case is unjust whereas the latter is just. But if there is a whole series of scenarios intermediate between the two that are arbitrarily close to their neighbors, do we not then pass imperceptibly from a judgment of unjust to a judgment of just, without having passed a clear dividing line between the two judgments? If we begin with the second case and run the scenario forward, it is possible that landownership will continue to concentrate; smallholders will occasionally lose their land, and large landowners will accumulate more land. At what point in such a process do we pass the threshold of injustice? But likewise, if we begin with the first case and start to reduce the degree of inequality in landholding, what is the basis of our stopping when we get to the degree of inequality of case two? Does the logic of the moral importance of improving access of the disadvantaged to productive assets mean that justice requires absolute equality in landholding—or perhaps some version of collective ownership?

In other words, we can ask whether the notion of a property-owning regime with moderate inequalities in ownership and ample opportunities for the propertyless to find economic opportunities is a stable one, either morally or institutionally. Morally, we may find that the logic of the position that defends moderate inequalities but condemns extreme inequalities is untenable. And institutionally, it may be that the moderate-inequality regime commonly shows a tendency to evolve into the extreme-inequality regime.

The institutional stability question gets some help from the policy tools that are available to the state. Taxation and inheritance policies can potentially be used as a brake on worsening inequalities in property ownership. But likewise, policies that aggressively enhance the human resources available to the nonpropertied class—education, health status, and equality of opportunity—should similarly moderate the growth of inequalities of property.

The question of the moral stability of the moderate-inequality position gains some leverage from Rawls's difference principle (see Rawls 2001: section 13). The difference principle maintains that a society should embody the least extensive inequalities consistent with maximizing the position of its least well off members. This formulation suggests that there is a threshold after all; it is the point along the curve of increasing inequalities where no further improvements in the well-being of the least well off results. At that point, and additional inequalities are unjust.

We can begin to devise a principled basis for limiting inequalities by examining the relationship between inequalities and the life prospects of the disadvantaged. Extreme inequalities of wealth usually create comparable inequalities of power and influence, and they generally result in economic circumstances in which the disadvantaged have extremely limited (and unequal) life prospects. So we might formulate a boundary principle on inequalities along these lines:

- Inequalities in wealth and income should not exceed the point where full democratic participation is impossible for the disadvantaged.
- Inequalities in wealth and income should not exceed the point where the ability of the disadvantaged to realize their human capabilities is impaired.

These principles do not provide a full theory of the justice of asset inequalities, but they set reasonable moral standards that can guide policymakers as they reform property institutions.

Property Reform

Entitlement and property reform has been a central recommendation advanced by experts concerned with "development with equity." Leading economists such as Irma Adelman and Hollis Chenery argue for a position that places a program of asset redistribution at the center of a strategy of just economic growth (Chenery et al. 1974; Adelman and Morris 1973; Herring 1983).

The advantages of entitlement reform are several. First, such reforms have the immediate effect of bringing about greater equality of income. As the poor are able to diversify their income opportunities, the distribution of income can be expected to narrow. Second, such reform can be expected to increase the equality of opportunity in society and to improve access to education, health care, and adequate nutrition. This result improves the overall well-being of the poor; it also enhances the overall productive capacity of the society.

Asset redistribution programs have immediate and enduring effects in reducing inequalities and increasing the share of income flowing to the poorest. The land reforms that occurred in Taiwan, Korea, and China had substantial impacts on both inequalities and poverty in each of those economies. Land reform, however, faces daunting problems of domestic political opposition, since it typically involves a transfer of wealth from the affluent to the poor. And land reform in the absence of corresponding support programs (e.g., provision of rural credit, appropriate price policies, marketing arrangements, and so on) is likely to leave the rural economy in a stagnant state. (See Herring 1983 for a detailed comparative study of Asian land reform programs.)

Adelman (1978) makes a strong argument for the redistribution of assets—*before* the period of rapid economic growth. Her argument is based on the postwar experiences of Taiwan and Korea, in which sweeping land reforms occurred prior to industrialization and agricultural modernization, with outcomes that were favorable for both inequalities and poverty. She argues that asset redistribution (land reform) is necessary in most developing countries because land is the chief productive asset in most poor nations and because development of agriculture without redistribution will lead to the bulk of rising incomes flowing to large farmers and landlords. Further, Adelman contends that redistribution should occur before development, for two reasons. First, the assets are still low in value at that point, so redistribution will be less politically and financially costly. And second, by redistributing in advance, it is all but guaranteed that development will lead to more evenly distributed income gains across rural society. (Adelman's article in Lewis and Kallab 1986 is a concise summary of her proposals on this issue.)

Adelman's position largely depends on notions of equity. But it is often argued that land reform is, in many contexts, a positive step in agricultural productivity due to its capacity to increase the yield of the land. This increase results from the fact that agriculture commonly involves few economies of scale; small farmers, with appropriate institutional support, are able to implement agricultural innovations and generally supply greater inputs of labor per hectare. So there is typically an increase in yields as a result of land reform. A second advantage of asset redistribution is the increase in demand that it creates for light-manufactured goods—thus providing an impetus to growth in the industrial sector.

Chenery offers a more modest proposal as a solution to the maldistribution of assets in the context of developing countries. He argues that direct asset redistribution is too politically contentious to be feasible in most instances (Chenery et al. 1974). Instead, he argues for a policy of "redistribution with growth," in which developing country governments will commit themselves to channeling a significant fraction of annual growth into building up the productive assets of the poor—for example, education, rural credit, irrigation facilities, or input subsidies. Chenery holds that this is a politically feasible means by which to gradually augment the asset base of the poor, without directly challenging existing property arrangements. (It ought to be noted, however, that the problem of keeping in place a redistributive program of this sort over a period of decades, in the face of the political opposition of elite and middle-class organizations, is not much less daunting than that of implementing land reform itself.)

These arguments suggest that land redistribution is critical and attainable in many circumstances. But the political context is critical; the strength of propertied elites is quite different in different contexts. In Brazil and the Philippines, landed elites are dominant in the political system; antielite policies cannot get on the agenda. In India, elites cannot block the agenda, but they can block the implementation of policies contrary to their interests. Thus, Atul Kohli argues that land reform is much more feasible in a multiclass setting, with elites in both urban and rural sectors, than is a transition to socialism in a two-class industrial setting. The central variable, according to Kohli, is the presence of a politically competent party with organizational capacity that is committed to development policies favoring the poor (see Kohli 1987). The obstacles are not class opposition so much as weak states and failures of administrative capacity.

Public Policy and Social Welfare

So far, I have focused attention on the institutions of the market and their distributive effects. Another crucial and large source of distributive outcomes is the state. Through its ability to collect taxes, the state is capable of creating institutions that deliver social goods to all or part of its citizenry, for a variety of reasons. The state can provide a system of free public education; it can create free or low-cost health clinics for the poor; it can create a backup system for food provisioning and food price subsidies for the poor; and it can create programs of social income insurance (supplementary income for the unemployed, elderly, disabled, or poor). Does justice require that the state provide any of these amenities? Or are these optional programs, subject to the state's discretion?

We might consider a spectrum of possible views of public policy programs designed for enhancing the welfare of the poor:

- A core set of public welfare programs is required by principles of justice.
- A core set of public welfare programs is desirable but not mandatory (to improve the welfare of the poor, to enhance the productivity of society, to reduce social tensions, and so on).
- A core set of public welfare programs is undesirable (because it creates perverse incentives, because it interferes with more efficient market mechanisms of delivery, because "people should only get what they earn").

I will take up the final position first. Throughout this chapter, I have emphasized the point that an economy is a wealth-producing engine that depends on the joint efforts of myriad persons and groups. All members of society have a positive stake in the workings of the economic system, and all deserve some share of the economic product. However, the market mechanism works poorly to handle problems of poverty and deprivation within a functioning society. The market does not provide an automatic mechanism for directing educational or health care resources toward poor communities or subcommunities; on the contrary, the tendency of the market is to direct those resources toward the groups most able to pay for them. This observation implies that the existence of persistent poverty and deprivation is akin to an "externality" within a market economy.

Second, I have emphasized throughout the book the centrality of social goods such as education, nutrition, and health care. The ability of children to realize their talents and capabilities is dramatically reduced if they are denied access to effective education, adequate nutrition, and an appropriate minimum level of health care. So these goods are crucially important for the realization of the central good of development—the realization of human capabilities.

Third, the state does in fact have the capacity to establish and fund effective systems for providing various goods. The examples of Kerala and Sri Lanka are instructive here; these are developing societies with high levels of human well-being in the context of low per capita GDPs. The best explanation of this anomaly is the provisioning of social goods such as education and health care through programs of public policy and public finance.

These points lead to the conclusion that the negative finding above is unjustified. The state ought to take on the responsibility of providing certain social goods for some or all of the population because the market mechanism cannot do so and because these goods are crucial for the full human development of some parts of the population. The state has the responsibility of adopting policies that further the public good, and it is plain that enhancing the human capabilities of the poor is a positive contribution to the public good.

All this suggests that public welfare programs are desirable. But are they in fact required? We can take a further step forward by noticing the close connection between at least some of these goods and the broader conception of equality of opportunity discussed in this chapter. Equality of opportunity is a requirement of justice, as was argued earlier. And it is plain that the broad provision of certain social goods is an essential component of equal opportunity. So we can hold that the state is obliged, on the grounds of the legitimate expectations of its citizens that they will be treated justly, to establish and maintain a suite of public policy programs aimed at securing these basic social goods for all. This conclusion in turn justifies the strongest position advanced earlier: that public policy programs are required by the demands of justice. All citizens have a right to demand that government agencies design programs to deliver certain core social goods to everyone in need.

What those programs should be is a large question. Is a citizen treated unjustly when he or she does not have access to affordable education or health care? Or is this another sort of social fault? Publicly funded education surely falls in this category. Governmental attention to widespread problems of malnutrition or famine does as well. The provision of clean water to all communities is likewise an essential component of public health. Thus, it would seem compelling that these services should be assured by government policy. How broadly to cast this net is an issue of legitimate debate, however. And the most important and most confident finding that we can reach in this context is the broad conclusion that the establishment of programs of public policy to supplement the market in the provision of social goods is a demand of justice. This demand is underwritten by the moral importance of the person and his ability to exercise freedom and develop his capabilities.

Conclusions

Considerations raised here prompt a whole series of diagnostic and policy questions when we consider issues of economic justice in a particular developing society. What are the institutions through which incomes are generated and distributed? Do these institutions treat all agents fairly? What is the scope of the inequalities that exist in the society—and are these inequalities sufficiently limited to permit the full and free development of all persons in society? What are the mechanisms that have spawned these inequalities? Are these fair processes of social competition? Do persons enjoy reasonable equality of opportunity in access to social positions—jobs, schools, and the like? Are there social resources in place that secure approximately equal life prospects for all citizens—adequate nutrition, adequate access to education and health care, and freedom of movement within society?

If the answers to some of these questions are unfavorable, we need to ask the therapeutic questions. What reforms are needed within the basic institutions and practices of this society? What steps can be taken by individuals, groups, and the state to move in the direction of greater fairness and opportunity? What obstacles exist to such reforms? How can individuals and groups take effective steps to advance such reforms? The main dimensions of reform that are implied by considerations of fairness and justice fall into several categories: reform of basic economic institutions to enhance equality of opportunity; establishment of effective human services (education, health, nutrition) that lay the groundwork for approximately equal life prospects; establishment and protection of basic labor rights, permitting workers to bargain effectively for a fair share of the economic product; and consideration of some form of entitlement reform.

What does this perspective on distributive justice leave out? One important gap involves the possibility that a given group or region may be economically marginal. Such a group will then receive ultralow incomes, consistent with the principles of distributive justice that we have explored here. Groups of this type are common in the developing world and include hill peoples, people in resource-poor regions, and handicapped and disadvantaged people.

Notes

1. John Roemer (1982, 1983) has offered several theories on the basis of which to make sense of this intuitive notion. These discussions reveal that there is an intimate connection between exploitation, coercion, and institutional structure.

2. See Albert Hirschman's use of this line of reasoning to evaluate political and economic institutions (Hirschman 1970). He introduces the important concept of "exit" to assess the citizen/consumer's level of satisfaction with existing institutions.

3. See John Roemer's analysis of the two conceptions of equality of opportunity (Roemer 1998).

5

Human Rights

Do ALL HUMAN BEINGS HAVE a set of universal human rights? In what do these rights consist? What gives rise to these rights? Are there "positive" human rights as well as "negative" human rights? Or is the moral force of the doctrine of human rights limited to civil and legal protections of the individual's person and freedoms? What consequences do human rights have for economic development policy? And is the concept of a human right a universal concept, or is it a specifically Western notion that has little relevance in other cultures? This chapter will consider whether a theory of human rights provides a strong basis for resolving the central problems of development ethics. I will take the position that a theory of human rights is indeed needed within development ethics but that many of the problems of development ethics may be better resolved on the basis of other normative resources.

What Is a Right?

I begin by surveying the moral terrain that is involved in the concept of an individual right. A right is an embodiment of a form of freedom. Individuals are deliberative actors. They have goals and purposes, they have the rational faculties needed to arrive at plans of action in pursuit of their goals, and they have physical abilities to attempt to carry out their plans. Individuals live in social groups, and they live within the boundaries of states with legal systems. Both states and social groups have the capability to coerce individuals—to use force and the threat of force to prohibit some actions and compel others.

125

An individual has freedom with respect to a certain kind of action if (1) she has the power and resources necessary to carry out the action, and (2) there is no coercive restraint that prohibits or compels the action. Coercion and threats, that is, represent limitations or abrogations of freedom. Rights, then, are the embodiment of freedom or liberty. When persons have effective and recognized rights with respect to certain kinds of action, they have the freedom to undertake those actions. The state's authority to create laws is an authority to coerce citizens. But the theory of individual rights stipulates that states and systems of law are subject to a higher requirement, analogous to a constitution, that lays out the system of rights that the state must respect. And liberal political theory holds that a constitution that embodies the correct set of rights and liberties is itself the embodiment of the freedom of its citizens (Rousseau 1983). Examples of important individual rights include the right to free expression, the right to liberty, the right to free association, the right to impersonal treatment within a system of law, and the right of bodily integrity.

The theory of individual rights as a foundation for the legitimate state finds powerful expression in the tradition of social contract theory, including particularly the writings of John Locke (1952), Immanuel Kant (1999), and John Stuart Mill (1989). The social contract tradition emphasizes the ideal of the free individual whose liberties are expressed within a bundle of individual rights. This defense of the importance of individual rights is associated with a developed conception of the intrinsic worth and dignity of the moral individual. Within this tradition, the individual is seen as possessing inherent worth, and it is of the greatest moral importance that each individual should be treated with respect. It is an inherent part of the moral definition of the person that he should possess freedom—the ability to choose his life plan and course of action. The individual's freedom is subject to justifiable constraints, and much of the content of liberal political theory assesses the nature of these legitimate constraints. But there is an overriding moral imperative that requires that the state respect individual rights and that it create a system of law in which these rights are embodied. Kant (1990) puts his theory of the person in terms of the principle that we ought to treat persons always as ends, not solely as means. To treat a person as an end means respecting his freedom, and this requires respecting his rights. Locke puts his theory in terms of the principle that individuals ought to have maximum liberty subject to the equal liberties of others. Maximum liberty is, then, equivalent to the idea of a system of rights that guarantees the same liberties for all citizens.

An individual right is thus a feature of the person's scope of freedom in choice and action. It embodies the individual's freedom or liberty. A right is a moral entitlement of one sort or another: for example, an entitlement to express one's thoughts freely and without interference, an entitlement to bodily integrity, or an entitlement to legality. To say that one is entitled to something is to say that others have corresponding obligations not to interfere with the object of this entitlement. If the individual has a right to X, then others have an obligation not to interfere with the individual's performance of X. So the fact that individuals have rights of bodily integrity entails that governments have obligations not to torture; to say that one has an entitlement to free expression entails that governments and persons are obligated to refrain from interfering with such expression. Rights and duties are therefore correlative; rights impose duties on others and on the state.

We can distinguish among rights along a number of dimensions. Particularly important is the distinction between institutionally defined rights (legal rights) and universal human rights (moral or natural rights). A legal system creates a vast system of institutionally defined rights for its citizens—for instance, the right to appeal a zoning board decision on the height of a proposed building, the right to exclude others from the use of one's intellectual property, or the right to apply for a passport. These rights—what might be called "juridical" rights—must be established through a political or legal process; absent such a process of legislation, the rights would not exist.

What, then, are *human* rights? A human right is thought to be a right that people have on universal moral grounds, not derivative from some act of legislation, contract, or personal action or choice. A human right is a right that people have solely by virtue of their moral status as human beings—irrespective of the character of the state within which they live.

We can also distinguish between negative and positive rights. Individuals in liberal democracies have a right of free speech. This is a negative right; it entails that others, including especially the state, have a duty not to interfere with the exercise of free speech. But our definition of freedom above referred to two factors: freedom from coercion and possession of the power or resources necessary to carry out one's actions. The positive theory of rights focuses on the latter point and maintains that individuals' freedoms are not truly embodied unless their ability to gain the necessities for carrying out their goals is assured. Thus, individuals in social welfare states are sometimes said to have a right to good health. This statement entails that others, especially the state, have a positive obligation to provide the necessary resources that provide the basis for good health. (Isaiah Berlin [1969] explores the parallel point with respect to liberties.)

The concept of human rights raises two separate issues: What is the moral foundation of a human right? And what specific rights are included in a valid enumeration of human rights? I will explore both issues in the next several sections.

Moral Foundations of Human Rights

Where do rights come from? What is the moral basis for attributing rights to persons? What set of facts provides moral force to the claim that "P has a right to X"? For certain categories of rights, answers to these questions are obvious. Legal and constitutional rights are created by a legislative or constitutional process within an organized state. They are established by some political process, and they are guaranteed by the coercive power of the state. (We can, of course, ask several deeper questions: What features of political institutions and legislative process are needed to create morally compulsory rights? And what constitutional protections does justice require of any just state?)

Another fairly straightforward source of rights is the act of promising or committing and, more generally, the free agreement among persons. If Smith promises Jones that he will mow the grass on Saturday, then Jones has a right to demand of Smith that he fulfill this promise; Smith has created a moral obligation for himself through his promise that constitutes a right of performance on the part of Jones. Normally, we expect such obligations to be incorporated into legal protections—through legally binding contracts, for example. But the obligations that surround such circumstances are independent from the legal system. In theory, individuals in the "state of nature" could make agreements among themselves that create obligations and rights for each other—though the issue of interpretation and enforcement of such agreements is a deep one. (Robert Nozick explores the scope of such voluntary agreements in *Anarchy, State and Utopia* [1974].) This idea can be expanded into the notion of a *social contract* as the source of individuals' rights and duties. It can be argued that certain rights exist because they were stipulated (or would have been stipulated) in a prior agreement setting the terms for a given range of social interactions.

But what about the most general and comprehensive notion of rights—moral rights or universal human rights? When we say that someone has a moral right or a universal human right, we are not presupposing a legitimate legal background that has stipulated the right. Rather, we are asserting that the individual has the right—and the state has a corresponding duty to respect the right—independent from the legal or constitutional order and independent from any agreements or promises that may have gone before. The assertion is that the individual has the right simply by virtue of his or her status as a moral being. What are the possible moral justifications for such claims?[1]

Two lines of thought in this regard have been of particular interest in political philosophy in recent years. The first is a generalization of the social contract argument in the direction of an analysis of fairness. On this approach, we take it that the moral situation of the individual ought to be framed in terms of the requirement of fairness. But what is fairness? Rawls's approach to this question stems from the insight that an individual is treated fairly if she is treated according to rules or principles that she would have accepted prior to the commencement of the activities in question. Do individuals have rights, or should their liberties be limited by the principle of social utility? We can answer these questions by asking whether individuals would have, *ex ante*, insisted on a set of arrangements that involved a core set of rights, or whether they would instead have agreed to a principle of utility (with its implication that the individual can be treated in any way whatsoever if such treatment leads to a greater overall utility). Rawls (2001) addresses this question with reference to a hypothetical "veil of ignorance," in which individuals deliberate prior to gaining specific knowledge about their own plans of life and the specific circumstances in which they will live. The argument is that individuals would recognize the moral centrality for them of their own purposes and plans, would recognize that their ability to pursue those purposes and plans would depend on their having rights, and would therefore agree on a set of principles that establishes a set of core rights. We can then extend the argument and ask what specific rights ought to be included in this core set of rights—such as the right of liberty, the right of expression, the right of private property, or the right to buy and sell commodity futures. And the general effort will be to determine which rights a rational person would insist on including in the bundle, prior to having specific knowledge about the circumstances of the society in which he would live. According to this approach, what makes a given set of rights "moral rights" is that all rational persons would prefer a political order in which these rights are respected to one in which they are not.

A second and more fundamental argument derives from the philosophical theory underlying the conception of the good for the person that was discussed in Chapter 1. This theory provides a basis for giving priority to the role of rights in defining the scope of the individual's freedom of choice. A particularly compelling view of the moral human being is that he is constituted by a plan of life and a bundle of individual rights that permit him to pursue the life plan. If we value the idea of the person engaged in free actions and choices along the path of realizing his capabilities and pursuing a deliberative plan of life, the concept of individual rights is almost inseparable from this ideal. Free expression and development require a zone of freedom protected by fundamental individual rights. The notion of an individual right thus emerges directly from a theory of the moral importance of the free individual.[2] But how is the freedom of the individual to be expressed and protected? It is logical to articulate the individual's freedom in terms of a set of rights establishing zones of noninterference in his choices and activities.

What does it mean to have the status of a moral person? In what ways is the moral status of a person different from that of nonhuman beings? It is to be worthy of being treated with respect and dignity, to be treated in a way that recognizes the inherent worth of this particular individual, and to be treated in a way that takes seriously the value of the individual's purposes and plans. We can argue that this perspective requires that we regard individuals as possessing a core set of rights—rights of liberty, freedom from enslavement and torture, freedom from coercion by individuals or the state, and freedom of expression and thought. If any of these rights are dissolved, then the individual is no longer being treated as a worthy and valuable person. Accordingly, a theory of moral rights would be derived as a component of a more general theory of the moral person. Rights are the moral means by which the dignity and liberty of the individual are secured. This line of moral theorizing owes a great deal of its force to the theories of Jean-Jacques Rousseau (1983) and Immanuel Kant (1999).

Both of these approaches attempt to justify the belief that individuals have moral rights by deriving that conclusion from some more basic or more initially credible proposition—for example, that individuals should be treated fairly or that individuals should be treated as moral persons. The arguments are intended to be morally and culturally neutral—that is, they are intended to depend only on general features of human life, including rationality, the diversity of life plans and values, the material limits that human activity confronts, and the possibility that some persons' choices may interfere unwarrantedly with the ability of others to act and choose unless all parties live within a set of principles that establish a zone of moral rights. I will return to the issue of cultural neutrality later in this chapter, but I need to confront one aspect of that issue here. It might be maintained that the moral circumstances of individuals are simply constituted by the set of moral values and structures that are embodied in their own cultures. If the culture emphasizes rights and liberty, then individuals have rights and liberty. If it emphasizes communal values, then individuals do not have rights, and they need to be socialized to accept sacrifices for the greater good of the group. On this approach, there is no such thing as general moral theory as a justification for specific moral principles; instead, there is only the empirical study of the many moral frameworks found in the world's many moral and religious systems.

The strongest possible response to this version of cultural relativism is the strength of the positive philosophical arguments we can put forward for affirmative moral positions. To the extent that we can make a credible, coherent, and cogent case for a conception of the individual and society in terms that emphasize compelling notions of the theory of the person and the well-ordered society, we will have significantly vindicated the position that moral and political values are not simply cultural variables. And if that set of arguments gives central importance to the notion of a core set of human rights within its account of the person, then we have a powerful moral argument for advocating the universal moral significance of human rights.

Issues for Moral Rights Theory

What is the relation between rights and other moral goods? Is the moral situation of the individual exhausted once we have described the bundle of moral rights that she possesses? Or are there other facts about the individual that create moral significance for others and for the state? This idea can be explored in several directions, including a further articulation of the theory of the person and an account of the moral qualities of the community. I will begin with the person. It seems highly compelling to suppose that the moral status of the person is not exhausted by the bundle of rights that we attribute to her. There is moral value in the individual's being able to realize her human potential—artistically, scientifically, communally. And this moral value in turn gives others a moral reason to facilitate these activities of self-actualization. When we realize that many children in Nigeria lack access to clean water, adequate nutrition, and elementary schooling, we can infer that their human capabilities have been limited by these circumstances. This gives us a reason to provide resources and infrastructure that will remove these obstacles. Such reasons lead to moral requirements for us to do more than simply respect rights; they lead us to an obligation to actively enhance the ability of these children to achieve their human potential. So the theory of individual moral rights takes us part way to an accurate understanding of the moral situation of the individual moral person, but it falls short of a complete theory of the person and the obligations that we have to others. Putting the point at the level of the state, we can say that the state has obligations of provisioning that go beyond the protection of individual rights. To the extent possible, the state has a positive obligation to create programs and opportunities that permit individuals to realize their human capabilities. From the perspective of political philosophy, the maxim for governments to "protect human rights" is morally important, but it is not the end of the responsibilities that governments have. Governments also have obligations stemming from the moral importance of the individual's ability to fully realize her human capabilities.

Another important issue concerning the theory of individual rights is the moral status of groups and communities. Do communities have moral values distinct from the values of the individuals who make them up? Do communities or groups have rights that are distinct from the individual rights of the people who constitute them? These are contested issues today. The theory of the person I have developed here suggests that moral worth is entirely invested in individuals. Groups have worth only in the derivative sense that they are constituted by individuals who have worth. There is no worth in the group that does not correspond to the worth of some of its members. This theory of the moral individual has been criticized from the point of view of communitarianism. According to that approach, communities and groups have value beyond the simple additive sum of the values of the individuals who make them up (Sandel 1982). So a moral theory that defines the value of a social group exclusively in terms of the rights of liberty of its citizens has missed an important moral factor. This critique can be extended to maintain that it is morally appropriate to limit individuals' rights for the greater good of the group or even that it is morally appropriate to regard "rights" as a legal fiction with no profound moral status.

A more limited critique of the theory of the moral centrality of individual rights questions the specific list of rights that an author or thinker puts forward. The critic accepts the general point that the individual has moral importance and that this moral importance is best identified as a cluster of rights but argues that certain of the rights enumerated have been smuggled in without appropriate justification. For example, democratic socialists would accept the notion that every citizen has rights of political association, freedom of expression, and freedom from unjustified punishment, but they would reject the idea that the right to own property is a genuine and fundamental right. The democratic socialist would argue that the property institutions of a given society are subject to legitimate moral variation and that "social property" (that is, property shared by groups or society at large) is a legitimate form of property institution (Walzer 1983; Gould 1988). From this vantage point, the question that should be posed is this: Which of the several possible property systems is best designed to permit the full and democratic development of the citizens of a society? The answer to this question must depend on a close analysis of the likely consequences of the several alternatives, measured from the point of view of the full and democratic development of the men and women who make up society. On this approach, then, the critic accepts the view that the individual has rights but disagrees about the particular enumeration of those rights.

A related criticism suggests that the enumerated list of rights that is commonly advanced by liberal theory is too limited. Critics in this group maintain that individuals have positive rights as well as negative rights—"rights to" as well as "rights against"—and that a fully satisfactory theory of individual rights must take these positive rights into account. For example, it is sometimes argued that every individual has a right to a livelihood. If accepted, this principle imposes a duty on the state to secure economic arrangements through which full employment is possible and to serve as the employer of last resort. I will consider this point more fully below.

Candidates for Universal Human Rights

I will now turn to the question of content. Are there specific rights that emerge from consideration of these powerful arguments linking freedom, the human good, and individual rights? What are the relevant individual rights— for example, a right to bodily integrity, a right to exercise free speech, or a right to hold and dispose of property?

Rights of the Person

An important bundle of human rights are those that pertain to the integrity and security of the individual: centrally, the rights not to be enslaved, killed, or tortured; the right to due process within the legal system; and the rights of freedom of thought, expression, and association. Why are these rights morally central? First, they are key because protections in these areas are prerequisites of respect for the value and dignity of the individual person. When the individual citizen is seized and tortured, his capacity to live as a flourishing person is obviously impaired or destroyed. And when citizens live in fear of arbitrary arrest and mistreatment, their freedoms are steeply devalued. So these rights of integrity and security are necessary preconditions for a decent human life. Second, these right are key because states and powerful organizations in the twentieth century were all too ready to violate these protections. Powerful organizations such as the state (but including many nonstate organizations as well) have immeasurable capacity to harm individual persons: Arrests in the middle of the night, political prisons, death squads, private militias, executions, and torture were both nightmarish and ordinary in the twentieth century. (It is worth seeking out some of the literature through which victims of such abuses have expressed their experiences. See, for example, descriptions of political arrest written by Arthur Koestler and Aleksandr Solzhenitsyn, accounts of the treatment of "class enemies" during the Cultural Revolution in China, accounts of survivors of massacres in peasant villages in Central America, or recollections of the human suffering created by McCarthyism in the United States [Koestler 1941; Solzhenitsyn 1974; Feng

1991; Schrecker 1986].) States are all too ready to employ their coercive powers to use and punish individuals for their own purposes. And so it is crucial that there be the strongest possible institutions to provide support to the individual's rights against these forms of abuse.

What about rights of freedom of thought, expression, and association? These rights are critical because of their relation to the meaningful exercise of human freedom. Throughout this volume, I have emphasized the moral importance of the free individual. To exercise freedom is precisely to be free to think, to criticize, to express one's thoughts, and to associate with others according to one's choices and preferences. So if persons are restricted in their exercise of these capacities, then their ability to develop and actualize their intellectual and political potential will be stunted. It is also credible, as argued by John Stuart Mill, that the "liberal" society—that is, the society characterized by extensive individual liberties of thought and expression—will also be the most effective society in arriving at new ideas, correcting false beliefs, and making progress on important social issues. Mill (1989) places great importance on the effectiveness of free and open debate as a tool for arriving at the truth on a particular issue, and we can only harness this engine of inquiry by securing extensive rights of thought and expression.

The inventory of the rights of the person often includes rights of property. Is the right to hold and use property itself a fundamental human right? Let me first canvass reasons for supposing that there is some important right lurking in this area. Centrally, the morally significant fact is this: Human beings have material needs, and their material needs can only be satisfied through some mediated exchange with nature and real physical property. Food can only be produced using tools, land, and accumulated seed stocks; clothing requires access to the materials and tools needed to assemble the clothing; and so forth. So a world in which individuals in general are denied all access to natural and fabricated products is one in which they quickly perish—or in which they are subject to irresistible coercive conditions. (If you have exclusive rights to all the water within a seven-day walk of the village, then I am entirely in your power. This point underlies the "Lockean proviso," according to which individuals are permitted to appropriate unclaimed natural products so long as there is as much and as good left for others [Locke 1952; Nozick 1974].) So we can infer that individuals have a right to some sort of access to the means of life—whatever form that access might take. And we can infer that individuals need to have a prima facie right to retain the material goods they have acquired through their material activities in support of their material needs. Thus, something like a right to hold and use property appears to be a fundamental prerequisite of a free human life.

The qualification that must be articulated is this. There are multiple possible property systems through which access to material goods can be mediated. A simple Lockean theory of private property holds (1) that all goods have private owners; (2) that individuals own a suite of forms of property, including real property, intellectual property, and labor power, talents, and skills; and (3) that individuals satisfy their material needs by exchanging rights of access or use of these various assets. Accordingly, individuals are treated justly if their full suite of assets (including labor time) is sufficient to permit them to sustain life. It is possible, however, to conceive of forms of "social property" through which at least some assets are held in common and for which there are fair and well-defined procedures for providing rights of access to the use and enjoyment of the social property. Two examples will suffice to make the point— fisheries and workers' cooperatives. As Elinor Ostrom (1990) has demonstrated in depth, there are socially feasible arrangements in which a "common property resource" such as a fish stock is exploited by a number of independent producers within the context of a stable community. In this instance, we have a combination of private property (nets and boats) and social property (the waterway and the fish stock), and we have a set of social rules that establish the terms of access and use that individuals will have to the common property resource. The example of workers' cooperatives illustrates a different point. Here, we are reminded that there are stable economic organizations that embody a type of collective ownership, in the form of a workers' cooperative. In this instance, the workers own the firm and its assets in common, and there is a set of rules through which the worker-owners determine the management of the firm and the distribution of the product (Elster and Moene 1989; Elster 1989a). There is extensive debate over the economic efficiency or viability of social property arrangements such as these. Concerning fisheries, there is the familiar argument that there will be overgrazing of the commons (Hardin 1968). And concerning workers' cooperatives (as well as communal agriculture), these arrangements are said to create perverse incentives such as "easy-riding," low average productivity, and lower than optimal employment of labor (Popkin 1981; Putterman 1985). My point here is not that social property regimes are superior but rather that they are possible. Therefore, what particular rules and institutions ought to govern the use of property becomes a matter of public debate. And the requirements of justice are satisfied if individuals have fair access to the use of natural and fabricated assets. So, on this account, the "right to property" should be understood at a more abstract level than the Lockean tradition would specify.

Rights of Political Participation

Rights of political participation include the right to express political preferences and beliefs, the right to support a political candidate or party, the right to exercise a vote within a procedurally fair democratic process, and the right to stand as a candidate for office. Why are these rights sufficiently fundamental to qualify as human rights? Our answer is analogous to the reasoning cited earlier, in that it begins in the requirements of freedom and results in the conclusion that these rights are essential to the exercise of human freedom. In this instance, however, the freedoms in question have to do with social decisionmaking rather than personal decisionmaking. The state does many things within society. It enacts and enforces laws, it establishes policies, it collects taxes, and it expends revenues in support of its policies. All of these activities affect individual citizens and groups of citizens. So how should the policies and activities of the state relate to the wishes, preferences, and values of the citizens? We cannot require that the state only adopt policies that represent the unanimous preferences of the citizens—because unanimity is unattainable. Likewise, we cannot permit the state to follow the preferences of one designated citizen—this is the "dictatorship" option. So how should public choice be determined? If we respect the dignity and worth of individual citizens, then it appears to follow that social decisionmaking should reflect the choices and preferences of all citizens; that is, democracy in politics appears to follow from the equal moral value of all persons.

This philosophical preference for democracy goes deeper than simply requiring electoral mechanisms; it gives a powerful basis for advocating a lively process of public debate as the arena in which public policy should be crafted. A very compelling strand of political philosophy contends that the freedom to engage in public debate and democratic decisionmaking is itself an important exercise of human freedom (Habermas 1975, 1979). Rousseau (1983), for example, argues that we are only genuinely free when we have entered into democratic moral community with others. In a constructive way, then, the exercise of the freedoms of democratic citizenship is itself a constitutive part of real human freedom. It is through this exercise that we constitute ourselves as part of a community of equal persons.

Second and equally important, the strongest guarantee that citizens can have that the institutions of the state will not exploit them or abuse them is to have full rights of democratic participation. The predatory and abusive state is made possible when citizens do not have the ability to advocate for policies, replace officials, and freely publicize their complaints against government. Consequently, for both intrinsic reasons and instrumental reasons, rights of political participation are essential to full human freedom; it is legitimate to call these human rights. (I will return to issues concerning the importance of democratic institutions in the final chapter.)

In what ways are these rights pertinent to the issues of justice in economic development? Is freedom from arbitrary arrest economically significant? Is the right to participate in elections an economically important right? These are economically important rights in ways that are not immediately obvious. Amartya Sen makes the point that rights of political participation, free expression, and a free press are critical in explaining the degree of responsiveness that various regimes show to the urgent economic needs of the poor. For instance, the fact that there is a free press in India, in the context of a democratic electoral system, explains that nation's success in avoiding famine since independence. Each national government has a powerful electoral reason to avoid famine, and it can be confident that the press will quickly uncover and publish the early evidence of famine. So Indian governments have been energetic in creating early famine warning systems and effective ways of addressing food crises in their earliest stages (A. Sen 1981; Drèze and Sen 1989). More generally, we can say that a society in which rights of political participation, inquiry, and expression are well developed will be responsive to the needs and interests of the poor and that public policies will reflect those interests. So political rights are crucial from the point of view of just development no less than from the point of view of political justice.

Labor Rights

Labor rights are critical in the developing world. Conditions of work directly affect the individual's health, safety, and well-being. And workers' ability to bargain effectively will determine the level of their wages, which in turn will deeply influence their ability to share in the economic product of society and to develop their human capabilities. Are there *universal labor rights* that ought to be established and defended everywhere in the world?

Consider this list of potential candidates for universal labor rights:

- The right to accept or reject a job
- The right to a nondiscriminatory employment process
- Freedom of association/the right to join a union
- The right to collective bargaining
- The right to a safe and healthy work environment
- The right to a nonviolent workplace
- The right to a workplace free from sexual harassment
- The right to a fair wage/living wage
- The right to reasonable limits on the workday
- The right to humane forms of supervision
- The right to employer subsidies for continuing education
- The right to a clean commissary for the lunch break
- The right to a fitness center and shower
- The right to a convenient parking space

Do these rights capture the main elements of what we would want to defend as a set of rights that ought to be mandatory in every setting? Are there items on the list that should be excluded?

The first several rights on the list are arguably fundamental.[3] By contrast, it is clear enough that the last four items are not critical to just treatment of workers but are instead amenities for which workers can bargain. Several candidates on the list may be controversial. Is the right to humane supervision a fundamental right, or is it a right that can emerge through the exercise of other rights (for example, the right to reject a job or the right to join a union)? What about the right to a fair wage or a living wage? What is the definition of *fair* in these circumstances? It might be reasonable to assert that a wage is fair if it is the result of a free and open competition among employers and prospective workers (as emerged in the discussion of fair institutions in Chapter 4). What if stipulating a right to a "living" wage leads to a substantial reduction of employment (and consequent worsening of the poverty of many potential workers)—particularly if we think of the living wage along the lines of the lifestyle of, say, a worker in Ann Arbor, Michigan? What about "reasonable limits on the workday"? Is there an absolute standard that can be used to interpret this requirement worldwide? Or is the limit on the length of the workday legitimately a subject of negotiation between employers and workers and their unions?

So some of these rights are either plainly or at least arguably not in the core. But it is plausible that the first half dozen or so are strong candidates for inclusion in that core set of universal labor rights. The right to accept or reject a job is, at bottom, a right not to be enslaved or physically coerced. Freedom of association is one of the rights identified above as an essential aspect of being a free person. The right to join a union and to bargain collectively is an exercise of the first two rights. The right to a safe and healthy work environment follows from a more general prohibition against inflicting harms on others. The right to be free from violence and sexual harassment derives from the same considerations that generated universal civil rights previously: the dignity of the person and the associated importance of respecting the physical integrity and choice of the person.

So I will put forward for consideration that the first seven rights listed here are strong candidates for universal labor rights and that the remaining rights are better seen as the potential outcomes of the exercise of these rights through negotiation between worker and employer.

What would be the effects of implementing such a core set of rights in a typical poor country? Would conditions for the whole body of society improve, remain constant, or worsen? First, it is plausible to suppose that working conditions and wages would improve. When workers are free to organize unions, they have a greater ability to influence the bargaining process toward their interests, and they are thereby in a better position to claim a greater portion of the value added during the production process. (It is, of course, possible that this greater power may lead to impasse rather than progress. In the medium and long term, productivity must improve if wages and working conditions are to improve. So it is in the interest of both parties to think creatively and flexibly about the organization of the production process.) Second, it is possible that the unit cost of production will rise (in the short term), reflecting the costs of improvements in the working environment that are required for the sake of health and safety. (Here again, though, there is the possibility of a countervailing effect: A healthier and safer workplace is likely to be a more productive workplace, so improvements in the quality of the work environment may be self-financing.) Third, it is possible or likely that profits will be lower, so the multinational firm may have an incentive to seek out a production location where these rights are less well established. Fourth, it is possible or likely that the firm will seek out labor-replacing technologies, thereby reducing the demand for labor and potentially increasing the number of workers forced into the informal sector.

These mixed results suggest that we cannot predict with confidence what the net economic effect would be on a country such as Mexico if core labor rights were effectively established. What we can infer is that a level playing field with respect to labor rights would substantially improve the condition of the poor in the developing world throughout the global economy. The additional costs associated with complying with these rights would be comparable across labor markets, so firms would not have an incentive to relocate. The rising human capital associated with better-paid workers would have positive effects on productivity and would give the firm a greater stake in its workforce. And rising productivity would give the firm the opportunity to expand production, thereby simultaneously reducing the unit labor cost and increasing the total amount of labor expended.

Rights of Well-Being

Henry Shue (1980), among others, argues that all human beings have basic rights that serve as the normative basis for international ethics: Regimes that disregard these rights are unjust. Further, Shue argues that a variety of economic rights are included among these basic rights; so that developing countries have a strong obligation to undertake development policies that most rapidly advance the ability of their citizens to satisfy their subsistence needs.

Do positive rights have the same status as negative rights? I will take the view that they do not and that they are better understood as statements of morally desirable outcomes that generate obligations and imperatives for governments rather than rights in the strict sense.[4] It is a profoundly good thing that every individual should have access to health, education, nutrition, and employment, and it is a moral fault when a government fails to take feasible actions to enhance its citizens' access to these goods when it is able to do so. But there is a great moral difference between the government that systematically violates the human right against torture and the government that fails to bring about maximum employment opportunities for the poor. Moreover, the world's most stringent efforts should be directed toward controlling the abusive behavior of states that violate their citizens' human rights through murder, torture, and arbitrary imprisonment.[5] I will therefore presume a narrow interpretation of human rights, according to which every human being has a core set of civil and political rights that all governments, agencies, and persons must respect: rights of life, security of person, basic freedoms, and equal treatment under the law. These rights follow from the core of the conception of the person and his or her relation to a just government. But the theory of human rights is not the whole of a theory of international justice; instead, it functions as a baseline set of guarantees that governments are urged to provide for their citizens, on pain of international censure.

The reader will note that this position is inconsistent with the United Nations Universal Declaration of Human Rights (UDHR) (discussed in the next section), which implies no such distinction in the moral status or compulsoriness of the list of rights it enumerates. The Universal Declaration includes both negative and positive human rights, including, for example, both the right against torture and the right to a job. The former rights include "civil and political" rights, and the latter include "economic, social, and cultural" rights. It is worth noticing, though, that subsequent efforts at institutionalizing the declaration within the United Nations proceeded by establishing two separate committees on human rights: the Human Rights Committee elected by the parties to the International Covenant on Civil and Political Rights and the parallel but weaker Committee on Economic, Social, and Cultural Rights (Donnelly 1998: 57). This division of responsibility came about in part as a result of political disagreements among signatory governments, but it also appears to reflect a version of the point made here—that we should confine our use of the notion of human rights in the strongest sense to the core rights of the person and pursue broader economic and social goods through other moral resources (theories of justice and equity, theories of the moral importance of human well-being).[6]

The Universal Declaration of Human Rights

So far, we have considered human rights from the perspective of moral and political philosophy. But human rights have also entered international politics in major ways since the 1940s.[7] International conferences have attempted to formulate sets of principles that all governments ought to honor in regard to treatment of their citizens. A general notion of human rights has played a central role in the theory of international law and ethics since World War II. The most important such effort resulted in the formulation and adoption of the United Nations Universal Declaration of Human Rights in 1948 (one of the first results of the newly established United Nations). The declaration is designed to provide minimal standards and protections that governments must provide for their citizens. Such rights include civil and political rights (freedom of expression and association, democratic rights of political partic-ipation), rights of personal security (freedom from arbitrary arrest, torture, or death), and (perhaps) economic rights (rights to health care, employment, or education).

The history of human rights institutions and practices in the twentieth century raises a number of difficult questions.[8] What is the moral force of an international declaration on human rights? Is the notion of a right itself an ethnocentric Western construct? What if practices in some countries (for in-stance, the practice of arranged marriage) flatly contravene the declaration—which norm trumps the other?

It is worthwhile noting that the declaration falls somewhere between a philosophical treatise and a legal document. A treatise puts forward the au-thor's conclusions or positions on one or more moral issues, along with a set of reasons designed to lead the reader to agree with these conclusions. A legal document is the result of a process of negotiation among legislators and is therefore a compromise document. Further, a legal document is designed to have compulsory force. It is intended to establish rules or principles that a political agency will then enforce with the coercive authority of the state. The UDHR is plainly a document that has emerged through a process of negotia-tion that is legislative-like; it reflects efforts by its various authors to accom-modate the concerns or objections of some of the signatories. So it is a document that has greater authority than a philosophical treatise, but at the same time, because the United Nations is not a state with full powers of en-forcement, the UDHR falls short of full legislative status (along the lines of the U.S. Bill of Rights, for example). The UDHR affords a point of moral leverage for citizens and groups whose rights have been abridged by their own governments or private organizations. It also provides a fulcrum within international law allowing groups to bring grievances to international tribunals such as the European Court of Human Rights or United Nations Commission for Human Rights.

I will now examine the content of the universal declaration. (The text is readily available on the World Wide Web at www.un.org/Overview/ rights.html.) The preamble to the declaration highlights the permanent importance of human rights and notes the language of the UN Charter to this effect: "Whereas the peoples of the United Nations have in the Charter reaffirmed their faith in fundamental human rights, in the dignity and worth of the human person and in the equal rights of men and women and have determined to promote social progress and better standards of life in larger freedom." The universal declaration is offered as an explicit articulation of understanding of the content of universal human rights.

The first fourteen clauses enumerating rights in the UDHR fall in the category of civil and political rights: freedom from torture, freedom from enslavement, equality before the law, freedom of association. The declaration then moves to rights of citizenship, family, and property (clauses 15–17); rights of conscience, thought, and religion (clauses 18–19); and rights of democratic participation and association (clauses 20–21).

The declaration offers an enumeration of positive rights in the final six clauses of the document: a right to social security and the means necessary to achieve dignity and full realization of his or her personality (clause 22), a right to work and to organize labor unions (clause 23), a right to leisure (clause 24), a right to subsistence and unemployment insurance (clause 25), a right to education (clause 26), and a right to intellectual property (clause 27).

We need to ask a number of questions about this long list of rights. First, do they all have the same moral standing? Are some more fundamental than others? Do some of these rights have a moral priority that demands response in the face of nonsatisfaction more than others? For example, is the right to be immune from enslavement or torture more fundamental than the right to a free elementary school education?

Many states in the developing world lack the fiscal resources to provide a level of social security consistent with clause 22. Should we consider such states as being morally at fault? Or is the right expressed in clause 22 an ideal rather than a strict requirement? Could the citizens of Ivory Coast make a claim against their government on the grounds that the state fails to provide universal free education? Could they make such an appeal on the grounds that the state arbitrarily arrests and imprisons its citizens for their political activities?

Second, what is the moral status of states that fail to secure some of these rights? The Guatemalan state has failed in recent years to guarantee the immunity of its citizens from killing at the hands of death squads, it fails to guarantee free formation of trade unions, and it fails to secure the circumstances of adequate nutrition for all its people. Are all these failures of equal magnitude?

I take the position here that the core human rights are included in the first fourteen clauses. The rights guaranteeing the civil, personal, and political rights of citizens of the world are most critical to their ability to function as free persons, and they are most likely to be assaulted by corrupt and powerful governments. So the full weight of international institutions—both governmental and nongovernmental—should be aimed at protecting these rights. The second batch of rights, the social and economic rights, are also important. But the good that they embody will be equally enhanced by a set of development goals that are constructed around the ideal of the full human person identified in Chapter 1 and the ideal of fair institutions advanced in Chapter 4. The positive rights, in short, are best honored by adhering to a good theory of other development goals and priorities.

Mechanisms of Enforcing Human Rights

The twentieth century witnessed massive state-sponsored assaults on the most basic human rights. The Holocaust, apartheid in South Africa, the Armenian genocide, secret programs of torture and murder on a large scale in Latin America, ethnic cleansing in Bosnia and Croatia—the twentieth century provided nightmarish evidence of the capacity and willingness of states to use violence, torture, and murder against their citizens in order to achieve their political purposes.[9] Are there mechanisms that citizens, governments, and nongovernmental organizations can employ to pressure repressive governments to respect human rights? The United Nations has established several committees and agencies that attempt to monitor compliance with the Universal Declaration of Human Rights—the aforementioned Human Rights Commission, the International Court of Justice, the International Criminal Court (established in 1998), and the Office of the United Nations High Commissioner for Human Rights. However, these agencies are limited in their scope and authority. They have gradually expanded their ability to investigate charges of systematic human rights abuses and to apply political pressure to offending governments, but they have no power of enforcement. A second important potential catalyst for change in the observance of human rights is the foreign policy agenda of developed countries. To the extent that powerful countries incorporate human rights performance into their foreign policy goals, they can wield significant influence over some governments. And there has been a perceptible expansion of the priority given to human rights concerns in U.S. and European foreign policy since 1980. However, the record is a mixed one, and the U.S. government showed a shameful passivity toward friendly Latin American governments (Argentina, Chile, El Salvador, Guatemala) during a period of terrible state-sponsored repression in those countries (Donnelly 1998). Nongovernmental organizations such as Amnesty International, Asia Watch, and Human Rights Watch have gathered the resources and reputations that permit them to monitor and publicize persistent violations of human rights.

How can citizens exert their influence on abusive states? Publicity, public opinion, sanctions, and foreign policy retaliation all have some effect on abuser states. And citizens can affect these factors by responsibly informing themselves of current abuses, by offering their support to NGOs that monitor and publicize human rights abuses, and by making their concerns known to their legislators to encourage stronger support within the government for a human rights-aware foreign policy. Through mechanisms such as these, ordinary citizens can press some of the levers of power by which abusive behavior by states is constrained. (When I discuss labor standards in the next chapter, more focused instruments through which "ethical consumers" can support labor rights in the developing world will be mentioned.)

The fifty-year struggle to create an international consensus on the importance and meaning of human rights and the parallel effort to create enforcement institutions that give strength to this consensus represent a significant advance in the ethical treatment of persons by states. But the experience of the past fifty years demonstrates just how uneven the struggle between predatory governments and citizens is. Governments and their armies and police forces have overseen massacre, imprisonment, torture, and genocide, and only rarely have they been brought to task for these crimes. There are many urgent needs for reform in the world today, to be sure, but the creation of stable institutions of government that respect the human lives and freedoms of their citizens is certainly near the top of the list. And the need for international institutions that have the ability to punish offending states is an urgent priority for international ethics.

Cultural Specificity of Rights?

Is a theory of human rights a Western construct that ought not be imposed on other cultures, or is it a genuine moral universal that applies to all people qua human beings? This topic has been the subject of particular controversy since the drafting of the universal declaration. The American Anthropological Association (AAA) issued a position paper on this topic in 1947. In commissioning this statement, the AAA urged the drafting committee to avoid the error of ethnocentrism, and it formulated several foundational propositions for the drafters to consider:

- "The individual realizes his personality through his culture, hence respect for individual differences entails respect for cultural differences."
- "Respect for differences between cultures is validated by the scientific fact that no technique of qualitatively evaluating cultures has been discovered."
- "How can the proposed Declaration be applicable to all human beings and not be a statement of rights conceived only in terms of values prevalent in the countries of Western Europe and America?"[10]

The third point, in particular, appears to suggest that the concept of universal human rights is culturally specific to the Western moral and political tradition and has no relevance to other cultures.

Alison Dundes Renteln (1990) takes on this topic at length, organizing her discussion chiefly around the issue of relativism and universalism.[11] Her approach proceeds on the basis of empirical cross-cultural study of the value systems of many of the world's great civilizations. She defends the position that ethical relativism is true as an empirical description of the moral practices of diverse cultures around the world. She takes this to amount to two things: that there is a great deal of moral diversity in different cultures and that there is no rational ground for maintaining that one culture's moral ideas are superior to another's. But if this is so, then what justification can there be for insisting on a doctrine of human rights, since this is (or may be perceived to be) an ethnocentric Western idea at odds with indigenous moral ideas and principles? In some cases, Renteln is content to say, so much the worse for human rights: "Women's rights and children's rights are problematic because societies do not all believe that these groups deserve special status. So, to assert the existence of universal standards for them is ethnocentric" (Renteln 1990: 60). But she has a more positive response as well. She holds that though there is no philosophical basis for asserting the moral primacy of human rights, it may turn out that there are empirical regularities across the world's moral cultures that permit us to argue that certain human rights are respected by all cultures. There may be what she calls "homeomorphic" equivalents to human rights in all moral cultures (Renteln 1990: 11). She describes these regularities as empirical universals and regards it as an important task for ethnography to identify such universals. Renteln illustrates this approach with an extended analysis of principles of retribution in a variety of cultures. She believes that a principle of proportional retribution is a plausible candidate for such a cross-cultural universal (Renteln 1990: 95) and one that may support international adherence to some human rights. Her conclusion, then, is that the theory of human rights should be restricted to requirements that are in fact respected by all the world's moral cultures. And she believes that there will be enough common moral substance to support a substantive doctrine of universal human rights.

This position gives too much to the moral relativist. The fact of moral diversity across cultures by no means entails the skeptical conclusion that there are no rational grounds for favoring one set of moral principles over another. The task of formulating a rationally supportable theory of universal human rights requires that we sort out acceptable cultural variation in practices, concerning which the theory of human rights should be silent, from valid moral constraints on states—such as "no torturing of prisoners"—that can be justifiably imposed whether or not indigenous moral beliefs sanction the practice. So Renteln is overly ready to accept the ethical relativist conclusion without making enough of an effort to canvass the philosophical resources available to support a substantive moral theory of human rights.

Rather, we can argue on philosophical grounds that there are rationally compelling answers to the moral relativism that underlies this critique of universal human rights. Of course, it is true that moral pronouncements often contain uncritical ethnocentric assumptions—that is, assumptions about how things ought to be arranged universally that really derive only from a parochial set of local beliefs. However, it is fallacious to infer from "sometimes there is the risk of ethnocentrism" to "always there is the fact of ethnocentrism." And in fact it is possible to offer criticisms of the practices, values, or beliefs of one culture from the perspective of other cultures. We can respect cultural differences without succumbing to the relativist notion that culturally embedded practices and values are beyond criticism. The Holocaust in Germany and Poland, the genocide in Rwanda, and the dirty war in Argentina all embody circumstances in which some important elements of the local culture maintain that "mass executions of enemies of the state are justified," but it is evident that these local beliefs violate universal moral truths. It is a fact that all human beings have moral worth; therefore, it follows that the genocide of Jews, communists, gypsies, and homosexuals is morally wrong. And these acts are morally wrong whether or not they are condoned by local values to the contrary. Cultures can be mistaken in their moral assumptions and practices. It is the function of philosophical ethics to attempt to arrive at justified beliefs about these universal moral truths.

This brings us to a measured position on the issue of ethnocentrism. We acknowledge the fact that moral pronouncements often conceal ethnocentric (or personal) bias. From this, we infer the importance of careful philosophical examination of our principles. But we affirm the possibility of arriving at justified moral judgments that permit criticism of practices that are sanctioned in other societies and cultures.

How, then, do we arrive at those valid cross-cultural principles? It is reasonable to argue that the Universal Declaration of Human Rights has successfully identified some of these; in particular, some of the principles articulating the core human rights—freedom from torture, right to free expression, right to a fair trial—are credible candidates for this sort of cross-cultural universality. The moral significance of the individual human being is an unmistakable moral fact, and from this fact derive these core human rights. Geoffrey Robertson (1999) makes this case with respect to rights against torture.

Viewed in this way, moral reasoning is both a part of a culture and an exercise in moral exploration. A culture's values are subject to self-scrutiny and criticism; thus, Western societies examined the moral implications of the then-accepted practice of slavery and found that their values were inconsistent with this practice. But a culture's values are also subject to scrutiny and criticism from the vantage points of other cultures as well. This scrutiny should proceed in all directions; so, for example, we may find that Confucian values concerning the family may provide a basis for criticizing and improving Western practices surrounding family relations.

The position being constructed here is designed to avoid both relativism and foundationalism, in favor of an all-around rational and critical examination of values and circumstances. We look to enhance the coherence of our beliefs and values, discovering points of inconsistency and revising some of our beliefs; we look to discover "considered judgments" in which our moral intuitions are relatively sharp; we look to survey and understand values from a variety of cultural sources; and finally, we look to formulating moral theories that do the best job of rendering coherent and explaining the judgments and intuitions that we have across a wide range of social circumstances. (Rawls [1971, 1993b] refers to this as the method of reflective equilibrium.)

Human Rights and Development Ethics

I have discussed a variety of types of human rights—rights having to do with the integrity of the person (freedom from torture and physical coercion), rights having to do with citizenship (freedom of association and the right of political participation), a range of positive rights (the right to a minimum standard of health care, education, and nutrition), and labor rights (the right to organize). Are these rights relevant to the issues of development ethics and distributive justice that are our concern in this book? Does a fully developed theory of human rights exhaust those moral considerations that should guide development choices?

Part of this issue depends on whether we include positive rights in the theory. It is plain that the positive rights enumerated here are relevant because they have direct consequences for how the state should organize its policies and finances. To honor these rights, states must deliver a significant level of social provisioning. This leads to direct improvement in the economic well-being of the poor, and it also arguably leads to more effective economic growth. If we conclude that individuals have a right to adequate health care, education, nutrition, and employment, then the theory is very broad and might credibly be thought to exhaust the relevant moral considerations in arriving at just development policies. The moral imperative to governments and policy actors on that approach would be: Respect people's human rights in everything you do. This approach absorbs the theory of the human good of development into the theory of human rights, so human rights theory serves to specify the goals of development as well as the limits on forms of treatment of persons that can be employed. But these rights are the most controversial among the rights we have discussed.

By contrast, if we conclude that it is better to define the theory of human rights more narrowly, as was argued above, giving greatest emphasis to the rights of the person and to political and civil rights, then the injunction "Respect rights" does not exhaust the moral domain of economic development. This is because we need guidance about what inherent goods public policy should be aimed at as well as the limitations on policies and actions that arise out of respect for human rights.

I take the view that human rights theory should be construed in the more focused fashion and that we should not include economic rights among the inventory of fundamental human rights. This position means that we will account for the moral importance of subsistence and human thriving in another way—as outlined in Chapter 1. There, it was argued that public policy ought to be aimed at maximizing the fulfillment of human capabilities (human development). This entails that there are moral goods that are independent from human rights; that human rights theory is not a comprehensive theory of just economic development; and, critically, that there may be circumstances in which the imperatives of human rights conflict with the imperatives of maximizing human development.

Finally, I have argued that there is a core set of labor rights that must be a part of our theory of valid human rights. Labor rights are also directly pertinent to economic development and the establishment of just and good outcomes within the development experience. An increasing proportion of every developing society takes the form of hired labor (as opposed to self-employment, peasant production, and the informal sector). When working men and women are able to advance their economic and social interests through effective organizations, it is logical that their conditions of work and life will improve.

Notes

1. See Dworkin 1977, Donnelly 1998, and Melden 1970 for efforts to provide a moral basis for universal human rights.

2. See Melden 1970 and 1977 for a careful discussion of the moral foundations of rights theories.

3. There is substantial convergence between the first several items on this list and those put forward by the International Labour Organization (ILO) in its Declaration of Fundamental Principles and Rights (International Labour Association 2000). The central rights enumerated in the ILO declaration include freedom of association and the effective recognition of the right to collective bargaining; the elimination of all forms of forced or compulsory labor; the effective abolition of child labor; and the elimination of discrimination in respect of employment and occupation.

4. For an argument against the idea that there is a right to work, see Jon Elster's arguments in Elster 1988.

5. Oxfam International (2001) bases its "global equity" strategy on the moral importance of these social and economic rights.

6. See Overseas Development Institute 1999 for a thoughtful discussion of this issue.

7. The 2000 *Human Development Report* focuses on the role of human rights in development (see United Nations Development Programme 2000). The volume provides an excellent summary of the human rights documents and policies that existed at the end of the twentieth century and of the importance of these issues for just economic development and poverty alleviation. A useful resource is the chronology of important developments in the evolution of human rights that is provided in the report (pp. 27–28).

8. Johannes Morsink (1999) offers a comprehensive historical interpretation of the Universal Declaration of Human Rights. See also Robertson 1999 for a passionate history of the vicissitudes of human rights in the past century.

9. Jack Donnelly (1998) provides detailed studies of many of these cases in his *International Human Rights*. See also Robertson 1999 for an extensive treatment of these cases and the efforts that have been made to limit such abuses.

10. Quoted in Morsink 1999: ix.

11. See also Messer 1993, Cohen 1989, and Magnarella 1994 for several recent anthropological discussions of the status of human rights.

6

Aid, Trade, and the Global Economy

SLUM DWELLERS IN KARACHI ARE affected by decisions made in Washington, Seattle, and Peoria. Sometimes the effects are highly mediated and invisible; sometimes they are positive and sometimes negative; and sometimes they are intended and sometimes unintended. When a teenager in Boston buys a soccer ball, he or she is creating demand for a product that is exported from Karachi, creating a small flow of foreign currency into Pakistan, supporting a business that offers employment to chronically underemployed people in Pakistan, and perhaps taking advantage of sweatshop labor and exploiting the labor of Pakistani children. When a corporate leader in Austin decides to establish a computer factory in Jakarta, he initiates a flow of money into the Indonesian economy, creates jobs for local people, and takes advantage of low-wage labor conditions in that country. When a business journalist researches the chain of production leading from coffee producers to the neighborhood coffee bar, she sheds light for the U.S. public on the conditions of work that are embodied in this chain of activities. When a World Bank committee approves a billion dollar infrastructure loan to the government of Brazil, it dams a river, controls flooding, displaces local people, and creates large opportunities for official corruption. When a telephone installer in Detroit contributes $100 to Oxfam, he makes a small but real contribution to the nutritional status of people suffering from malnutrition or famine and helps make possible the total food programs of that organization. And when the U.S. government approves a total development assistance package of $800 million to Egypt, it pursues a combination of humanitarian and self-interested motives.

These examples all fall within the general rubric of the "globalization" of the world's economy: increasing financial and trade integration, increasing communication and transportation, and increasing interaction among people in widely separated parts of the world. These interrelations within the global economy give rise to important moral relationships among persons and groups who are physically, socially, and culturally very far apart. Several facts about globalization are especially salient from a moral point of view. First, citizens of wealthy nations have the ability to come to know a great deal about the life circumstances of poor people in the developing world, through improved communications and information flows (including information on the Internet). Second, citizens and governments in the wealthy nations are able to take specific actions that can have a measurable effect on the well-being of poor people in developing countries. And third, citizens and governments in wealthy countries are in fact benefited by the economic activities of the developing world—we drink the coffee, we wear the clothing, and we watch the televisions that are produced in poor countries, and we do so at a cost that is less than it would be if we did not have access to the economic activities of those countries. So we have (or can have) reliable knowledge about conditions of human deprivation in the developing world; we have the ability to improve those conditions; and we ourselves benefit from economic structures that help to create those conditions of deprivation. These facts are ethically central. Taken together, they create significant obligations on our part toward people in poor countries. The globalization of economic activity also implies the globalization of moral relationships among the people of the earth.

In this chapter, I will consider mechanisms of international influence through which conditions of life are affected in the developing world and the obligations that these mechanisms create for citizens and governments in the industrialized world. I will begin by addressing issues of trade and investment that have accelerated the process of globalization. Then, I will look at the issues surrounding international development assistance, both governmental and nongovernmental—the topic of foreign aid directed toward stimulating development, alleviating poverty, and responding to humanitarian crises such as famines and refugee movements. This discussion will also consider development lending through such development banks as the World Bank and the Asian Development Bank. In each instance, I will focus on the issues of justice and obligation that arise in the context of these institutions.

Globalization

A powerful impulse in the world today is hastening the process of international economic integration. Economic integration means greater interdependency among countries, greater international trade, greater market integration in commodity prices, and more extensive flows of investment and revenues. The process of globalization incorporates a number of factors: the extension of international trade, the increased mobility of capital through liberalized financial markets, the enlargement of foreign direct investment in developing economies, the extension of manufacturing into global labor markets, the diffusion of technology, and the expansion of activities that affect environmental quality in the developing world.

Economic development—poverty alleviation and consistent improvement of the quality of life in developing countries—requires the growth of employment opportunities and growth in labor productivity. When labor productivity is low, wages will be low as well; so one of the chief goals of economic development strategy must be to achieve sustained growth in productivity and enhanced human development, leading to rising wages and improved conditions of work. These facts imply that it is generally desirable for a developing country to encourage international investment in modern factories and manufacturing sectors. Poor countries need greater access to investment capital; they need easier access to emerging technologies (manufacturing, communications, agriculture, transportation); and they need the stimulus to economic growth that increased global demand for their products can create.

But when international investors choose a locale for new manufacturing capacity, one of the features they are looking for is a source of reliable low-wage labor. So these firms have an interest in keeping wages low. The picture is not altogether bleak, however, because there are countervailing pressures that give the multinational employer incentive to raise wages and improve working conditions. First among these is the need for high-quality products, which implies a manufacturing process that involves increasingly skilled and committed workers. The second is the imperative that "ethical consumers" have begun to create for corporations to establish codes of labor and environ-ment that they implement throughout their manufacturing operations worldwide. It is worth emphasizing that a labor environment can be simulta-neously low-wage and decent; the employer can continue to offer low wages while at the same time observing standards of work hours, health and safety, and fair treatment.

Critics of globalization have emphasized several central themes in recent years. Does globalization involve the exploitation of poor countries by rich countries? Do multinational corporations acquire too much power in an in-creasingly globalized world? Does the pace of globalization create economic processes that lead to environmental harms—perhaps disproportionately in poor countries? Do these processes foster conditions of labor throughout the world that are inconsistent with reasonable standards of human development and well-being? And does the process of globalization intensify inequality, both between rich and poor countries and within developing countries themselves?

Some critics have criticized globalization on other grounds, having to do with cultural factors rather than economic factors. It is sometimes claimed that the globalization of products through marketing and sales is itself a bad result, whereby a few products drive out the valuable diversity of local varia-tion. The mass culture of global marketing extinguishes local culture and val-ues—again, a result that many critics condemn. Local arts, culture, and ceremony are diminished as Hollywood and Bollywood (the Indian film in-dustry) create a global mass culture. And traditional cultures—Native Amer-ican culture, aboriginal cultures, the various regional cultures and languages of Europe—are preserved only in theme parks. These criticisms begin to con-verge on a general critique of the goals of modernization and material im-provement that underlie the whole project of economic development.

In the pages that follow, I will examine some of the international institu-tions and trends that have led to an increasing pace of globalization since the 1980s.

The Theory of Free Trade

The underlying economic theory in favor of free trade depends on the idea of "relative advantage" and the economic benefits of "getting the prices right." The theory of relative advantage reflects the idea that each nation has a specific configuration of economic characteristics—natural resources, skilled labor, agricultural land, industrial knowledge, and transportation advantages—that enable the national economy to produce certain goods more efficiently than other economies can do. Country A has limited arable land and extensive skilled industrial labor; country B has abundant arable land and limited skilled labor. Country A has a relative advantage in producing finished consumer goods (shirts), whereas Country B has a relative advantage in producing food (corn). The theory of relative advantage holds that both countries are better off if each produces the goods for which it possesses a relative advantage and they then trade goods to satisfy the needs of consumers in both countries. Each country makes the most efficient use of its available resources, and each reaches a situation in which the consumption bundle for its population is maximized at lowest cost. In other words, free trade between two countries optimizes the use of the resources in each in a way that maximizes the standard of living of both populations.

Now suppose that A and B introduce a tariff on the other's chief product. This action has the effect of increasing the price of corn in A and the price of shirts in B. These increases then give an incentive for producers in A to shift from shirt production to corn production and for producers in B to shift from corn production to shirt production. Both systems now reach a new equilibrium—but one in which a smaller total output is achieved in both corn and shirts (because more of the production in each sector is taking place in the country that is less efficient at producing that good). Overall, this has the effect of reducing the standard of living for people in both A and B.

This simple theory leads to a global conclusion. Reduction of barriers to trade will increase the overall efficiency of the global production of all traded goods, thereby increasing the standard of living for every population. (This conclusion does not imply a reduction of inequalities across nations; rather, it implies that the results for each population would be even worse if trade barriers were established.) Albert Fishlow and Karen Parker (1999: 9) identify a host of specific benefits for the United States of the global integration of goods, capital, and labor markets: lower-cost consumer goods, growth of U.S. exports, expansion of the aggregate quantity of higher-skilled, better-paid jobs; and increasing productivity.

What are the possible harmful consequences of free trade? Several specific concerns have been particularly prominent among critics of globalization:

that globalization is environmentally harmful, that it leads to deterioration of labor standards in many places, that it takes jobs away from some countries by moving production toward low-wage environments, and that it exacerbates inequalities and poverty in developing countries.

Trading Regimes

Free trade regimes such as the General Agreement on Tariffs and Trade (GATT), the World Trade Organization (WTO), and the North American Free Trade Agreement (NAFTA) have made significant steps forward in the extension of free trade agreements among trading nations since World War II. These regimes have had the goal of lowering the barriers to trade among nations by reducing or eliminating tariffs and quotas on goods. The 1990 *World Development Report* put the point this way: "Open trade relations are ultimately in everybody's interest. Protection in the industrial countries preserves only a small number of jobs, and at great cost to consumers" (World Bank 1990: 21). Since 1990, however, free trade issues have been at the center of antiglobalization protests. It has been held that free trade is the strongest single factor leading to poverty alleviation, on the one hand, and that it is a source of continuing exploitation in developing countries, on the other. The central criticisms of free trade revolve around possible effects on poverty, environment quality, and labor standards. Critics have also maintained that these trading regimes are weighted against the interests of poor nations in favor of rich and powerful nations—an allegation that gains some force when we consider the lagging progress of free trade in agricultural goods and fibers.

What is the reality? Does free trade harm the world's poor, or does it help—through stimulating economic development throughout the world, permitting countries and regions to make the most of their comparative advantage, and giving the ethical consumer greater leverage on the conditions of work and environment in the developing world? How do trade regimes work? In what ways do they stimulate economic growth? What good and bad effects do they have? In what ways are they thought to harm the poor and powerless? Are they exploitative?

The free trade agenda is geared to lowering the barriers to trade throughout the world or throughout specific regions. The impulse toward barriers to trade stems from governmental and private efforts to "protect" domestic producers against foreign competition. Barriers to trade include quotas and tariffs. A nation may choose to protect its domestic industries by forbidding or limiting import of goods in that industry, or it may attach a tariff to the import of the good (so that the domestic producer has a price advantage in selling the product to the domestic consumer). Examples of quotas include the U.S. policy on sugar importation; the United States imposes a tariff-rate quota on sugar imports in order to protect domestic sugar beet producers. Examples of tariffs include the proposed new U.S. tariffs on imported steel. When the United States places a 30 percent tariff on imported steel, the action increases the effective cost of imported steel relative to domestic steel within the U.S. market, thereby permitting U.S. producers to sell their product at a higher price.

International trading regimes emerged after World War II to set a framework for international trade. The General Agreement on Tariffs and Trade evolved after the war as a framework for nondiscriminatory trade practices among contracting parties. The overall purpose of the organization was to reduce or eliminate barriers to international trade, including quotas, tariffs, and preferential trade agreements. The World Trade Organization is the successor to GATT, and it has moved to eliminate quotas and bilateral agreements in favor of uniform (low) tariffs on sectors of goods (Overseas Development Institute 1995). The establishment of the WTO through the Uruguay Round of trade negotiations significantly extended the importance of GATT for developing countries. The WTO widens the scope of trade agreements to include clothing and agricultural products—which were excluded from GATT. (Textiles and clothing were separately negotiated and were included in separate agreements under the rubric of several Multi-Fibre Arrangements [MFAs].) And developing countries have significantly increased their share of manufactured exports on world markets. The Overseas Development Institute estimates that developing countries contributed 7 percent of manufactured exports in 1970, 12.5 percent in 1986, and 20 percent by 1990 (Overseas Development Institute 1995). So trade reform is increasingly important for developing countries.

The European Union (EU) and the North American Free Trade Agreement are both important developments in the establishment of large free-trade zones in Europe and North America, respectively. Each embodies environment and labor standards (a feature that the WTO has promised to address in future negotiations).

Possible Distributive Effects of Free Trade

An important potential harmful effect of free-trade regimes requires a more detailed analysis of the winners and losers within each domestic economy. Even if we accept the inference that the domestic accounts overall will increase for each country as a result of free trade, it is likely that this result will lead to a transfer of income from some sectors of the domestic economy to other sectors. Consider a stylized narrative based on U.S.-Mexico trade following NAFTA, and suppose that only two industries are involved, banking and auto assembly. Mexico has a relative advantage in auto assembly, whereas the United States has a relative advantage in banking. Lower-wage, skilled industrial labor is available in Mexico, and it would be predicted that the equilibrium will be one in which more auto production occurs in Mexico and less in the United States, whereas more of the banking activity will take place in the United States. This is good for both the United States and Mexico; cars will be cheaper for consumers in both countries, and banking transactions will reflect lower transaction costs. But this scenario may involve a shift of jobs from the United States to Mexico in the area of auto assembly, and a shift of banking jobs from Mexico to the United States. So this scenario is not good for autoworkers in the United States and banking workers in Mexico. Moreover, there will be interregional consequences within the United States that create benefits for some regions and net losses for other regions. The Michigan economy may be a net loser of jobs and income in this scenario, whereas the Connecticut–New York–New Jersey region may be a net gainer.

A second important effect of the globalization of trade is most pertinent to issues of human well-being in Third World countries: the effect of globalization on the extent of poverty and the range of inequalities in these nations. Globalization is a blind economic process that is not inherently sensitive to human suffering and well-being. In this way, it is somewhat similar to laissez-faire capitalism in the nineteenth century—a system that created great wealth but also great poverty, great deprivation, and extensive inequality. Most industrial countries recognized the need for the establishment of a social safety net to protect individuals from the harms created by rapid economic change (Kapstein 1999). The social welfare state attempted to buffer citizens against the shocks of economic change and to prepare them for productive roles within expanding economies. Public education, unemployment insurance, job-training programs, and programs of aid to citizens unable to earn incomes are examples of the efforts made by the social welfare state, and these programs can be seen as part of a large social compact assuring that all citizens benefit from the economic change made possible by free markets and industrial and commercial development (Esping-Andersen 1985; Lindblom 1977). Social welfare programs require taxation. They are financed through the ability of the state to redistribute wealth and income within society in such a way as to fund programs for the disadvantaged. And here we encounter an immediate challenge for just globalization: It is national governments that have the ability to tax individuals and corporations, but globalization creates the opportunity for individuals and corporations to locate themselves beyond the reach of specific national fiscal regimes. Moreover, the negative social consequences of a given country's business activities are just as likely to occur in another country—so the social welfare programs of the first country will not improve the lot of those most severely affected by such activities. The social welfare state, then, faces two difficulties in the face of globalization: a competitive process through which social spending is forced to fall (because businesses will resist higher taxes by threatening to relocate offshore) and a global distribution of the harsh effects of global business that operates beyond the reach of the national welfare state.[1]

Free trade and the globalization of business activity have been under way at least since the 1950s. What effects have these processes had on inequalities and poverty in the developing world? Globalization appears to have left poverty and inequality essentially unchanged in Latin America since 1980 (Ocampo 2001; Ocampo and Franco 2000). It is a familiar story: Growth in economic activity does not inherently favor the poor, and it does not inherently work to reduce inequalities. Rather, public policy must entail specific choices that will propel economic processes in ways that are socially desirable, and public policy programs and regulations must establish the public good in zones of activity that are not well served by market processes.

Global Economic Activity

Here, I will turn from issues of trade and investment to issues of the globalization of production. The other mechanism of globalization is through the multinational company that conducts its business in many countries. Corporations make investments in foreign countries, they sometimes establish production centers in offshore locations, they market and sell their products in many countries, and they gather revenues and profits into the corporation's control.

It is possible to estimate the overall employment and revenues of multinational companies. In a report on multinational corporations, the International Labour Organization (2002) finds that "in 1996, the total revenues of the 500 largest companies globally were $11.4 trillion, total profits were $404 billion, total assets were $33.3 trillion, and the total number of employees was 35,517,692." These figures have increased dramatically since 1970. The world's economy is more interconnected, and a relatively small number of large corporations handle a larger percentage of the volume of business activity and employment than ever before. Is this a good thing? How would we begin to answer this question?

One criterion for answering these questions involves asking whether the welfare and incomes of the workers involved in this global system are improving over time. In addition, we can ask whether the presence of multinational production in a national context (for example, in Indonesia) has multiplier effects on economic development. Does the presence of a relatively well-paying shoe factory in Jakarta stimulate demand and raise wages for other sectors in the region? A somewhat more difficult question is whether these improvements are themselves more substantial and rapid than those in other sectors of developing economies. And an even more hypothetical question asks whether there is a different pathway of development that would have had greater and more rapid effects than either of these alternatives.

Consider this favorable scenario. Multinational investment in a developing economy leads to the establishment of relatively modern production capacity. It leads to expanded employment in the country, at wages that are low by developed country standards but higher than domestic standards. Labor conditions (health, environment, length of the working day) are, on average, better than in the local domestic industry. The presence of the multinational factory introduces a competitive pressure that results in improvement of wages and conditions in other industries as well. As wages rise, the demand for consumer goods rises as well, leading to increased production and employment. The standard of living of the working people rises, and unemployment and underemployment fall. In this scenario, multinational business activity in a developing country is a progressive force.

Now consider an unfavorable scenario. The multinational company seeks out low-wage opportunities worldwide. It structures its investments in such a way as to take advantage of low wages as long as the low-wage environment persists. Managers pursue a cost-minimization strategy that leads to persistently poor labor conditions, including long hours and poor environmental, health, and safety conditions. When domestic conditions begin to change—the domestic government imposes more restrictive safety and health standards, wages begin to rise—the multinational company closes its factory and seeks out another low-wage destination. The standard of living of the working people is essentially unchanged, and employment levels are static over time. This scenario is plainly not one that leads to sustained improvement in the quality of life in the country in which it takes place.

There are real examples of both scenarios. So to make significant progress in debates over the human consequences of globalization, we need to have a substantially better understanding of the real effects of international business activity in many different locations in the world. This approach to evaluating the overall benefits and harms of globalization focuses on human well-being. It gives a positive evaluation to a given process of change if it results in higher and broader standards of living and better conditions of work and life. And it faults the process if its effects in these areas are neutral or negative.

Foreign Direct Investment

Foreign direct investment is an important avenue of globalization. Businesses and corporations in one country invest in plants and facilities in another country and produce goods that are then traded in world markets. Foreign direct investment would appear to be a very direct engine of economic development in poor countries. The total volume of nongovernmental investment in the developing world dwarfs the volume of official development assistance; in 1998, the net private flow of capital to developing countries exceeded $268 billion (World Bank 2001b: 190), compared to $60 billion in official development assistance from Development Assistance Committee (DAC) countries. Foreign direct investment (FDI) is defined as investment by foreign corporations in the domestic economy. When it establishes a factory in a developing country, when it develops mining capabilities in a developing country, or when it invests in land and farming for export, a corporation is making a

business decision that promises profits for the corporation and that stimu-
lates employment and exports for the host country.

However, the flow of foreign direct investment is very unequally distributed among the poorest countries in the developing world. A recent briefing
paper by the Overseas Development Institute provides data concerning the
profile of foreign direct investment across low-income countries between
1986 and 1995. China was the recipient of the lion's share of FDI in 1995,
with 86 percent of the total. Nigeria and India were the next largest recipients. Significantly, the poorest countries of sub-Saharan Africa and Latin
America received almost no foreign direct investment during these years.
The report cites small domestic markets, small GDPs, and low levels of
openness as the most significant obstacles to foreign direct investment in the
poorest countries. Economies that have higher levels of exports generally attract higher levels of FDI. Low labor costs, adequate infrastructure, political
stability, and dependable rule of law are identified as incentives to FDI
(Overseas Development Institute 1997). The report concludes with a gloomy
observation: "For the vast majority of low-income countries, however, FDI is
minimal."[2]

Labor Standards

The internationalization of production and manufacturing has cast new and
critical light on the labor standards that are in place in various developing
countries. Manufacturers look for suppliers who can provide parts and finished products at the lowest possible cost, so there is a powerful incentive for
large companies to seek out production capacity in ultra-low-wage countries.
Multinational firms produce finished goods and components in many countries for a global market. The soccer ball sold to the Boston teenager may have
been sewn in a shantytown home in Pakistan, assembled in a factory in
Sialkot, and sold in a Cambridge, Massachusetts, sports shop. The conditions
of work under which men, women, and children undertook various stages of
this process varied widely, from decent and fair to exploitative and destructive. Likewise, the coffee sold in the multinational coffee shop on the corner
may have been cultivated and harvested under reasonable conditions of employment or under abysmal conditions. We know with confidence that bad
labor conditions are epidemic throughout the developing world, and we
know that labor performed under these conditions is embodied in the con-

sumer products that we buy. Moreover, we know that improvement in conditions of labor is possible, even inevitable, over time. The question is whether we can identify strategies and structures of incentive and regulation that have significantly greater efficacy in bringing about these improvements in a shorter period of time.

How are we to think, then, about issues of sweatshops, limited labor rights, child labor, and toxic workplaces? Are there justifiable and feasible "standards of labor" that ought to be applied universally throughout the world?[3] Are there feasible strategies through which we, as ethical consumers, can encourage the promulgation of these standards more and more widely throughout the world? And can we be confident that establishing such standards would be a net good thing, all effects considered?

It is sometimes said that it is difficult to influence labor conditions in the developing world because of globalization. Multinational firms are insulated from national regulations, some say, and therefore succeed in evading labor standards. The question of the feasibility of improving labor standards globally arises out of the global nature of the contemporary manufacturing system. Today, manufacturing is performed on a global, cross-border basis, and the regulatory reach of any particular state is limited. So how is it possible to exert influence on the global workplace in such a way as to prevent the worst abuses of Third World labor? In this perspective, labor standards in the developing world might be thought to lie beyond the zone of feasible inspection or regulation.

There is another valid perspective on this issue, however, that is substantially more hopeful. One could argue that labor conditions in the developing world are substantially *more* accessible to intervention from progressive organizations than are other areas of human rights abuses. When military dictatorships or authoritarian countries violate the civil and political rights of their citizens, there are almost no levers of influence that exist for nongovernmental organizations and ordinary citizens. But when indecent labor conditions are exposed in the developing world and they are linked to large, multinational corporations, the ethical consumer has a very significant lever of influence. It is precisely because the multinational corporation has the power to change labor conditions in the developing world and the ethical consumer has the power to influence the behavior of the corporation that labor rights are more accessible to change than civil and political rights.

Work conditions vary substantially across the world and within particular countries. A great proportion of labor in the developing world is dehumanizing and exploitative. Special areas of abuse include ultralow wages, coerced labor, child labor, toxic working conditions, limited or absent rights of labor organization, and unregulated work hours. Bad conditions of labor constitute a critical issue from the perspective of development ethics because of the direct linkages that exist between employment, income, and human development. The labor environment itself creates a hazard for the development of the normal human being, and an ultralow wage guarantees the extremes of poverty that make full human development impossible. When children are forced to work at an early age, their health and educational status is compromised, and their development capabilities are stunted. When men and women are compelled by economic necessity into unsafe and toxic places of work, their liberty, their human dignity, and their physical well-being are affronted. And when workers are paid ultralow wages, they are confined to a continuing cycle of poverty and constrained opportunity.

So bad conditions of work are a direct source of human ills. They are also implicated in the injustice of coercion. Persons do not freely choose to work in sweatshop conditions. Rather, they do so because the alternatives available to them are even worse. Extreme poverty—involving, as it does, malnutrition, homelessness, bad health, and lack of education—compels individuals to accept conditions of work that fall far short of decent, fair standards.

In a national economy, it is possible to restrain these cruel choices through regulation. The state can set standards of fair labor practice, and it can enforce these standards through inspection and monitoring. In an economy in which effective regulation of the work environment exists, poverty may persist, but labor standards are honored in the workplace. Effective regulation and monitoring activities are enormously more difficult in the global economy. No single government has the authority to establish labor standards (or economic standards, or standards of gender justice, or standards of other areas of social importance), and there is no effective power capable of directly enforcing standards.

Consumers in the developed world have gradually come to a clearer appreciation of the relationship between the goods that they consume daily and the conditions of work in which these goods are produced. Consumers and activists in the developed world have made a variety of organized efforts to improve working conditions in the developing world.

A number of monitoring organizations have been established since 1990, and ethical consumers and activists have attempted to elicit agreements from major apparel manufacturers to abide by the protocols of one or more of these organizations. The general approach that these organizations take is to use consumer concern about unfair labor practices in the developing world as a means to induce major apparel corporations to enter into agreements that stipulate a code of labor standards and a monitoring and compliance regime. These include the Fair Labor Association, Workers' Rights Consortium, and Social Accountability International (for some useful websites, consult www.fairtrade.org.uk, www.fairlabor.org, www.fairtrade.net, and www.workersrights.org). What these organizations have in common is an effort to influence multinational manufacturing labor practices by gathering information about those practices and mobilizing consumers to make choices based on comparative performance in labor practices. Firms want to avoid the label "sweatshop producer," and they are subject to exposure of bad practices through monitoring efforts. Over time, according to this approach, we would expect gradual improvement in the conditions of labor in the developing world.

A particularly innovative concept in new regulatory regimes suitable to the global economy has been advanced by Archon Fung, Dara O'Rourke, and Charles Sabel (2001). These authors advance a concept that they refer to as "ratcheting labor standards" (RLS) that attempts to bring together the separate business interests of the manufacturers, the evolving character of the supply chain in "lean" manufacturing, and the rising interest that many consumers have in assurances that their products have been manufactured in a nonsweated environment. They propose a system in which manufacturers are encouraged to subscribe to credible monitoring firms (analogous to accounting firms). The monitors would assess labor conditions within the total manufacturing process and make their findings publicly available in a way that permits comparison with other firms. And consumers and activists would then make purchases and decide on strategies of pressure depending on their assessment of various firms' performance. Fung, O'Rourke, and Sabel argue that such a system would have a justified form of flexibility—in that it would permit comparisons of like circumstances—and would gradually improve the global workplace as firms compete for high ratings in a dimension that consumers care about (the quality of labor standards involved in production of the commodity).

Protecting the Global Public Good

Within a single political and economic system, it is well understood that the state has a number of important social functions. The state needs to collect funds to finance public goods and amenities (roads, schools, health clinics). It needs to provide a social safety net to prevent citizens from falling into destitution as a result of illness, age, or loss of a job. It needs to establish a set of laws and regulations that secure the public health and safety—health and safety regulations in the workplace, environmental regulations, regulations governing contracts and conditions of labor, and so forth. And perhaps it needs to engage in some degree of income and wealth redistribution in order to keep inequalities within an acceptable range.

Globalization poses a serious challenge to this paradigm of government and the public good. Much economic activity now falls beyond the jurisdiction of states that have the interest and ability to appropriately regulate the actions, policies, and behavior of corporations and to assure the well-being of the people who are affected by that behavior. The harms created by a French corporation may be significant but may be imposed on the citizens of Senegal—and the government of Senegal may lack the will or capacity to regulate those effects. "Weak states" may be unable to establish effective regulatory schemes—or they may lack the political will to do so.

This analysis implies that developing countries are likely to be characterized by weak regulation and minimal safety nets. But, as Ethan Kapstein (1999) points out, the circumstances of globalization may push back even into the domestic political and economic system of wealthy countries in such a way as to undermine regulation and social security in the wealthy country. Competition between regulated and unregulated zones in the world create a business imperative to reduce the tax burden in the regulated zone. This situation imposes pressure on the regulatory regime and on the social safety net—with the result that future citizens in even the wealthy countries may find themselves with less effective protection against harmful business activities and less security in the face of life's emergencies.

The issue of regulation for the public good is particularly important. Effective regulation is needed to establish decent conditions of life for the citizens of the world. Otherwise, unregulated profit incentives will push economic activity into more and more harmful forms (along the lines witnessed by nineteenth-century industrial development). This need includes regulation of environmental harms, resource depletion, use of oceans and atmosphere, and conditions of labor. Is it possible to establish regulatory regimes that transcend national borders? And is it possible to create fiscal systems that collect revenues beyond the national level?

International institutions that provide a basis for establishing regulatory regimes governing these sorts of issues do exist. Negotiations within the World Trade Organization, for example, involve interstate negotiations over the terms of environmental protection and workplace standards that the signatory states will agree to. Institutions such as the United Nations, the Universal Declaration of Human Rights, or the International Labour Organization represent interstate agreements about schemes of regulation and the protection of citizens' rights and well-being. The Achilles' heel of such agreements is the problem of enforcement, however. And the most favorable strategy for global improvement in regulations and compliance is the establishment of more interconnected institutions that shift the balance of incentives against the national "scofflaw." On this score, then, the future well-being of the citizens of the world depends heavily on the success of international processes and regimes that create an environment in which there is a higher level of national compliance with international norms.

Let us turn now to the international fiscal issues that must be addressed if supranational social goods are to be financed. Many of the economic activities involved in the global economy today are beyond the reach of national taxation. So it is reasonable to ask whether there are global taxation schemes that could be adopted that would serve to benefit the development of the global economy, provide a basis for development investment in poor countries, and serve as a social safety net for those affected negatively by globalization. There are several such alternatives. The most prominent is the "Tobin tax," a small tax on currency transactions (Haq, Kaul, and Grunberg 1996). The Tobin tax idea was developed by the Nobel Prize–winning economist James Tobin. It would serve two purposes. First, it would provide a break to short-term currency speculation; Tobin argued that such speculation imposed a serious risk to the financial security of the global economic system. And second, it would generate some $100 to $300 billion that could be used to solve the problems of poverty alleviation, environmental protection, and adjustment that we have examined throughout this book.[4]

Conclusions on Globalization

What conclusions can we draw from these points? It is not justified to conclude that globalization is inherently unfavorable to the poor or that progressive people should oppose free trade and global business activity. Rather, we
need to find ways of addressing the fact that globalization is blind to public
goods. Analogous to the creation of the welfare state in the early twentieth
century, ways of addressing public welfare in the twenty-first century must be
identified and defined (Kapstein 1999). Central to this task is the issue of enhancing the human capabilities and productive talents of the poor in the developing world. Consequently, states need to put a high priority on education
and the other elements of social infrastructure through which human capabilities are developed.

In addition, processes of globalization need to be linked with effective public institutions—local, national, and international—that will buffer the hardships created by blind market forces—unemployment, increasing
inequalities, and pockets of poverty. Citizens therefore should work toward
establishing and maintaining such institutions through their investment
choices, their consuming choices, their political influence within their own
democracies, and their engagement in international organizations.

Further, when the partnership between the market and institutions of public policy falters, the bonds of civil society are threatened. Harmonious social
life depends on a broad confidence in the justice and fairness of underlying
institutions. All citizens need to be confident that their interests are being
fairly served through existing economic and social institutions. This confidence will not be sustained in the face of persistent and debilitating inequalities and poverty.

International Aid

Let us turn now to the question of international assistance. States, nongovernmental organizations, and citizens provide money to help stimulate
economic progress in poor countries. Why should developed nations provide
aid to the developing world? Why and at what level should citizens of these
countries support such aid? Should normative considerations play a role in
national decisions about the level and character of aid? How much aid should
be given? Should aid be transmitted through bilateral channels, or is multilat-

eral assistance preferable (for example, via the United Nations or the OECD)? What form should aid take? How important is food aid in the development process? How significant is aid administered through nongovernmental organizations (Oxfam, Food First, and the like)? What obligations do citizens of developed countries have to support such organizations with funds, services, or participation? The goal of this section is to draw out a discussion of the implications of the normative theories discussed in earlier chapters for governmental policy and for the political choices and activities of citizens in wealthy countries.

The Obligation to Render Aid

Several relevant moral principles are raised by the facts of globalization in support of an obligation to render aid:

- *Altruism:* When we are in the presence of human suffering and have the ability to alleviate that suffering at a reasonable cost to ourselves, we have a prima facie obligation to do so.
- *Fairness:* When we benefit from the activities of others, we have a prima facie obligation to take steps to assure that those others receive fair benefits from the cooperation as well.
- *Nonexploitation:* When we benefit from an unfair system of exchange with others, we have an obligation to take steps to end the pattern of injustice.

One important answer to the question "Why give aid?" stems from the humanitarian obligations that derive from the extreme conditions of human suffering that are associated with the poverty and inequality that exist in many parts of the world today. Kant refers to these as "obligations of benevolence." It is a bad thing for people to live within circumstances of extreme deprivation. When a person has knowledge of a situation of extreme deprivation and has the capacity to reduce that deprivation, he or she has a prima facie obligation to provide assistance. Persons living in the developed world generally have both knowledge and capacity to help. Therefore, such persons have a prima facie obligation to provide assistance to the poor in the developing world.

It is reasonable to argue that the circumstances of poverty and human deprivation that are current in the world today give rise to a general obligation of rendering aid. The depth of human suffering in the developing world makes it compelling that wealthy countries and their citizens provide assistance to less developed countries. This obligation derives from the requirements of altruism. Where does the moral force of this principle come from? A central intuition throughout this book is the moral significance of the human person. It is an inherently good thing that people live in circumstances that permit them to live full and satisfying lives; conversely, it is a morally bad thing when people live in circumstances that systematically block their ability to live full and satisfying lives. So to recognize the human reality of poverty is to immediately have a moral reason for taking steps to alleviate that poverty. (Thomas Nagel [1970] offers a profound argument in defense of altruism along these lines.)

It has sometimes been argued that there are no effective actions available through which it is possible to ameliorate these forms of deprivation or that no such intervention has lasting consequences. (Perhaps the total sum of human deprivation continues to increase in spite of these interventions.) However, the sources of doubt appear entirely unjustified. It is plain that individuals and groups can take actions that improve the life circumstances of other persons in poor countries. And therefore, the obligation of altruism is a binding one. It is important not to make mistakes of moral mathematics and disregard small benefits (Parfit 1984).

A related point derives from the breadth of material inequalities that exist between wealthy countries and poor countries (and between the representative life circumstances of individuals within each category). The prosperity of wealthy countries in the modern global economy depends unavoidably on the contributions, resources, and labor of persons in the developing world. The global economy is a system of economic cooperation. So there is a background requirement of fairness in the distributive outcomes that emerge from this cooperation. And it is difficult to reconcile the extreme inequalities that exist between wealthy countries and poor countries with the idea of fair distributive results of a cooperative process. This concept is a generalization of the principle of fair institutions developed in Chapter 4.

The "nonexploitation principle" depends on a prior finding of exploitative relationships within a system of exchange. A clear example of international economic exploitation is that of colonialism. A system in which a poor country's resources are forcibly extracted and exported to the colonial power is plainly exploitative; it confers benefits on the colonial power at the expense of the subject nation, and it depends on the use of coercion to bring about the transfers of wealth and resources. Colonialism ended with the formal independence of colonial states following World War II (though inequalities of power persist). It can be argued, however, that wealthy countries continue to exert unfair economic power over formerly colonial states and thereby create favorable terms of trade for themselves. (Are fibers, textiles, and foods treated fairly within the General Agreement on Tariffs and Trade and the Multi-Fibre Agreement, for example?) To the extent that this is a justified conclusion, the principle of nonexploitation would give citizens of wealthy countries a direct obligation to take appropriate steps to restore the just claims of citizens of exploited states.

A related answer falls under the rubric of "restorative justice." If we come to the conclusion that the poverty of the developing world is systemically related to the wealth of the First World—and that the deprivation of specific persons is the necessary condition of the affluence of other persons—and if we judge that these results have come about through unfair or exploitative circumstances, then we have a strong obligation to correct the effects of injustice and to restore the current victims of these injustices to something like the condition they would have attained in the absence of past injustice. This conclusion has force in the case of the current effects of past injustice; it is all the more compelling in the case of continuing injustice or exploitation. As was argued in Chapter 4, not all forms of inequality are unjust. But those inequalities that have emerged as the consequence of unjust social arrangements are themselves a current injustice, and we have an obligation to attempt to remedy the injustice. Effective aid can be one important mechanism through which we attempt to achieve this goal of restorative justice. (There are other mechanisms as well. For example, universities and colleges could take it as part of their mission to provide education to young people from developing countries who will in turn facilitate economic and social development in their home countries. Medical schools could encourage young physicians to devote part of their time to improving health care systems in developing countries. Corporations doing business in developing countries could devote a percentage of their revenues to development of the local social infrastructure.)

These arguments have to do with obligations we have as individual citizens. But these obligations in turn give rise to moral imperatives for tax-based government aid programs to developing countries.

It is also clear that aid should be rendered for reasons of enlightened self-interest. A more just world is a safer world, and a world in which hundreds of millions of men and women in poor countries believe that they are treated unfairly within the global system is one that is ripe for devastating conflict. Consequently, wealthy countries have a direct interest based on their long-term security to help design a smooth process of economic growth, poverty alleviation, and improvement of the circumstances of justice in the developing world.

Thus, there are a variety of moral reasons why wealthy countries should provide development aid to poor countries. The harder questions are how much and in what form. And we need also to ask how effective development assistance is (World Bank 1998).

How Much Aid?

The issue of "how much" can be addressed from two points of view—the donor's and the recipient's (or, put another way, in terms of the supply and the demand). From the donor's perspective, we can ask what percentage of income (GDP or personal income) is it reasonable to expect to be provided as aid. For example, the United Nations has recommended that OECD nations should contribute 0.7 percent of GDP to official development assistance. Religious groups sometimes advocate a practice of "tithing"—offering 10 percent of one's income to charitable purposes. Peter Singer (1972) has advocated the principle of giving up to the point at which the marginal utility of the last donation is equal for self and other. This principle would drive the individual's income down to the level of that of a reasonably well-off citizen of a developing country. Several of these principles are somewhat arbitrary: Why make it 0.7 percent of GDP? Why make it 10 percent of personal income? The Singer principle is logical but strenuous beyond what we can reasonably expect of ordinary ethical persons. Mahatma Gandhi and Francis of Assisi may have been willing to live up to this standard, but most of us are not.

We might pursue a slightly more principled approach on the "supply" side through an argument along the following lines. In current circumstances, the need for resources to assist in poverty alleviation is essentially unlimited. Each person has a right to give some level of priority to his or her own needs and desires and those of family and friends over the needs and desires of remote strangers. But ethics requires that the individual give some weight and recognition of the urgent needs of others as he or she makes expenditure decisions. In other words, personal and familial consumption is a legitimate priority, and recognition of the human reality of others is an ethical necessity. So the ethical person will make financial plans that satisfy the condition that the expenditure profile should result from deliberation that gives weight to both personal and extrapersonal needs. The requirement is simply: Take seriously the urgent needs of others. One person may do this by tithing; another may do so by establishing a personal budget that includes basic needs, nonbasic preferences, personal savings, gifts to family, and contributions to poverty alleviation. With this approach, what ethics requires is that the individual should have deliberated about how he or she ought to distribute income across these categories and should have assigned some measurable weight to the final category. This approach assumes that there is no ethically mandatory answer to the question of "how much" but rather an imperative: Give weight to the interests of others.

This analysis focuses on the individual's choices in the distribution of his or her income. What about the corresponding question for national governments? Governments collect taxes from their citizens, and they spend these revenues on a series of national priorities arrived at through a political process of deliberation. Such priorities include national defense, government operating expenses, social welfare expenses, infrastructure expenses, law enforcement expenses, and international aid. Almost all these categories fall plainly within a narrow definition of *public interest*—that is, they are forms of public expenditure that serve the interests of the citizens whose tax payments are the source of funds for the expenditures. What is the rationale for making use of tax revenues to further the interests of nations and persons outside the country's borders?

Several answers are possible. First, most fundamentally, one can argue that the same moral considerations that give rise to the obligation for an individual to render aid also create a moral obligation for states to do so. "Pay attention to the urgent needs of human beings," "don't exploit," and "compensate others for harms imposed on them" all appear to be relevant principles to guide state action.

Second, we can approach the issue from the perspective of the citizens' own priorities and preferences. When legislators enact spending priorities

within a democracy, they are theoretically expressing the priorities and preferences of the citizens. If citizens place some degree of priority on poverty alleviation and international justice, then it is appropriate for legislators to
transform that citizen interest into spending priorities. From this point of
view, the same arguments that lead to conclusions about individual spending
behavior can be mobilized in favor of a democratic process of aggregation
leading to political decisions that allocate public resources for Third World
development.

Third, one could argue that it is in the national interest to contribute to
poverty alleviation and economic development in the developing world:
Greater democracy, greater peace and security, and reduced international
conflict will result. On this approach, international aid is an instrument
through which national interests, broadly construed, are pursued.

Consideration of the "demand" side leads to a different line of reasoning.
We can ask "What outcomes are we trying to achieve, over what period of
time, and what level of assistance is necessary to get us there?" From the recipient's point of view, we can ask what we are hoping to achieve over what
period of time and then determine the cost of this scenario. The approach
taken by the OECD in setting development goals for the coming fifty years is
a powerful illustration of this approach (World Bank 2001b: 5).[5] Once we
have identified the outcomes, we can investigate the multiple strategies that
will be necessary to achieve these goals. This step will imply a "budget" of development assistance for countries and for individual charitable giving.

The issue of the form that aid should take is equally complicated. There is a
tension between the impulse that aid should be structured in such a way as to
bring about specific outcomes (poverty alleviation, environmental improvement, human rights, democracy) and the notion that the recipients should decide what their priorities and goals are. In one sense, it is reasonable to expect
that aid should be structured so as to bring about the donor's goals—poverty
alleviation, human rights, democracy, environment. From another perspective, it can be argued that it is better to allow the recipient to determine the
priorities and goals—to provide the resources and permit recipients to come
to their best judgments about priorities. And, as recent discussions within the
development community have increasingly emphasized, the success of a set of
development strategies depends crucially on the degree to which the recipient
nation and its citizenry have participated in the formulation of its goals.

It is useful to consider how things are different when the issues we are confronting are found within a single nation. A national government has the ability to tax its citizens to achieve high-priority goals. And it is possible for a country to establish as a goal the achievement of a high minimum standard of living for all its citizens: adequate nutrition, health care, education, and job training. So a national government has the ability to establish policies that involve a degree of redistribution of income and resources from the wealthy to the poor. Inequalities within a state can take the form of class, racial, or regional inequalities. The political philosophy of social democracy articulates this approach to political institutions. But how extensive a redistributive program is it politically feasible for a democratic regime to sustain? (For an extensive discussion of the politics and principles of the welfare state, see the essays included in Gutmann 1988 and Gilbert 1983.) Let us consider some of the central mechanisms through which development assistance occurs in the developing world today.

Official Development Assistance

The leading multilateral development assistance entity through which official development assistance flows is the Development Assistance Committee of the Organization for Economic Cooperation and Development. The OECD, an international organization of democratic industrialized countries with market economies and political systems, was established in 1961 with several goals: to facilitate economic growth and employment, to enhance economic and social welfare, to organize member states' development assistance efforts, and to stimulate nondiscriminatory international trade. Functional agencies of the United Nations are another important source of multilateral development assistance (UNDP, World Food Programme [WFP], and United Nations Children's Fund [UNCF], for example, which distributed $3.8 billion in 1988; see World Bank 1990: box 8.4).

Bilateral assistance represents a larger overall flow of aid from wealthy countries to developing countries. In 1987, for instance, bilateral aid represented 64 percent of the total aid, with multilateral aid representing 22 percent and nongovernmental aid representing 14 percent (World Bank 1990: figure 8.2). But bilateral aid is often driven by political and military interests rather than by a focused assessment of world development needs, and it is often criticized for its failure to contribute as effectively as possible to poverty alleviation.

Official development assistance declined significantly during the 1990s (World Bank 2001b: figure 11.1). In the early 1990s, donor nations provided approximately 0.33 percent of their GDP in development assistance (Development Assistance Committee 1992: table 2), less than half the level recommended by UN resolutions on development assistance (0.7 percent of GDP) (UN Resolution 3201, 1974). This figure dropped to about 0.22 percent in 2000—during a period in which donor nation GDP per capita increased by about 14 percent. There are significant disparities in levels of giving among donor nations, ranging from 0.10 percent for the United States to 0.80 percent for Sweden and 0.32 percent for France (Development Assistance Committee 2001: table 4). Japan's level of giving in 1999 fell in the middle, at 0.28 percent of GDP. The experience since the early 1990s, then, has been a gloomy one from the point of view of international assistance; wealthy countries experienced significant growth in national incomes but at the same time significantly reduced their contributions to official development assistance to the developing world. (See the 1990 *World Development Report* for a summary of official development assistance patterns [World Bank 1990: box 8.4].)

Nongovernmental Organizations and Aid

Nongovernmental organizations provide a meaningful but small share of the world's development assistance to developing countries. In 1998, NGOs distributed or administered about $10 billion in development assistance. This amount consisted of about $5 billion in NGO funds and about $5 billion in DAC funds provided by donor governments to be administered through NGO institutions (World Bank 2001b: figure 11.5). This number compares to approximately $43 billion in official development assistance in 1998 (World Bank 2001b: figure 11.3) and $268 billion in private capital flows to developing countries (World Bank 2001b: 190).

NGOs provide two important qualities not available through the official channels of development assistance. First, the priorities and goals of NGOs are not governed by the strategic or geopolitical interests of states. The nongovernmental organization is free to articulate its goals—the alleviation of hunger, the enhancement of education or health, the preservation of human rights—in a way that is not overridden by the larger political concerns of developed states.

Second, NGOs give ordinary citizens a significant opportunity for engagement in important issues—justice, poverty, human rights, democracy, or environmental quality—at a variety of levels. Citizens of the developing world can contribute money to the pursuit of these goals, they can offer their services as volunteers in developing countries, and they can lobby public opinion and government officials on behalf of these values.

Third, NGOs are more capable than governmental bodies of forming the engaged and interactive relationships among citizens of developing countries that are most likely to produce meaningful change in those countries. NGOs can provide significant organizational support for groups of citizens who are otherwise powerless in their societies—women and members of ethnic, racial, or geographic minorities—and can enhance the effectiveness of these local organizations through access to communication and other international resources.

It is reasonable to conclude, then, that NGOs have a significant role to play in the development process and that this role goes beyond the monetary contribution that NGOs make to developing countries.

Food Assistance

One important type of international assistance falls in the category of food aid. A particularly direct symptom of poverty is hunger, either chronic or episodic. So food assistance is an especially direct way of addressing the human costs of deep poverty. Food security is a crucial dimension of the most pressing needs of the poor in the developing world. Food aid represented a total of about $2.5 billion in 1989 and was just under 20 percent of total U.S. foreign assistance in that year. There are, however, significant issues concerning the effectiveness of food aid in addressing poverty alleviation in nonemergency circumstances (World Bank 1990: box 8.7).

Concessional Lending and Debt Forgiveness

A critical factor in the process of economic development in poor countries is access to credit. Poor countries need to develop health care and education infrastructures, construct roads as well as power and communications networks, and provide sources of credit for domestic enterprises. So international lending agencies—the International Monetary Fund (IMF), the World Bank, and various regional lending agencies—play a central role in economic development. How do these agencies work? How are they funded? Do they represent a net transfer from north to south, or are they revenue-neutral? Do these agencies have the ability to influence policy choices within target developing countries? Can they offer governments incentives to give priority to improving the human welfare of the poor?[6]

Concessional lending through the World Bank and the several regional development banks is a critical component of official development assistance. The major multilateral lending institutions include the World Bank and the four regional development banks—the African Development Bank, the Asian Development Bank, the Caribbean Development Bank, and the Inter-American Development Bank. Each of the development banks offers a concessional "window" through which it provides low- or zero-interest loans to poor countries. Concessional lending is restricted to the poorest countries and is provided at substantially below-market interest rates. The IDA, the concessional arm of the World Bank, distributed $7 billion in concessional lending in 2001, and the regional development banks distributed another several billion dollars.

Issues that have arisen concerning the World Bank's policies include effectiveness, attentiveness to poverty and environment, the liberalization agenda, and the harsh effects of structural adjustment policies that the bank imposed as conditions for further lending.

Debt relief has emerged as a major issue for developing countries and their advocates in North America and Western Europe. The *1990 World Development Report* gave attention to the problems of severely indebted nations (World Bank 1990: 19–20), but it placed much of the responsibility for resolution of the problem on the debtor nations themselves: "For all the severely indebted countries the main challenge is to design and implement credible policy reforms to foster growth." Attention since 1990 has given more priority to the responsibilities of donor nations in addressing the problems of poor-country debt. This debate has focused on "severely indebted low-income countries" (SILICs) and the strategies of debt relief or debt forgiveness that would help these countries make sustained progress on poverty alleviation (Overseas Development Institute 1995). Some thirty-two countries are classified as SILICs, and twenty-five of them are in sub-Saharan Africa.

The level of debt (and annual debt service payments) in many poor countries has grown dramatically since the 1980s. World Bank data show that many poor countries devoted more than 20 percent of their government funds on debt payments in the late 1990s and that these funds competed directly with spending on education and health programs (World Bank 2001b: 201). The Enhanced Heavily Indebted Poor Countries (HIPC) Debt Relief Initiative, approved in 1999, is designed to provide effective and equitable debt relief to the most severely debt-burdened poor nations. This initiative is intended to provide debt relief in a context in which new resources are targeted to poverty reduction and in which effective accountability institutions will assure that these resources are not diverted into other sectors (World Bank 2001b: 203).

A Role for the Ethical Citizen

How should the ethical citizen engage with the processes of globalization and international aid? Several imperatives and strategies seem particularly important. First is an imperative of concern. It is all too easy to turn one's eyes away from suffering in other countries—poverty, repression, malnutrition, and brutality. But it is morally critical for each person to remain sensitive to the human situation of people in other parts of the world, to recognize their human reality, to give moral importance to their suffering, and to assume both a motive and an obligation to aid.

Second is an imperative of being well informed. The processes of economic development, political change, and democratization that are under way in the world today are complex and interdependent. So the efforts that are offered as strategies of improvement must reflect accurate understandings of the dynamics of these processes. Slogans cannot replace clear thinking. Being well informed is costly—we need to find the avenues of information that exist to let us form an understanding of the state of affairs in various parts of the world, and we need to exercise our intelligence in evaluating and organizing this information. And it is a highly critical element of the process of progressive change. If citizens are well informed about the conditions of labor that are embodied in the various products they consume, they can then apply effective pressure on abusive producers. The World Wide Web provides a highly effective tool for gaining information about the global economy and global poverty.

Third is an imperative of reflective consideration of the possibilities for action that are open to us as ordinary citizens. What are some of those possibilities? Think of the various roles we play and the opportunities for change that these roles create for us. We are consumers. Therefore, we have the ability to choose among products based on knowledge of the circumstances under which these products were made. We are citizens. Therefore, we have democratic rights of participation that permit us to form associations aimed at influencing our governments in the direction of well-considered, progressive action. We are wealthy, relatively speaking. Therefore, we can contribute our financial resources to support progressive development—famine relief, financial support for children, and financial support for effective NGOs active in the developing world. We are intelligent, productive people. Therefore, we have the ability to lend our own labor to help people in the developing world—through the Peace Corps, Doctors Without Borders, civil engineers who provide volunteer assistance in developing local water resources.

Citizens are also consumers, and consumers have power. A consumer is a person who purchases goods to satisfy needs and preferences. An ethical person is one who makes decisions with appropriate consideration of the principles and moral goods and bads that are involved in the choice at hand. What, then, is an ethical consumer? It is a person who takes principles and values into account as she or he makes choices about purchases of goods. The central idea underlying the ethical consumer concept is the notion that the consumer collects information about the production history of the products he or she consumes and selects among available products on the basis of favorable ratings on these criteria. Have the producer and its subcontractors observed reasonable labor and environmental standards? Have the raw materials for the product been acquired through fair trading agreements with primary producers? Have farmers, miners, or fishermen been treated fairly in the commercial relations that govern the sale of their products?

Collecting this sort of information for even a few products is difficult and costly. The product does not come labeled with a description of the labor or trade conditions through which it came to be. However, two developments in recent years have made ethical consuming more feasible. First, a variety of nonprofit organizations have emerged that have taken on the task of monitoring conditions of production and trade in specific consumer industries. These organizations commonly certify specific products or brands as having complied with a given set of criteria, and they offer the consumer the assurance that a given product conforms to minimal standards of fairness in its production history. An example is Fairtrade Labelling Organizations International (www.fairtrade.net). FLO surveys conditions in the product markets of coffee, drinking chocolate, chocolate bars, orange juice, tea, honey, sugar, and bananas and licenses particular producers that conform to a specific set of standards. Other examples of product monitoring organizations are easily found on the World Wide Web.

Another major innovation that shifts the balance toward the ethical consumer is the proliferation of resources available on the Web. Monitoring organizations can quickly make public the data that they collect on particular industries, and consumers can quickly collect that data as they make choices about alternative products they will consume in their consumption lives.

The credibility and independence of information sources is critical to their effectiveness. Information that is collected through a process that is strongly influenced by any of the parties—the growers, the producers, the farmers' associations—will be suspect and potentially biased. Information that is collected to "prove" a particular point of view—whether the fairness of free trade, the negative environmental impact of globalization, or the positive or negative character of labor standards in the world today—will not provide an objective basis for making comparisons across products or processes. Ideally, we would be in a situation in which a few organizations have emerged that have the resources necessary to provide effective monitoring of a given industry; an institutional commitment to fair and unbiased analysis; and a track record of accuracy, comprehensiveness, and credibility in its reports over a number of years. This is precisely the situation in which we live with respect to human rights organizations; for example, Amnesty International has won high praise for its investigations and reporting on human rights issues throughout the world over several decades.

These two developments substantially change the information costs associated with choosing products. Normally, consumers can collect information about price, quality, and consumer satisfaction about the products they are considering. Organizations such as Consumer Reports provide quality and satisfaction data (financed by consumer subscriptions). The emergence of organizations that collect information about the conditions of labor, environment, and trade that are involved in the production of various consumer goods and the emergence of a communications medium (the Web) through which these sources are easily accessible have made it possible for the consumer to take this set of factors into account at a reasonable cost (in terms of time, effort, and money).

It is possible, then, for the consumer to collect information at reasonable cost about the conditions of production and exchange through which a given product arrives in the local marketplace. Two sets of questions arise. First, are consumers willing to make choices based (in part, at least) on this sort of information? Are they willing to pay higher prices for goods with higher "production fairness" ratings? And second, is there evidence or theory that support the potential efficacy of such choices? Can the overall fairness of global production and commerce be enhanced by the emergence of "ethical consumer" behavior?

Survey data concerning North American and Western European consumers supports the conclusion that consumers would take such information into account and that they would be willing to pay higher prices for products with high production fairness ratings.[7] If the cost of acquiring the relevant data is high, we would expect only a few consumers to do so, but if the cost of the data is low and falling (as suggested earlier), then we may find a basis for optimism that ethical consuming may become substantially more prevalent. In other words, it is entirely possible that large numbers of consumers may come to differentiate among products on the basis of their production and trade histories.

This scenario suggests a possible answer to the question of efficacy. If large numbers of consumers express a preference for goods with superior labor or environmental ratings, we can expect a competition among producers to enhance their ratings in these areas. Higher ratings contribute to higher sales. And if we can have reasonable confidence in monitoring organizations, the only way to raise the rating is to improve conditions in the production process. This would suggest, then, that there is a credible economic mechanism linking ethical consuming to improvement in the life and work conditions at the point of production (the worker or farmer).

And, indeed, we can see some manifestations of competition among producers along these lines. Large producers in the sports apparel industry direct part of their marketing efforts toward establishing that their production processes comply with appropriate standards for labor and environment. And through organizations such as the Fair Labor Association and the Workers' Rights Consortium, it is increasingly possible for consumers to assess the veracity of such claims. So it would appear we can see the earliest stages of "ratcheting" of labor standards in the sports apparel industry.

A similar process appears to be under way in the high-end coffee industry. Large providers of consumer coffee are including the theme of "fair prices to producers" in their marketing and advertising—clearly acknowledging the consumer's preference for this feature. And organizations are emerging that are capable of monitoring conditions in the field that allow the consumer to evaluate the veracity of these claims.

These are the easy cases, however: large, visible corporations with a substantial investment in reputation. It is credible that Nike or Starbucks would be increasingly vulnerable to negative publicity deriving from information concerning factory conditions or coffee farmers' conditions and would therefore have compelling business reasons to give intense scrutiny to associated production process. This means that the strategy of ethical consuming may be effective in these special cases. But what about other types of commodities—groceries, automobiles, computers, cell phones, furniture, clothing? Is it credible to suppose that the consumer will evaluate all of the hundreds of products he or she purchases at the grocery store every week? Will consumers choose one brand of automobile over another because of better performance in terms of labor standards among some of the suppliers the company uses? (Here, the answer appears to be yes with regard to environmental performance.)

Assessment: The Moral Importance of Aid

There are multiple moral considerations that lead to the conclusion that citizens of the developed world have obligations to attempt to improve the life conditions of citizens of the developing world. These obligations derive from altruism (recognition of the human reality of other persons), unjustified current inequalities (distributive justice), and past injustice (restorative justice). The obligations imply several more specific duties. First, each of us in the developed world has a duty to contribute some level of material support aimed at improving the condition of people in the developing world. (At what level? we might ask.) This duty involves making choices in the expenditure of income that affects personal consumption and savings. Second, we have a collateral duty to press our governments to provide effective and generous development assistance. This duty involves effective political advocacy for the expenditure of tax revenues for the purpose of development assistance. Third, we have an obligation to assess the effectiveness of the programs and organizations through which development assistance occurs—both NGOs and public agencies.

A different set of obligations stem from the duty to refrain from doing harm. We have a duty to refrain from benefiting from the unjust or exploitative treatment of others. We have a duty to refrain from benefiting from unsustainable environmental actions. And we have a collateral duty to collect the pertinent information about our current practices and consumption that will permit us to determine whether the "do no harm" principle is honored in our consumption and savings.

These duties have special relevance for aid, trade, and lending.

Concerning aid: Individuals, NGOs, and governments of the developed world ought to provide generous and effective development assistance to developing countries. That aid ought to be targeted to poverty alleviation, preservation of human rights, and enhancement of environmental values. It ought to be intelligently designed and administered so that the intended benefits are achieved. And it ought to flow in volumes that are sufficient to contribute to sustained and measurable progress toward poverty alleviation in the developing world.

Concerning lending: Citizens need to monitor the lending practices of multilateral lenders. They need to assess the priorities that underlie these practices. And they need to assess the effectiveness and sincerity of the lending programs that these institutions conduct. (Good examples of this sort of scrutiny can be found in Fox and Brown 1998, where contributors look very carefully and rigorously at the World Bank's policies and practices with respect to poverty, environment, and gender issues.)

Concerning trade: Citizens ought to assure themselves that the institutions of trade treat developing countries and peoples fairly. They ought to determine that existing and proposed trade institutions secure adequate benefits for all parties. They ought to exercise diligence in selecting products that meet appropriate labor and environmental standards. They ought to be "responsible investors," making meaningful efforts to select investments based on an assessment of corporate behavior with regard to labor and environmental standards and other forms of in-country behavior.

Concerning all three areas of obligation: There is an overriding obligation to collect pertinent information. To act ethically in the domain of international economics, it is necessary to acquire reliable information about institutions, corporations, and practices. We need to know the nature of the effects that are created by these institutions and practices, and we need to be able to assess the overall goodness or badness of these effects. I have emphasized the complexity of economic development throughout this book. There are multiple causal factors involved in the world economic system, and the effects of a given intervention are often difficult to determine. The fact of unintended and unanticipated consequences is common, and the imperative that we can only determine what we should do when we can assess the consequences of the choices with some accuracy is an important one. It is entirely possible that well-intentioned and antecedently plausible policy choices in fact turn out to have perverse and undesirable effects. Pranab Bardhan (2001) provides an example of one such effect in his discussion of labor standards in the developing world: Standards that lead multinational companies to avoid child labor may have the effect of driving Third World children into even more damaging work, including harsh conditions of sweatshop labor and child prostitution. So it is imperative that we evaluate moral positions on international development on the basis of accurate assessments of the likely consequences of policy alternatives.

Notes

1. See also Dani Rodrik's careful attempt to answer the question of the distributive effects of globalization on wages (Rodrik 1997). Rodrik concludes that the benefits of international trade outweigh the risks; however, he also cautions about the importance of establishing institutions that compensate losers in order to secure the basis of social stability.

2. Michael Twomey (2000) provides a valuable historical account of foreign direct investment over the past century.

3. See, for example, the Declaration on the Fundamental Principles and Rights at Work adopted by the International Labour Organization in 1998 (International Labour Association 2000). These rights include freedom of association, the right to collective bargaining, elimination of forced labor, abolition of child labor, and elimination of employment discrimination (World Bank 2001b: 73).

4. For valuable information about the Tobin tax initiative, consult www.ceedweb.org/iirp/.

5. The goals adopted by OECD nations include these: reduce extreme poverty, ensure universal primary education, eliminate gender disparity in schooling, reduce infant and child mortality, reduce maternal mortality, ensure universal access to reproductive health services, and implement strategies for sustainable development (World Bank 2001b: 6).

6. There is a large literature on development aid and debt reduction; see Fox and Brown 1998, Sanford 1989, Burnside and Dollar 1997, Harrigan and Mosley 1991, Hyden and Reutlinger 1992, and Opeskin 1996.

7. See, for example, the Eurobarometer study, entitled "Attitudes of EU Consumers to Fair Trade Bananas" (European Commission 1997b). The study finds that EU consumers would be prepared to pay a premium for bananas that are labeled "fair trade," that there is only a low level of consumer knowledge about fair trade labeling, and that both variables show significant variation across European countries. The Netherlands population shows the highest participation in both measures—highest awareness of fair trade labeling and highest willingness to pay a price premium for the goods carrying this label.

7

Development and the Environment

MOST PEOPLE WOULD AGREE THAT preserving the environment is a good thing and that development policies need to give proper attention to environmental conservation. But why is this so? What are the values that are involved in environmental preservation? And how should the goods associated with the environment be compared with other goods of development (including particularly the good of enhancing human welfare)? Answers to the first question range from the prudential—environmental protection is necessary to preserve resources and a livable environment for future generations—to the intrinsic—the environment is inherently valuable, independent of human welfare. The chapter will consider a range of such views and will then turn to the question of how to handle conflicts between the value of environmental conservation and other important goods of development—in particular, the good of enhancing the quality of life of the poor and the near-poor. Some degree of conflict between long-term environmental conservation and medium-term poverty alleviation seems unavoidable, since more rapid development of natural resources harms the former while potentially benefiting the latter. How should these conflicts be resolved?

Like economic development itself, environmental ethics is an area in which there is an important interaction between value analysis and factual analysis. I will begin with an analysis of some of the empirical issues that define the challenge of environmental preservation and then turn to the value questions.

The Issues of Primary Environmental Concern

Let me begin with a practical discussion of environmental issues within economic development. The evidence concerning the direction and rate of change in global environmental quality is alarming. And the negative effects that are now visible in environmental change are themselves the more or less direct consequence of the combination of population increase and economic development. The United Nations Environment Programme published its third annual report on global environmental change in 2002 (United Nations Environment Programme 2002), and its global assessment is bleak. Water resources are under severe stress in some parts of the world, biological diversity and coastal ecosystems are predicted to suffer severe damage by 2032, soil erosion and degradation continue at a rapid pace, acid rain and the production of greenhouse gases continue to give rise to major climate and forestry changes, and the unplanned and rapid expansion of extremely poor cities throughout the developing world creates enormous stresses on the surrounding environment. The next thirty or so years may witness both a degree of economic progress toward the improvement of the standard of living of the world's poorest people and a severe degradation of the global environment—resulting in an impaired ability to make further economic progress and a diminishment of global quality of life. The report attempts to evaluate the environmental consequences of four possible scenarios for economic and political development in the next thirty years. These scenarios are: "markets first," "policy first," "security first," and "sustainability first" (United Nations Environment Programme 2002: 12). The authors find that the likely environmental effects of the market-first and security-first strategies are likely to result in further rapid degradation of the environment. The best prospects for the global environment appear to derive from a combination of the policy-first and sustainability-first scenarios, but significantly, neither scenario results in a stable or improving environmental future in this report.

What are the aspects of the environment that demand our attention? First, the earth is the sole source of the natural resources that human communities need to sustain their economies and technologies. These resources include fossil fuels, metals, minerals, and gases, as well as the biomass capacity of soils and waters. The fish stock of the planet's oceans, the agricultural potential of its cropland, and the fecundity of its forests fall in the same category: resources that can be consumed today or tomorrow or can be conserved over many generations. When we use a ton of iron ore to produce an automobile, that resource will not be accessible to future generations for their own uses. This situation can be referred to as the problem of *resource depletion*. Not all resources are subject to depletion, but the total global stock of fossil fuels, metals, and gases is finite. The world's supply of timber, by contrast, is not limited to a specific quantity; we can choose to invest in more tree farms and produce more timber.

A related issue is the preservation of water and air quality and prudent provision for effective *waste management*. Groundwater, oceans, and atmosphere are directly vulnerable to human activity, largely as a result of the dumping of waste products from human activities: combustion, sewage, chemical by-products, hot waste water, agricultural waste runoff, and the like. Waste is always created as a by-product of activity, and it is always possible to remediate waste through more or less costly means. Production processes can be redesigned to produce fewer by-products, scrubbers can be incorporated to reduce harmful particles and gases, holding ponds can be implemented to allow hot waste water to cool off, and so forth. However, these remediations are almost always costly: They add costs to the process of production and therefore increase the price of the good and/or decrease the profitability of the activity. Ultimately, this means less consumption for the sake of greater protection of the environment. More intensive agriculture, for example, is an important response to the important goal of boosting rural incomes and increasing food security, but it also imposes significant stress on soils and groundwater.

The emission of waste is a classic example of a *public harm* or *externality*. When a producer or consumer dumps wastewater into a public waterway, he or she avoids the cost of proper disposal and simultaneously imposes a cost on the public. The challenge for public policy is to develop regulations that protect the public from these harms—which private markets will not do. (Public harms are discussed more fully below.)

A specific area of great current concern is the prevention of catastrophic climate and atmospheric effects as a result of large-scale production of greenhouse gases and other harmful gases: global warming, ozone depletion, and air pollution. There is a direct causal relationship between economic activity and the production of greenhouse gases, through the expansion of the use of fossil fuels. So developing countries are likely to greatly increase their production of greenhouse gases during the process of intensive economic growth; yet the choice of slowing down or deferring economic growth is hard to reconcile with the goal of increasing the material well-being of a population. It has been very challenging to design stable international regimes that elicit cooperation from all nations on the production of greenhouse gases, and the mixed record of the Rio Treaty is the leading example of these difficulties.

Another large issue of environmental concern relates to the preservation of forests, wetlands, and other "natural" land uses. The clear-cutting of forests for timber and paper, intensive use of trees for firewood, and extension of development of cropland or businesses into hitherto natural areas are predictable consequences of economic and population growth. Yet, these tendencies represent a clear harm to the future stock of environmental goods, they represent a reduction of habitat for numerous species, and they shrink further the scope of undeveloped land and water that will be available for the enjoyment of future generations.

This process might be called the problem of "*encroachment*"—the process through which human settlements transform wilderness or undeveloped areas into habitation and other spaces for human activity. This process illustrates a clear tension between the interests of the present generation and the interests of future generations. The core of the issue is a simple one. It involves the exploitation and consumption of resources in order to satisfy the consumption needs of the people of the present at the expense of the availability of these or similar resources for the people of the future. This dilemma is distinct from the problem of waste; a society with a stable population and a zero net economic growth would not "encroach," but it would still "waste."

Finally, we turn to the problems of species preservation and *biodiversity*. Human activity presents a serious threat to species at every scale. Large predators such as cougars, wolves, and bears are subject to extinction as a result of the sprawl of human activity into previously wilderness areas. Reduction of the expanse of rain forest threatens the extinction of insect and plant species through the removal of habitat. Fish populations are imperiled as a result of overfishing and the obstruction of spawning rivers.

We can have many reasons for thinking that biodiversity and preservation of species are good things. There are good reasons to believe that the pool of genetic information represented by biodiversity is an important potential source of medical innovation; likewise, the diversity of grasses in the world to some extent protects us from the risk of a catastrophic disease that destroys the rice or wheat crop. And we have come to understand the complexity of ecological systems well enough to see that the extinction of one class of organisms may have large consequences for the rest of the organisms in that system. But most fundamentally, many reflective observers put it forward that species are valuable in and of themselves: The world is impoverished when the last spotted owl dies or when the Asian elephant is no more.

These issues represent a series of areas of particular environmental concern. They are especially salient because each of these processes is directly related to economic growth and development. How are we to think of these issues in the context of development planning and development ethics? It would appear that there are two chief avenues along which a people can go wrong, environmentally speaking. First, it may be "intergenerationally imprudent," in that it imposes costs on the environment (through encroachment and waste) that would be unjustified if we were giving fair consideration to the interests of future generations. And second, it may be excessively humanocentric, giving little or no weight to legitimate nonhuman environmental values. An example of the first sort of mistake might be the permanent destruction of a virgin forest for the short-term good of building a village; by this choice, the planner has created a short-term advantage for the present population but has forever denied future generations from enjoyment of the forest. An example of the second sort of mistake might be choosing to hunt bison to extinction for their hides; through this choice, the planner has privileged a relatively trivial human need over the permanent extinction of a species.

The Value Issues

I now begin a discussion of some of the underlying value issues in environmental policy and ethics. First is the issue of intrinsic versus instrumental interpretations of environmental values. Does the environment—or the ecological system or the inventory of species currently inhabiting the earth—have intrinsic value, or does it have value insofar as human beings need to have access to environmental resources? And if the environment or the ecological system has intrinsic value, does this mean that there are limits to the steps that we can take in the present to alleviate poverty? Suppose the cost of ending poverty within fifty years is the extinction of dozens of species and the reduction of wetland and rain forest by another 30 percent—is this a morally acceptable outcome? How do we reason about tradeoffs between incommensurable intrinsic goods?

Second is the issue of conflicts of interest between the present and the future. Americans of the year 2200 will likely to be profoundly influenced by the choices that we make today concerning the use of the world's resources—yet they cannot express their interests or needs directly. So we have obligations to persons distant from us in time and space as we make choices that affect the global environment. We will turn to the topic of intergenerational justice in a moment.

Third, there is an important cultural and regional dimension to environmental ethics. There are often fundamental conflicts of valuation about environmental values across cultures and regions in the present. Chinese people may place a different weight on environmental quality and economic development than Americans in the year 2000. These differences may stem from differences in wealth between East Asia and wealthier nations. When incomes are low, it is understandable that citizens and states may prefer to assign greater weight to improving incomes than preserving the environment. But it is also possible that there are cultural differences among the great civilizations of the world on this set of issues. This means that the choices that are taken by the German government, the Brazilian government, and the Chinese government may be driven by different underlying theories of the value and importance of environmental quality. The policies of one country may in turn lead to outcomes that adversely affect the citizens of the other countries, given the value framework within which those citizens evaluate alternative states of the world.[1]

Is Environment an Intrinsic or Instrumental Good?

Let us consider the nature of the value that the environment represents. What gives the environment a value within public policy and ethics? Why should we attach any weight to the conservation of the environment as we formulate plans, goals, and policies?

There are at least two families of answers to this question:

- The environment is a critical input into human well-being for all generations and for all persons—present and future. Therefore, present

generations should treat the environment as an important asset to be conserved and preserved for future generations.
- The environment is intrinsically valuable and should be conserved for its own sake—independently from human well-being.

The first line of thought begins in the moral value we attach to human well-being, and it notes that key environmental qualities are essential to the attainment of human flourishing: access to clean air and water, access to natural resources, and a sustainable system of agriculture to start and, at a loftier level, access to the beauty of nature. The environment is valuable because it is important to the realization of human needs, and human needs are intrinsically important. On this approach, environmental values can be folded into the value of enhancing human development.

This approach has an unmistakable logic. It is certainly true that the satisfaction of future human needs depends on the quality of the environment in which the people live. And it is true that choices made today will significantly affect the ability of people in the future to achieve the quality of life that we have seen to be the highest good in economic development in earlier chapters. So the quality of the environment has profound and pervasive importance that derives from its relationship to the intrinsic value of human flourishing. But note the implications of this view. It implies that any policy that enhances the overall quality of life of the people of the future will be justified—no matter what its environmental consequences. If environmental quality is exclusively instrumental, then ethics require that we carefully assess the overall consequences of a given set of policy choices and then choose that option that maximizes human well-being. Human well-being "trumps" effects on the environment.

From this perspective, we can look at environmental ethics from the point of multigenerational prudence: the adoption of policies on the use of environmental resources that would be considered fair from the vantage point of all generations, present and future. And from this perspective, the reason to pay attention to environmental values in our economic development choices today is that we owe such consideration to the people who will come in future generations. Our choices today should respect the moral importance of the generations to come, and therefore, we should act prudently with regard to our interests and theirs.

This approach can avoid an excessive materialism—the error of arriving at development choices on the basis of a narrow consideration of the income effects of various policies—by noting that future human interests will in fact reflect the importance of the environment. In particular, we note that humanity has a long-term interest in enjoying and exploiting the environment. We then come to a more enlightened treatment of the environment that takes into account the interests of future generations more fully in our current policymaking. A concern for future human interests allows us to consider environmental factors in a way that identifies just one central set of values—human well-being and development—but notes that environmental policy affects the long-term interests of people over time in ways that extend beyond income and the physical standard of living.

The second line of thought on environmental ethics criticizes the first as being unacceptably humanocentric. On the second approach, the natural environment has intrinsic value and should be taken into account independent from facts about future human well-being. (A central advocate of this approach is Aldo Leopold; see Leopold 1966 and Leopold and Schwartz 1966.) Species, biodiversity, habitat, forests, waterways, and the natural environment are all elements that have been advanced as having independent, intrinsic value. To say that entities such as these have intrinsic value is to say that they are not trumped by a finding of enhancement of human well-being, no matter how slight. Instead, the finding that an entity is harmed—habitat, waterways, species—must be assigned some weight in choosing policies.

This approach requires that we make substantive choices in balancing competing intrinsic goods as we adopt policies that affect both environmental qualities and features of future human well-being. The approach does not assume that the intrinsic good of the environment trumps the good of human well-being. But it does require that we provide reasons for the choices we make; in particular, it requires that we give fair consideration to the incommensurate intrinsic values that are inherent in a given policy choice.

And in fact it is plausible to find that environmental values are *not* exclusively instrumental and dependent for their value-worthiness on their contribution to human well-being. Is it really acceptable to suppose that even a slight overall improvement in human well-being would justify the extinction of a dozen species or that a slight reduction in poverty would justify the destruction of the earth's rain forests? But if we find these trade-offs unacceptable, then we are implicitly accepting the point that there are environmental qualities that possess intrinsic, not instrumental, value.

However, the position that the environment has intrinsic value has raised difficult problems within moral theory. Philosophers have asked, What would be the source of the intrinsic value of environmental features? We have a clear understanding of the value of human well-being; likewise, we understand clearly what is involved in a nonhuman entity as having instrumental value along the road to enhancing human well-being. And through our understanding of sentience, we may have an understanding of the moral importance of nonhuman animal pain and suffering. But what possible sources are there for establishing the intrinsic worth of things wholly unrelated to human well-being? Andrew Brennan (1995) provides a thoughtful discussion of this point of view. He and others focus the question along the lines of duties: Do we have duties to aspects of the environment—animals, species, ecosystems, rain forests? But the most promising way of justifying the notion that "X has a duty toward preserving Y" is to argue that Y has intrinsic value; so there is an intimate connection between duty and value. This approach, consequently, does not appear to succeed in clarifying the nature of the intrinsic environmental values.

It is relatively easy to motivate the moral importance of animals as sentient beings. Pain and suffering are bad things, whether experienced by human beings or sentient nonhuman beings. This point gives some justification for the intrinsic value or moral importance of animals. However, this line of reasoning does not extend to plants, ecosystems, or other nonsentient environmental categories. Elliott Sober (1995) provides a careful analysis of the philosophical difficulties with attributing value to the environment. He comes to the conclusion that the intrinsic value of the environment is ultimately best understood as an aesthetic value: We humans prefer the world in which there are multiple species, beautiful forests, and clean waterways to that in which the world has been scorched and polluted.

These are difficult philosophical issues within the theory of value. However, for our purposes, it is not necessary to come to a conclusion on the foundational issues. Instead, we can begin midstream and simply acknowledge that many of us do in fact assign noninstrumental value to at least some environmental goods. We prefer certain long-horizon scenarios about the future of the earth over others, and we may suspect that future generations will have similar preferences. If this is the case, it gives us a basis for holding that economic policy needs to take these environmental values into account. This approach remains human-centered in that it ultimately places the seat of environmental value in the assessments that we humans make about alternative outcomes in the environment. But the position is strong enough to support the conclusion that environmental factors ought not be simply subsumed within the calculus of choice that leads to the enhancement of human well-being or economic growth. (This approach puts environmental ethics into the domain of what Rawls [1993b] calls "political liberalism"—a set of values that are negotiated among a citizenry as a shared basis for policymaking.)

If we take the view that some environmental values are intrinsic, we are confronted with the ethical issue of tradeoffs—decisionmaking in circumstances in which there are multiple independent goods to be achieved and the task is to strike an appropriate balance in the attainment of all the goods. We might take the view, for example, that animals such as cows, hogs, or chickens have some moral value; that the human need for food has moral value; and that the morally appropriate balance of these independent but competing goods is to permit human consumption of animals but to require humane treatment of animals. The process of rearing and slaughtering animals therefore ought to minimize unnecessary pain and suffering. Or we might take a more extreme view and conclude that the moral importance of animals is on a par with that of human needs and that vegetarianism is the only morally acceptable position.

If we take the view that there are some elements of environment that have intrinsic value—say, the preservation of species and the preservation of habitat—then we must address the issue of how to honor this value in development planning. I have argued throughout this book that the first value of development ought to be the fulfillment of human capabilities, so how might the real but subordinate values of species preservation or ecological equilibrium be brought into our calculus about the future?

Intergenerational Justice

Let me turn now to the topic of intergenerational justice. Central to environmental reasoning is the fact that environmental choices impose substantial effects on future generations—good and bad. We make choices today, those choices have the power to enhance or harm the life prospects of people in the future, and those future people are not able to lobby for their interests in our deliberations. So how should the policymaking process reflect the interests of future people? What is involved in treating those people fairly?

I begin by noting that policy formation tends in practice to be myopic—particularly within a democracy, in that decisionmakers and citizens generally focus on the more immediate consequences of policies rather than the more distant consequences. This means that the interests of the present generation and near generations have greater weight than those of more distant generations. A second relevant consideration involves the uncertainty of our beliefs about those citizens of the future. The more distant the persons are from our own circumstances, the greater the uncertainty we have in deliberating about their interests. We can be confident that future generations will need food and shelter. But we do not know what innovations in technology and science may affect the means through which these needs will be satisfied.

What types of issues would be of interest to future generations? When we reflect on the needs of future generations, several environmental factors rise to special prominence: resource utilization and conservation, preservation of air and water quality, preservation of wetlands and rain forest, sustainable patterns of urbanization and urban development, and sustainable population policies. People in the future will have an interest in accessing a share of the world's physical resources, an interest in the level of air and water quality that they inherit, and an interest in not living in a world that is overburdened by population. However, these interests are silent in policy debates because citizens of the future cannot directly express their interests and preferences. So it is up to the current generation to calculate the legitimate interests of the future generations and to adopt policies that give fair consideration of those interests.

The reason that environmental issues pose a challenge at any time in history derives from the basic tension between consumption and savings and between present interests and future interests. Individuals and societies make choices that divide their resources and productive efforts between providing for a current standard of living or quality of life and providing for a future standard of living. Environmental conservation is costly. Treating waste products, seeking out resource-conserving technologies, and limiting personal consumption are all costly examples of the consequences of taking environmental values into account, and each choice imposes a sacrifice on today's quality of life in order to support an enhancement of future persons' quality of life.

Consider the following thought experiment. Suppose that it is known that crude petroleum has a current use (energy production) and a future use (a reservoir of complex hydrocarbons that can be the basis of powerful new technologies for chemistry and medicine). Moreover, suppose that a national energy policy based on petroleum use will substantially exhaust the petroleum reserve within fifty years. Finally, assume that the latter would have great effects on the well-being of people who benefit from that technology. A critical question is the timescale of the choice; if the new technology is two centuries in the future, our reasoning is probably different than if it is twenty years in the future. But let us suppose that the new technology can confidently be expected between fifty and sixty years from the present. This takes the benefit beyond the enjoyment of the present generation; at the same time, we can demand that ethical decisionmakers give consideration to the interests of future persons. So how should this tradeoff be determined? Should the current generation sacrifice some degree of its currently feasible quality of life (through costly investment in alternative energy sources) in order to enhance the quality of life for the future generations who would benefit?

We note that the present generation—whichever generation that is—inevitably makes choices that affect the quality of the environment for future generations. If this generation uses 10 percent of the available fossil fuels, then future generations will have proportionally fewer fossil fuels for their needs. If this generation allows the quality of air and water to decline in order to achieve savings on manufacture and energy production today, future generations will either be forced to expend significant wealth to remediate these harms or will have a lesser quality of life as a result of these choices.

On this approach to the problem of environmental stewardship, an ethically satisfactory solution is a planning principle that gives fair consideration to environmental values insofar as they affect the quality of life of future generations of humans. And the principle ought to be such as to embed an unlimited time line for this consideration (along the lines of the principle of "generational induction" described later in this chapter—a principle that requires that planners give explicit consideration to the interests of the next three generations, a planning horizon of sixty years).

How can we rationally and morally incorporate consideration of the legitimate future interests of humanity and the interests of future generations into a just and rational planning process today? What does ethics require in making choices about the interests of future generations? In what ways should we take the interests of persons of the future into account in our current policies and choices?[2] The central moral fact that underlies intergenerational ethics is the fact that persons are morally significant, whether they are close or distant from us. This is so whether we consider distant strangers in the present (victims of famine on another continent, for example) or persons who will exist in the next century in our own cities. This fact implies that our choices ought to take these morally significant interests into account in a significant way. Each generation should take a moral interest in the well-being of the next. So the policies adopted today should be broadly consistent with the interests of future generations; today's policies ought not guarantee harm for future generations.

How can the interests of the future be incorporated into today's decision-making process? One possible solution is for our ethical theory to define the scope of consideration to a manageable number of generations—for example, three generations, or about sixty years. This requirement would establish a condition of planning rationality that we might term *generational induction*: If each generation of planners is charged to make prudent decisions that give fair consideration to the interests of persons sixty years in the future, then over time, we can infer that all generations will be given fair consideration. This is a principle that gives some degree of intergenerational consideration. But it is possible that some choices made today could go beyond this time frame—choices that might impose harms on people living two centuries from the present and that would be uncorrectable at any future time. Some have made the case that the storage of spent nuclear fuels creates this sort of intergenerational hazard.

Consider an example. Suppose we are confronted with two development choices. The first policy package leads to an immediate and gradual improvement in the welfare of the poor, followed by slow but steady growth over the next fifty years. The second policy package leads to some decline in the position of the poorest 40 percent of the current population, then gradual improvement and medium steady growth for the next fifty years. Finally, suppose that the welfare of the poor on the second plan passes that of the first plan after thirty years. Considered with strict temporal neutrality, the second plan is preferable to the first; for a historically brief time, the first dominates the second, whereas for the rest of time, the second dominates the first. The gains achieved by the future poor vastly (perhaps infinitely) outweigh the sacrifices of today's poor.

By contrast, we might reason along the following lines. The needs of today's poor are extremely urgent: Infant mortality is high, morbidity is high, literacy is low, nutritional status is compromised, and so on. Today's poor need immediate attention. Tomorrow's poor deserve consideration as well, but their condition will be better than that of the poor today. Therefore, we should give first priority to poverty alleviation for today's poor and then turn to improving the prospects of later generations.

Both these arguments have a certain amount of force. (Ideally, of course, it would be preferable to adopt the poverty alleviation strategy for the first thirty years and then switch effortlessly to the growth strategy. But this may not be feasible; the technological and institutional innovations needed for the first may not support the second.) So how are we to resolve the issue? Shall we maximize utility over time—thus favoring the growth strategy? Or shall we maximize the welfare of today's poor—thus favoring the poverty-first strategy?

One possible line of analysis involves introducing a time discount function. If we discount future utilities by even a low rate, then large gains in the distant future will not outweigh small gains in the near future. Moreover, if we do not discount future utilities, then we should always favor investment over current consumption—at every point in time. So a time discount is mandatory. But setting the discount rate high or low is a substantive moral issue, and we need to have a justification for our choice.

The way we treat this issue makes a great deal of practical difference in the kinds of development plans that we favor. On the one hand, if the present generation gets strong priority, then there will be less investment in productive assets and more in current consumption—food grain subsidies, free health care and education, and the like. On the other hand, if we favor future generations very heavily over the present generation (as might be justified by a temporally neutral social choice approach considering a large number of generations), then we will choose a mix of strategies heavily biased toward long-term investments in productive assets.

Public Goods, Public Policy, and Future Interests

Environments need state protection; a high-quality environment is not one of the effects that even the strenuous advocates of liberal economic regimes claim for the workings of the market. Why is this so? There are two related reasons, each having to do with the nature of private decisionmaking in economic activities. First, environmental goods and bads are typically public goods or common goods and not easily converted to private goods and bads. A public good is an effect that is costly to achieve, requiring contributions from numerous agents, but concerning which no individual can be excluded from access. An example of a public good is public radio. A specific group of individuals, firms, and government sources provide the resources necessary to fund the production costs of the broadcast, but everyone—contributors and noncontributors alike—are able to enjoy the good once it is made available. Public goods are notoriously difficult to achieve, since there is an ever-present incentive to become a free rider on the good. This means that there will be a chronic tendency toward underfunding of public goods, with the result that providers of public goods often fail (Mueller 1989, 1976). Public harms are the opposite of public goods. They are harms that are costly to avoid but where the effects of the harmful behavior are broadly distributed over harm producers and harm avoiders alike. An example of a public harm is smoke emissions from wood-burning stoves in a valley community. The air quality of the valley reflects the sum of emissions from all homes that use wood-burning stoves. Each resident would prefer higher air quality, but the effect of one individual reducing emissions on the overall air quality is negligible. Therefore, no resident has a direct incentive to reduce emissions—though all have an incentive to urge their neighbors to do so.

Government regulations are a way of protecting the common good by promoting the production of public goods and discouraging the production of public harms. In the most general terms, we can regard the market as an effective agent of certain kinds of collective goods—for example, efficient allocation of resources through competitive price mechanisms—and the state as an effective agent of certain other kinds of collective goods—for example, the prevention of public harms. Evidently, we need effective organs of public policy to work against the effects of purely private decisionmaking in many areas of economic activity.[3]

A further complication in the case of environmental harms comes from the intergenerational aspect of environmental decisionmaking. The negative consequences of current economic activities are commonly imposed on future generations rather than the current generation. Government regulation is a way of protecting future common interests against the effects of purely present-centered decisionmaking. We need to ask our governments to adopt fair and prudent policies that protect the legitimate interests of future generations and then to adopt policies that effectively constrain private activities so as to respect those policies.

When the harms in question are global rather than national, we are faced with an even deeper public goods problem. Problems such as ozone depletion or global warming have global causes and global consequences. But there are important conflicts of interest among the nations that are affected by these consequences, there are important differences in the ways in which nations contribute to the causes of these processes, and the problem of establishing effective international regimes that provide for prudent protection of the environmental interests of future generations is a deeply difficult one. The unilateral withdrawal of the United States from the Kyoto Treaty is an example; at the other end of the scale, the grassroots protests against the WTO and globalization of the economy draw much of their energy from the widespread concern that firms with global reach are essentially unregulated in their environmental behavior.

Clearly, the challenge of creating effective and prudent international regimes for protecting global environmental interests, present and future, is critically important and deeply difficult.

Goals

What must a theory of environmental values offer within the context of economic development thinking? It needs to give us guidance in the design of plans for future choices for investment and activity; further, it needs to provide a basis for choosing among diverse goods and bads, some of which are environmental. The discussion to this point suggests a few guiding principles.

First, development strategies need to be compatible with the need to sustain the agricultural carrying capacity of the planet. That is, the ability for societies to grow food is a fundamental material prerequisite for present and future human well-being. So agriculture must be sustainable, in a fairly direct and uncontroversial sense: Soils need to be preserved and renewed in terms of nutrients, groundwater needs to be protected, and so forth.

Second, prudent regard for the generations of the future requires that we make sensible choices that conserve important nonrenewable material resources (metals, minerals, gases). This endeavor may entail finding production techniques that minimize the use of various potentially scarce metals, or it may mean manufacturing techniques that maximize the recycling potential of the object.

Third, prudent regard for the legitimate interests of the future requires that we sustain (and enhance) air and water quality to preserve human health and enjoyment. It would appear unacceptable on its face, in a neo-Kantian sort of way, to benefit from industrial or agricultural practices, that, if universalized (that is, continued indefinitely), would lead to an uninhabitable world. So our goal should be to reach a point of equilibrium at which air and water quality are no longer deteriorating and are perhaps even improving.

This observation suggests that we can get quite a lot of mileage for environmental ethics from the premise of intergenerational fairness. But what about other environmental values—the importance of preserving species and biodiversity, for example? These values can partially be justified on the basis of intergenerational justice; the species may turn out to be valuable or important to the people of the future in ways we cannot foresee. But more important, it appears that we can appropriately reach for a moderate principle of "the moral importance of animals" to argue that policies ought to take species preservation into account. What we have not settled, however, is a principle for weighting the moral importance of various environmental values and the importance of values having to do with human development and well-being.

Sustainable Development

Is it possible to formulate a general theory of a prudent and intergenerationally fair environmental policy? The concept of sustainable development has been central to discussions of this topic since the early 1990s, and it corresponds very well to the requirements of intergenerational justice that highlighted previously. Sustainability came into central focus in discussions of global environmental policy at the 1992 United Nations Earth Summit in Rio de Janeiro. One definition of this concept incorporated the following points:

- Modes of material human activity should be constrained in such a way as to assure that the use of resources and the production of waste can be continued indefinitely.
- Sustainable development is development that satisfies the needs of the present without compromising the needs of the future (Brundtland 1987: chapter 2).

The preceding definition disregards the possibility of technical change, so the principle might be amended as:
- Modes of material activity should be constrained in such a way as to assure (1) that the current use of resources and production of waste can be continued indefinitely, or (2) that new technologies and materials can be envisioned to take the place of resources and assets that are depleted through the activity.

We saw above that agriculture and industry would need to increase manyfold to accomplish economic development; likewise, the use of resources such as fossil fuels, minerals, and timber must increase dramatically, and the production of waste will increase concomitantly. Is the goal of progressive economic development (or, indeed, any form of sustained economic growth) compatible with the principle of sustainable development? It is not obvious that we can answer this question affirmatively; indeed, if we exclude the possibility of large-scale new technological discoveries in the relatively near future (fifty years), it is probably more justified to conclude that progressive economic development is *not* compatible with sustainable development over the course of a half century. In other words, to pursue the goal of progressive economic development, we may have to accept the consequence that the earth's environment will continue to degrade over time and in ways that are not reversible in the medium term.[4]

Nonetheless, the goal of sustainability is the only credible position we can take, given the duties we have to future generations. The need for economic growth for the sake of poverty alleviation and the rising use of resources that this will entail together imply that things will get worse for the environment and that we have a strong moral obligation to seek out policies and behaviors that will permit the emergence of sustainable environmental strategies at some point in the not too distant future (when population has stabilized and when new technologies in agriculture, energy production, and materials have made sustainability achievable).

Conflicts Between Environmental Goals and Economic Development

It is important to recognize that the most basic threats to environmental quality—population increase, urbanization, and the use of land for more and more intensive purposes—are part and parcel of modernization, economic growth, and the enhancement of global human well-being. This fact creates the likelihood of conflict between environmental values and the goal of poverty alleviation.

I have identified a series of objectives that an environmentalist program would wish to see honored within the context of economic development in the coming fifty years. Why are these goals especially challenging within the context of a world undergoing significant economic development and in which an absolute majority of the population lives in conditions of absolute poverty? Environmental goals and economic development goals are almost inevitably at odds with one another in this setting. Economic growth requires a change in the character and level of human activity in a region, it requires increasing use of natural resources, it implies more intensive land use, it implies rapid increases in energy consumption, and it gives rise to activities that produce waste in vastly greater quantities than traditional means of economic activity had done. (In the grandest scale, one might even say that the conflict between environment and economy is an implication of the laws of thermodynamics relating activity [the creation of local order] to the production of greater entropy [in the form of heat].)[5] Economic development therefore leads inevitably to increased depletion of nonrenewable resources, increased pressure on land and water resources, and ever-increasing production of waste products (household waste, industrial waste, chemical by-products, and heat released into air and water systems).

One important dimension of the conflict between economic activity and the quality of the global environment is demographic: With increasing human population, even the goal of sustaining a given level of consumption requires more intensive and extensive use of resources. If we keep production technology and individual consumption levels fixed, an increase of 5 percent in the population implies a 5 percent increase in energy use, fossil fuel use, metals and minerals use, timber and agricultural products use, and so forth. At present, the global population is increasing at a rate of more than 1 percent per year. It is predicted that developing nations will undergo a demographic transition similar to that witnessed by the developed countries over the past fifty years, with the hope of a stable global population of 9.0 billion in the year 2050. However, this equilibrium, if it occurs at all, will not come about for fifty years. So population growth itself will be a major driver of environmental degradation.

More profoundly, however, the goal of economic growth and the goal of poverty alleviation that I have identified throughout this volume as being a leading priority within economic growth are intimately related to sustained increases in the use of resources and the creation of waste. The ultimate goal of economic growth is to increase the consumption bundles available to human beings. When a person becomes less poor, this means that he or she will be able to consume more of the economy's finished products: food, shelter, clothing, books, education, electronic goods, and so forth. So the goal of economic growth implies a rising per capita output of the global economy. Here, we can put concrete terms on the goal of reducing the poverty of the Indonesian farmer: We would hope that economic development will give him or her the opportunity of gaining access to a more varied and satisfying diet, better clothing and shelter, and access to a broader spectrum of the goods through which human capacities are amplified. These goals, however, require a higher per capita level of industrial and agricultural production in the global economy and higher per capita use of resources such as metals, petroleum, or paper.

If we put these two trends—global population increase and global economic growth—together, we can derive a theorem in the environment-economy sphere. The inference that we can draw is that—other things being equal—the next fifty years will reflect greater usage of natural resources, more intensive and extensive use of land and water, and greater overall production of waste products.

Fortunately, it is not quite the case that all things are equal. For a central goal of environmental policymaking is to improve the efficiency of the "exploitation of nature"—that is, to improve the efficiency of energy production, distribution, and consumption; to improve the efficiency of the use of raw materials in the production of useful items; to arrive at agricultural techniques that make more efficient use of inputs and permit sustainable land use over multiple generations; and, in general, to produce more with less. To the extent that efficiency gains are possible in some or all of these areas, we can hope that the rate of increase in the use of resources and in the creation of waste will be lower than the rate of increase in per capita consumption times population increase. Technological change is the dimension that has permitted the globe to avoid a Malthusian crisis, and it is likely that technological change will continue to moderate the tension between demand and supply in the world production system. (It is dubious, however, that efficiency gains along these lines can be achieved indefinitely; rather, it is probably more reasonable to hypothesize a period of efficiency improvement, followed by a constant level of energy costs.)

It is worthwhile to attempt to model these several effects simultaneously, to attempt to work out the consequences of the assumptions we have been making about sustained economic development. The model is designed to probe the question of what is required of the process of economic development if there is to be sustained improvement in the material quality of life of the world's population (including especially the poor). And what are the implications of such growth on energy and resource expenditure? The model summarized in Figure 7.1 makes very simple assumptions:

- An increase in the quantity of goods in the consumption basket over time
- An increase in the efficiency of each production technology over time (falling coefficients of production)
- An increase in energy and resource efficiency (leading to lower production costs)

It is possible to estimate the resource consumption and waste production levels associated with a hypothetical equilibrium in which population is stable and the whole population has achieved a high minimum standard of living. (At this point, we could reasonably assert that the human imperatives of economic development have been satisfied.) The resource budget of this high-level human welfare equilibrium is represented (in a highly imprecise way) in Figure 7.1. (Note that this is not a sophisticated effort to model future resource use; it is simply an attempt to take account of very crude assumptions about consumption and project them forward.)

The implications of this effort at compiling a "resource budget" for progressive economic development are profoundly sobering. This analysis sug-

210

	2000	2050	change
Population (million)	6,000	9,000	50%
GDP per capita (1998 $)	$5,000	$15,000	200%
GDP for global economy (million $)	$30,000,000	$135,000,000	350%
Minimum income	$1,000	$8,000	700%
Gini coefficient	0.700	0.500	-29%
per capita			
Energy (tons of oil)	1.70	2.75	62%
Metals	500.00	1000.00	100%
grain (kg)	250.00	500.00	100%
meat (kg)	33.00	75.00	127%
fish (kg)	50.00	75.00	50%
total output			
Energy (million tons of oil)	10,200	24,750	143%
Metals (million)	3,000,000	9,000,000	200%
Grain (million kg)	1,500,000	4,500,000	200%
Meat (million kg)	198,000	675,000	241%
Fish (million kg)	300,000	675,000	125%
agricultural output			
grain per hectare (kg)	3,000	4,500	50%
meat per hectare (kg)	700	1,000	43%
fish per hectare (kg)	800	1,200	50%
agricultural land use			
Grain (hectare)	500,000,000	1,000,000,000	100%
meat (hectare)	282,857,143	675,000,000	139%
forests	3,540,000,000	2,500,000,000	-29%
agricultural land	782,857,143	1,675,000,000	114%
fish ponds	375,000,000	562,500,000	50%
Total agricultural land	1,157,857,143	2,237,500,000	93%

Figure 7.1   High-level global human welfare equilibrium

gests that the goals described as desirable throughout this book would entail a doubling in agricultural land use (implying a dramatic reduction in uncultivated land, wetlands, meadows, and forests); a two-and-a-half-fold increase in global energy use; and a tripling in the use of metals (implying even more intensive mining than the present). In short, progressive economic development poses an agenda for the world that implies profound stress on the natural environment.[6]

Population Size and the Environment

There is a deep connection between the goals and processes of economic development and a concern for population policy and demographic pathways. I have emphasized the moral importance of enhancing human well-being through development. But maximizing human capabilities does not entail maximizing human population. Our goal should be to stabilize population growth at a level that permits all human beings to fully realize their capabilities at a high level. That in turn means that we need to achieve a high level of access to education and sufficient income to permit individuals to have material welfare compatible with the realization of their capabilities—thereby removing or reducing the incentives toward large families on the part of households in poor countries.

Arguments presented to this point come very close to establishing the following conclusion: The goals of progressive economic development, conjoined with standard demographic models, entail that sustainable development is not attainable in the next fifty years and that the environment that would result from such a process would be one in which there was substantial resource depletion, depletion of forest and meadow, and degradation of water and air quality.[7] Moreover, the central line of normative reasoning offered in this book would accept this outcome, in that I have privileged human well-being over other goods (including environmental quality). It is better to have an impaired environment if that is the cost of eliminating global poverty.

There is another possible solution, however, that forces us to contemplate another large set of normative issues. For it is possible to imagine a world in which all human beings are supported at a high level of functioning, a world in which the globe's resources are treated in a sustainable way. This is a world in which the equilibrium population is smaller than what we currently expect—not 9 billion, but—perhaps—5 billion.[8]

Put it the other way around: What is the equilibrium population size that emerges as a solution to the constraints created by sustainable progressive economic development? This number would be an estimate of the carrying capacity of the global economy, based on the minimum consumption levels implied by the goals of progressive economic development.

It should be clear to all that this solution to the problem—ultimately, controlled human fertility—is by no means an easy one; in fact, the social disruption and negative welfare created by poverty may well be less pervasive than the social problems created by aggressive population policy. However, it is essential to recognize that the central values underlying the arguments advanced in this book are silent on absolute population size. To value human well-being is not to prefer a larger over a smaller population.

This is, in one way, an alternative statement of an old debate between "average" and "sum" versions of utilitarian ethics: Do we maximize happiness by creating a large number of somewhat happy people or a smaller number of very happy people? Maximizing the average welfare seems, in general, to be a more defensible moral position, and this intuition has immediate implications for the problem before us. A preliminary conclusion appears to emerge, therefore: that development policy must be highly engaged in population policy as well and that the target equilibrium of global population ought to be one constrained by appropriate conditions of sustainability and human well-being.

Means of Preserving Environmental Goods

What are some of the chief means to establish sustainable environmental practices on a global basis? First, we have seen that a major source of stress on the environment has to do with energy production, including particularly the use of fossil fuels in transportation and the production of electricity, heat, and steam. Yet, energy production is directly related to economic growth. As poor societies increase their levels of economic activity in agriculture, manufacturing, and consumption, they will also increase their need for abundant energy. And this need is likely to increase nonlinearly; if economic activity increases 10 percent, it is likely that demand for energy will increase by more than this percentage. Consequently, energy use is one of the most fundamental environmental challenges we face. The reservoir of fossil fuels is finite, so there is a direct reason to attempt to conserve a fair share of this resource for future generations. And combustion of fossil fuels create the waste products that result in massive environmental harm to the atmosphere, including the production of greenhouse gases and the intensifying of global warming.

Increased energy efficiency—in automotive fuel efficiency standards, the efficiency of power plant technology, and the efficiency of home heating systems—has the dual effects of reducing the use of the energy resource (petroleum, coal, natural gas) and reducing the emissions that are produced. Efficiency improvement can be achieved on both sides of the equation: The energy production process itself can be enhanced, so that more of the potential energy in the fuel is converted to useable kinetic energy, and the process being driven by the energy can be increased in efficiency—by reducing the weight of the vehicle, by reducing wastage of energy within the process (friction, for example), or by redesigning the manufacturing process so that it requires less energy overall.

Parallel to efforts to improve efficiency are attempts to enhance clean combustion, reducing by-products that are released as exhaust products. Research efforts to perfect fuel cell technology promise to lead to progress on both these goals because this technology promises to yield higher usable energy and lower exhaust waste per unit of fuel.

A related research effort with positive environmental effects involves the development and refinement of alternative energy sources that reduce reliance on fossil fuels. These sources include the various means of collecting solar energy (solar panels, wind farms, hydroelectric plants), next-generation nuclear technologies, or geothermal energy production technology (Cooper and Layard 2002).

Greater efficiency in the production and use of energy and greater progress toward energy production systems that are cleaner overall can have very significant effects on the slope of two crucial curves: the curve tracking the increase in per capita energy consumption on the globe and the curve tracking the increase in the output of harmful by-products (including greenhouse gases). Both effects are critically important for the well-being of future generations. But nothing in the remedies we have surveyed here suggests that it is possible to reduce the slope of these two curves to zero. This would reflect a stable equilibrium in which demand for energy (at least per capita) is no longer increasing and the emission of waste products is no longer increasing (again, per capita). This result, it appears, would only come about in the context of zero net economic growth per capita, and this result is inconsistent with the overriding goal of enhancing the well-being of the poor and the near-poor in the next fifty years.

Let me turn now to another key environmental need and consider what remedies exist for this need. I noted above that the supply of metals, minerals, and gases is finite on the earth. And yet, economic activity is dependent on the prodigious use of these resources. Two scenes illustrate the situation. First, consider the case of a major integrated automobile plant, where freighters deliver mountains of iron ore and coke, steel is produced, and finished vehicles are delivered at the factory exit. The plant transforms raw materials, through labor and machinery, into finished vehicles. Next, consider the vast automobile graveyards that exist throughout the United States, where vehicles have ended their useful lives and their component materials are rusting away. This scenario describes a unidirectional process that is obviously unsustainable over many centuries. The valuable resources—iron ore, copper, other metals, and so on—that were collected from the mines in northern Michigan have been transported, in an unusable form, to the junkyards of the United States. And these valuable resources are no longer usable by future generations.

A preferable scenario is one in which there is effective and economically viable resource recycling on a massive scale. Can we reconceive the picture so that, instead of freighters delivering raw iron ore, we find a massive vehicle disassembly plant at the entrance to the factory, in which the components of the vehicle are restored to a usable form and used as inputs into the next generation of vehicles? This is a challenge that manufacturing engineers and environmental scientists are beginning to confront. To what extent is the ideal attainable? To what extent can the design of the product and its manufacturing process be reconceived so that component resources can be captured and reused?

A fourth large area of environmental policy falls in the area of land use, deforestation, and wilderness and wetland preservation. Human activities in local and regional land zones have had massive consequences for the ecologies of continents. The clearing of forests associated with the "second feudalism" in the fifteenth century is a good example, with the transformation of vast forests into cultivated land through the use of the axe and the plow (P. Anderson 1996). The transformation of the Great Plains from prairie to farmland is a similarly sweeping example (Cronon 1991). A more familiar contemporary example is the phenomenon of "periurban sprawl" through which business and residential developments creep outward from cities and towns into the farmlands, forests, and wetlands that surround them. The expansion of human activity—whether based on population growth, migration, economic growth, or all of these factors at the same time—creates powerful tendencies toward erosion of previously undeveloped zones or transformation of low-intensity zones into medium- or high-intensity zones. But this process has massive consequences for habitat, ecological stability, and the stability of wild populations of birds, animals, insects, and plants. Poverty alleviation entails expansion of human activity—in agriculture, manufacturing, services, transportation, communication, and consumption—and these processes can be expected to apply continuing pressures on land, forest, and wetland resources. So how are developing countries to adopt appropriate and effective policies concerning the development (or nondevelopment) of these resources?

A final set of strategies that can ameliorate environmental harms has to do with large-scale behavioral change on the part of consumers and citizens. Is it possible for a society to reconfigure public expectations about consumption patterns in such a way as to ameliorate environmental harms and reduce the rate of resource use? Many examples of such potential changes come to mind. Consider transportation as an example. The private automobile is an especially energy-intensive way of moving people from one place to another. For short distances, pedestrian and bicycle traffic is more efficient; for long distances, mass transportation such as the railroad is more efficient. However, Americans have adopted a set of preferences about transportation that lead us to choose the automobile over the bicycle and railroad. Is it possible to set in motion a program of "preference shifting" that would lead Americans toward more energy-efficient modes of transportation? A second example has to do with diet and food. Through the history of economic growth, greater affluence has typically led to diets that shift in the direction of more meat and less vegetable and grain. But the production of meat is much more resource-intensive than the production of grain, so this shift in preferences can be expected to will give rise to a surge in the consumption of agricultural resources in the coming fifty years. This shift has often had negative nutritional and public health consequences for the population. Is it possible to imagine a social process through which people come to have food preferences that are both more nutritionally appropriate and less resource-intensive? Finally, what about the set of values that equates affluence with massive consumption? Is it possible to initiate a process of values transformation through which human needs and consumption are more realistically related? And can such a shifting of consumption preferences foster a dampening of the growth rate of resource consumption, energy consumption, and the creation of pollution? Can whole populations be brought to an understanding of individual well-being that is less defined by the volume of consumption and more defined by the full exercise of human creativity and capability?

It should be noted that all of these instrumentalities have an economic cost, and there are relatively clear limits to the positive effects they would be able to produce. In treating waste gases exiting from a smokestack, for instance, it costs nothing (directly) to allow the gases to escape without treatment, it costs $X to remove 90 percent of the particles, and it costs $3X to remove 95 percent of the particles. There is a point of diminishing returns in any process of enhancement of a good; the hard question is where to set the standard.

Many of these examples suggest the importance of new forms of cost accounting that allow more specific enumeration of environmental costs in the production and use of a given product—whether or not these costs are reflected in the balance sheet of a producer or consumer. Rational decision-making requires that we be able to provide good estimates of the costs, benefits, and risks associated with various possible actions. And if all costs and benefits are measured through the market prices of inputs and outputs, then environmental values are likely to be systematically underserved. The accounting discipline has made significant progress in developing tools that attempt to incorporate environmental and nonmonetary costs into the discipline of managerial accounting under the general rubric of "social and environmental accounting."[9]

Finally, public policy is an essential element of effective environmental policy. This fact derives from the public harm aspect of environmental change. Market mechanisms do not capture environmental costs, so an effective and prudent system of public policy must be in place that can create regulations and institutions that serve important collective interests in environmental preservation. This is all the more true when it comes to global environmental processes. Individual states can take the "free-riding" option on environmental policy, so it will be necessary to craft effective and binding international institutions if we are to have any hope of arriving at stable and sustainable environmental policies worldwide.

Notes

1. An important series of conferences on the subject of ecology and the world religions took place in the 1990s under the auspices of the Harvard Center for the Study of World Religions, and a number of signification publications were produced. See Tucker and Williams 1997, Chapple and Tucker 2000, Tucker and Grim 1994, and Tucker and Berthrong 1998 for important contributions to this topic.

2. A particularly important philosophical discussion of the issue of the rights of future generations is provided by Joel Feinberg (1974). Norm Daniels (1988) addresses the issue of intergenerational justice with a shorter time frame.

3. Government regulation is not the only possible solution to public goods problems, however. Elinor Ostrom (1990) documents community-based solutions to "common property resource" problems. These are quasi-voluntary arrangements through which a community of users (fisherman, grazers, irrigators) are able to manage the resource collectively, and control violators, in such a way as to preserve the resource over time. See also Baden and Noonan 1998 for an important set of perspectives on "managing the commons" and solving common property resource problems.

4. See van den Bergh and van der Straaten 1997 for a formal model pertinent to efforts to project the environmental effects of sustained global growth.

5. H. E. Daly makes this point in *Steady State Economics* (1991).

6. See Cooper and Layard 2002 for an extensive discussion of the conceptual and methodological difficulties in projecting the future values of any of these important variables (population, energy use, global climate change). See Grossman and Krueger 1995 for a discussion of the linkages between economic growth and environmental degradation.

7. This conclusion is very consistent with the findings of the third United Nations Environmental Programme report (United Nations Environment Programme 2002). The most common basis for disagreeing with this view is the prospect that technological advances in the future will offset rising pressure on the environment. See Starr 1996 for a survey of this view.

8. See Keyfitz 1993 for further discussion.

9. See the U.S. Environmental Protection Agency website on "Environmental Cost Accounting"—www.epa.gov/opptintr/acctg/.

8

Democracy and Development

IS DEMOCRACY INHERENTLY A GOOD thing? And do democratic institutions facilitate economic development? Do they have positive effects on the achievement of some or all of the characteristics of progressive economic development? Does a transition to stable electoral democracy in a developing society help to facilitate economic development "of the right kind" in that society?

This chapter will consider both the normative and the empirical aspects of these questions. I will argue that democracy is morally important because it embodies the idea of freedom in the context of social decisionmaking. But the answer to the last question is an empirical one, and there is debate within the development field about the effects of electoral democracy on the development process. Some argue, for example, that the experiences of Korea, Taiwan, or Indonesia show that a strong authoritarian state is better able to engineer a successful process of economic development than an electoral democracy such as India (because of its inability to discipline fractious demand groups).

I will argue, first, that democracy is inherently desirable—for poor countries and for rich countries; second, that the empirical record of authoritarian developing states is about as mixed as that of democratic states; and finally, that only democratic institutions give any promise of tilting economic development policies toward the interests of the poor. We will find that democracy is an important instrument of progressive economic development because it is an institutional assurance that the policies and laws

created by a government will have a reasonable fit with the fundamental interests of the people.

So democracy is a desirable component of just development—at least, this
is what the moral intuitions of a liberal Western philosopher would assert.
But before we can have great confidence in this utterance, we need to look
more closely at the meaning of democracy and democratic citizenship—particularly in the context of the developing world. And we need to consider several important empirical questions: Do democratic institutions facilitate
economic development of the right kind? And do democratic institutions
guarantee or even make probable the result that government policy and law
will reflect the fundamental interests of the people?

What Is Democracy?

Let me begin by asking, What is a democracy? We can represent the central
characteristics of a democracy from two points of view: that of the individual
citizen and that of the political institutions through which the values of
democracy are realized in a particular social context. At the level of the citizen, we can say that persons conduct their lives within the context of a set of
political and legal institutions. These institutions constitute the state and the
system of law and government. The modern state wields enormous power. It
creates laws and regulations, it creates police and military forces, and it creates systems of taxation for funding the work of government. The citizen has
several chief concerns with regard to the state. Does the system of law establish an appropriate and generous range of rights and liberties? Is the state
guided by the common good? Is the state responsive to the interests and preferences of citizens in the establishment of laws and regulations? And is the
system of taxation a fair one?

Several elements distinguish a political group from other forms of association. For instance, the political unit is empowered to coerce its members
through the collection of taxes, restrictions on the use of property, and the
imposition of regulations and laws. Moreover, the authority of the unit does
not depend on the continuing voluntary consent of the individual for the exercise of its authority. The citizen may sometimes vote with his or her feet (by
departing the jurisdiction), but while resident within the jurisdiction of the
political unit, the citizen can be compelled to act according to the laws, poli-

cies, and decrees of the political authorities. And laws have the invariable characteristic of restricting freedom; that is, they inevitably work to prevent people from acting on choices they otherwise might have made.

It is sometimes debated whether there is ever a moral justification for coercive legislation by the state, but I will not enter into this debate here.[1] Rather, I will join with Hobbes, Locke, Rousseau, Mill, and Rawls in stating that the individuals within a society require some central authority in order to establish a system of law, to prevent violence, and to enact policies in the common good. Society requires a state. And democratic theory attempts to provide the most general blueprint possible for the legitimate state.

Several central and defining normative commitments jointly define the political theory of a democracy. In the briefest possible way, a preliminary definition of democracy can be presented in these terms:

- A *democracy* is a polity in which collective decisions (laws, policies, procedures) are the expression, direct or indirect, of the preferences and choices of the collection of equal citizens of that polity.
- A *constitutional democracy* is a polity in which an explicit set of principles defines the scope of collective decisionmaking, including especially the definition of a fundamental set of citizens' rights that cannot be overturned by democratic action.
- A *representative democracy* is a polity in which citizens express their preferences through regular elections of legislators and executive officers (governors, prime ministers, presidents). Legislators in turn adopt legislation through a majoritarian process.

These definitions emphasize several important elements: self-rule, individual preferences, equality of citizenship, elections, and constitutionality. Democracy is a set of collective decisionmaking institutions through which individuals assert themselves in the public sphere. As such, it incorporates the ideal of citizen self-rule of a politically constituted social group. Many alternative sets of political institutions embody this set of ideals. And for each proposed alternative institutional design, we can ask the question, How well does this design express the values of equality, constitutionality, and liberty?

Tenets of Normative Democratic Theory

Some of the central tenets of normative democratic theory follow:

- All adult members of the collectivity ought to have the status of citizens (that is, there should be no restriction in political rights for different groups of people within the polity; the *universal citizenship principle*).
- All citizens ought to have the broadest set of political rights and liberties possible, compatible with the extension of equal rights to all (that is, there ought to be full political equality and the broadest possible liberty for all citizens; the *liberty principle* and the *equality principle*).
- Legislation ought to reflect the principle of the sovereignty of the people. When and where legislation is required, it should result from a process that involves the meaningful expression of interests and preferences by all citizens (the *popular sovereignty principle*).
- The legislative process ought to weight no individual's or group's preferences more heavily than those of any other individual or group (the *equal weight principle*).
- Finally, a democratic society is one that is fully subject to the rule of law: Legislation rather than personal authority produces limitations on individual liberty, and legislation is neutral across persons (the *legality principle*).

What is a citizen? A citizen is, to begin with, a person, and so the thick conception of a person described in Chapter 1 is a good starting point here as well. A person is a moral individual, possessing a plan of life, a conception of the good for him- or herself, a set of needs, a set of rights and liberties, and finally, a set of preferences that derive from the needs and the conception of the good. The individual's preferences represent the embodiment of his or her wishes with respect to a given set of outcomes or choices. A citizen is also a person who is an active member of a political community, with the capacity for participation and autonomy that this involves.

These principles leave many questions unsettled. What is the role of parties? How are powers of government divided (legislative, executive, judicial)? How do elections take place? What institutions govern the process of legislation? These principles do not serve as a full theory of democratic government. Rather, they are intended to establish the groundwork that any set of political institutions must satisfy if it is to be judged democratic.

Democratic Institutions

These principles represent the chief desiderata of a democratic polity. But they do not dictate a specific implementation. Rather, it is necessary for a given polity to design a set of political institutions through which the principles of liberty, equality, and sovereignty are realized. There is a logical gap between the principles and the institutional implementation, in the sense that people can always debate whether the particulars of proposed institutions adequately realize the relevant underlying values. It is likely, moreover, that different institutional arrangements represent different ways of accommodating the underlying values and offer different types of trade-offs among them.

Two institutions deserve special attention in the consideration of democracy. First is the idea of a *constitution:* a stipulation of first principles that set limits to the state's authority to establish laws. A constitution may be thought to express a set of moral first principles that pertain to the ultimate good of the individual and the state—for example, the priority of a core set of individual rights that cannot be abrogated by the will of the majority.[2] Second is the idea of a *majoritarian process:* a process through which choices are presented to the citizenry, citizens' preferences are recorded, and the choice receiving the majority (or plurality) of preferences is selected as the collective choice. This idea captures the notion of popular sovereignty, the requirement that collective choice should reflect the will of the people.[3]

A democratic state is a complex system involving multiple features (electoral institutions, parties, constitutional protections) and embodying multiple goods (individual liberty, effective legislation, secure property rights, popular sovereignty). Institutions can be designed de novo, or they can be adjusted through a series of corrections and reforms. And as we consider the process of adjustment of an institution, it is necessary to consider carefully the "objective function" by which we intend to guide the adjustment and reform process. Are we willing to make trade-offs among the goods embodied by the institution—for example, give up some popular sovereignty in order to achieve more equality of assets? Or do we mean to accept only Pareto-improving innovations—that is, those that improve at least one good without reducing any other good?

In addition to the institutions of constitution, elections, legislation, and executive action, a political system has a surrounding cluster of supporting institutions: mass media, political parties, political fund-raising, and legislation regarding the electoral process. Once again, for any particular configuration of institutions of these sorts, we can ask the question: How well do these institutions establish and implement the central values of democracy?

Finally, we need to find a place within our theory for the "instruments of coercion" in a society—the military and police and the organs of private violence. A modern state—whether developed or developing—marshals the capacity for a significant level of coercion. It is possible for political authorities to make use of this capacity for their own political purposes; likewise, it is possible for military and police authorities to use coercion and the threat of coercion to political purpose.

This brief discussion serves to establish the abstract topography of a democratic polity: constitutional definition of the status of citizens, constitutional establishment of basic rights and liberties, establishment of an electoral process through which representatives are chosen, establishment of a majoritarian legislative process through which legislation is brought into being, establishment of an executive power that has the authority and charge to implement and enforce legislation, and establishment of a judicial authority responsible for interpreting the law and judging lawbreakers.

Consider this institutional sketch of a democratic system. The polity adopts a constitution that defines maximal political rights and liberties for all citizens and defines the status of citizenship. The constitution prohibits the establishment of laws that limit the constitutional rights and liberties of citizens or create inequalities in basic rights among different groups of citizens. The constitution further creates a legislative process through which elected representatives engage in a majoritarian process of debate and legislation. Representatives are elected and can be removed by the electorate, and the legislative process is itself governed by majoritarian voting rules. Legislation cannot contravene the constitution, and a separate supermajoritarian process for revision of the constitution is established.

This sketch embodies each of the values indicated above: universal citizenship, maximum liberties, and popular sovereignty. The sketch corresponds fairly closely to the political theory of liberal democracies. Note that this sketch privileges liberty and equality (by placing the constitution above the legislative process). As a result, it restricts popular sovereignty. Even if a majority preferred legislation that restricted liberties (for all or for a group), such legislation would be unconstitutional.

We can imagine other institutional sketches as well. We might imagine building a polity on the popular sovereignty principle first: All legislation emerges on the basis of the majority vote of all citizens, and all legislation is in principle possible. Such an approach would privilege popular sovereignty, but it would potentially interfere with the liberty principle or the equality principle (since it is possible that a majority would prefer to reduce liberties or undermine equality).

For any species of democratic government, we can always ask the fundamental question, How well do these institutions work to establish and implement the values of universal citizenship, maximum liberty, full equality, and popular sovereignty?

Social Democracy and Producers' Democracy

Thus far, I have concentrated on political democracy—the institutions through which citizens express their interests and preferences via legislation and the conduct of government. Several other important dimensions of democracy should be highlighted as well. First, there is the long tradition of social democratic thinking that has emphasized the responsibility of the state for establishing the social prerequisites of freedom and human development. The social democratic state takes on the social obligation of providing education, access to health care, and a substantial social security safety net for those members of society whose status in the market economy is compromised—children, the elderly, the unemployed, the educationally disadvantaged, or the physically disabled. (See Esping-Andersen 1985, 1990, and Przeworski 1985 for eloquent expositions of the history and normative theories that underlay these developments in Western Europe.) On this approach, the freedoms represented by democracy include both the political freedoms associated with citizenship and the social freedoms associated with the exercise of one's human capabilities (and the social resources needed to actualize those capabilities). The impulse toward social democracy in the late nineteenth century and the twentieth century (largely in Western Europe) derived from the growing recognition of the limitations of the market as a general solution to the problem of securing universal human well-being. Markets work well for a portion of the population (perhaps the majority) by providing employment and incomes that are sufficient to support a decent and healthy standard of living. But there are segments of the population who are not well served by the market. And social democracy accepts the obligation that society as a whole needs to establish institutions that assure all citizens a decent minimum standard of living.

It is apparent that the viability of social democracy within the context of political democracy requires a high level of social consensus about the underlying values of equality and universal human well-being. The social welfare institutions that social democracy requires—universal health care, universal public education, unemployment and disability insurance, retirement plans, and programs for disadvantaged children, to name several—are costly and can only be funded through taxation. Given that citizens control the level of taxation within a political democracy, the stability of a social democracy requires active education and mobilization concerning the importance of these underlying values. Otherwise, citizens will withdraw tax support for these programs, the welfare of the least well-off in society will decline, and the bonds of civility and commonality within society will diminish. So a widespread consensus about the importance of social justice and a widespread social solidarity among citizens appear to be necessary prerequisites for stable social democracy.

A second important strand of democratic thought concerns what we might call "workplace democracy." Are self-control and self-determination important human values? Do we value the equality of persons in all important settings?[4] And if so, what implications do these values have for the organization of work? I note, to begin, that the stereotypical factory is a profoundly antidemocratic place. Owners command, managers direct, supervisors implement, and workers perform accordingly. Workers have one essential freedom in the workplace—the freedom to quit the job. But they do not have the right to participate in decisions about the organization, content, or pace of the production process. Is it possible to design institutions of work that involve greater self-determination for workers? And is it possible that more democratic work arrangements might in fact be more productive and flexible? Carol Gould (1988) addresses this set of issues in *Rethinking Democracy*. Twentieth-century capitalism has witnessed several institutional experiments in the direction of greater workplace democracy.[5] This topic raises a series of complex questions about possible alternatives. Are these alternatives efficient? Are they more equitable than existing institutions? Are they compatible with an efficient or just property system? And through what sort of political process might a liberal democracy arrive at such institutions?

Both topics legitimately fall within the scope of deliberation within a political democracy. The question of the nature and scope of the social safety net is an issue for citizens to debate. It involves important social values about which citizens may disagree, and it presents an opportunity for parties and organizations to bring forward their positions for public consideration. So the question of the extent of the social welfare state is a topic for public policy and electoral process to resolve. And the burden falls on the advocates of a broad social welfare state to make the case for the social benefits that follow from these institutions—benefits that may lead to greater productivity, stronger communities, and a greater extent of social cohesion and harmony.

The institutions that define the circumstances of work are legitimately the object of negotiation between owners and workers. We have seen that it is crucial for the state to set a minimum standard of health and safety in the workplace. Markets do not assure safe and healthy work environments. Beyond these minimum standards, the issue of the degree to which workers have input into production decisions can be negotiated. And as long as the conditions of fair bargaining are respected, we can foresee that a variety of institutional outcomes will emerge in different industries and regions. Evidence supports the notion that greater involvement of workers in decisionmaking is positive for enterprise productivity; workers have higher morale and higher commitment to the goals of the enterprise, and managers are able to gather together the expert knowledge of line workers in redesigning the process. So greater worker involvement in the management of the production process may be an important part of the achievement of economic growth. (The current interest in "lean manufacturing" within the automobile industry reflects this intuition; see Womack et al. 1990.)

Authoritarian Government

Authoritarian government—the alternative to democratic government—is just as complex in that there are many different ways of institutionally implementing a system in which the few govern the many. I will lay out a simple model of authoritarian government that is common in the developing world. I will focus on what is sometimes called "bureaucratic authoritarianism." Important variants include military dictatorship, party dictatorship, or "strongman" dictatorship. (See O'Donnell 1979 for an account of bureaucratic authoritarianism in Latin America.) In the bureaucratic authoritarian state, a strong leader rules the state, making use of a complex bureaucratic organization to create legislation and policy and an extensive coercive apparatus (army, police) to enforce government policy. The state and its forms of power function as an instrument for carrying out the ruler's objectives.

This account emphasizes the use of state power to realize the objectives of the ruler. But since both bureaucracies and police organizations are complex social organizations, autocrats have less than absolute power. They confront classic "principal-agent" problems in inducing the various organizations to do their bidding. So there is some looseness in the lineages of power from the center to the administrative peripheries of the polity. In addition, most societies contain nonpolitical centers of power with which the autocrat must contend—landowners, businesspeople, financiers, unions. Finally, even the most autocratic regime must give some weight to the preferences of the masses of the population. Coercion has its limits, and the autocrat must remain aware of the potential of popular unrest in response to unpopular policies (increases in staple prices, increases in taxes, reduction in customary rights).

What are some of the common characteristics of authoritarian regimes?

- Frequent use of force and threats of force against the population
- Predatory treatment of the national economy—taxation, access to positions of wealth, rent seeking
- Corruption
- Bureaucratic interference with the market (especially financial markets)
- Tendency toward capital-intensive growth
- Low ability to moderate and negotiate ethnic or nationalist conflicts

Transitions to Democracy

It is common in recent history to find developing societies in a state of transition from authoritarian to democratic regimes. Military dictatorships, bureaucratic oligarchies, and other authoritarian regimes have found themselves subject to irresistible forces that compel them in the direction of a degree of progressive democratic reform: extension of political rights to citizens, establishment of limited electoral processes, extension of the ability of independent parties to organize themselves, extension of some degree of freedom of press, and so forth. Here, a series of questions demand answers. First, to what extent is it possible for skillful elites and rulers to orchestrate the process of democratic liberalization in such a way as to preserve their power and privilege within the resulting regime? Second, what are the features of institutions that best serve to bring about effective democratization? Third, is there a relatively clear distinction between effective democracies and sham democracies? Finally, what, if anything, can we say about the progressive features of hybrid political systems—polities that are intermediate between authoritarianism and democracy? Are the steps along the road to democracy unambiguously positive with regard to individual freedom and other democratic virtues?

Why Democracy?

Is democracy a morally important institution? Should we include democratization within the set of fundamental values and goals of development? Democracy is a crucial aspect of human freedom. Fundamentally, it is a good thing because it facilitates free human choice and furthers the good of political participation. Democracy is a necessary component of the individual's ability to live freely and autonomously. And democracy is a political form that pays appropriate heed to the inherent worth and dignity of the person. Thus, democracy is a central constituent of the individual's ability to live freely and autonomously as a human being. This is no less so in poor and developing countries than it is in the North and the West.

To respect the dignity of the individual is to acknowledge her autonomy in choosing a life plan and deciding on a series of actions designed to bring this plan to fruition. And within the polity, the dignity of the individual is recognized through the equal rights that all have to participate in the process of public deliberation and decisionmaking and the right to a process that recognizes the equal weight of each individual's preferences. A person is politically free when she is empowered to participate fully in public deliberations that affect the public well-being and when the institutions of decisionmaking give equal treatment to the preferences and points of view of all citizens. Conversely, the person who is free to choose in private matters but is prevented from participating in public affairs is doubly unfree: She has been prevented from participating in decisions that will affect the achievement of her life plan, and she has been blocked from the expression of the freedom of citizenship (participation in the polity).

There is thus an intimate connection between democracy and freedom. People are free when they are able to pursue plans and objectives without (unjustified) interference from others. Freedom of choice and action is the way in which individuals define and express themselves as moral beings, and it is a good thing for people to experience freedom. And democratic institutions embody freedom in several senses: They commonly result in legal and constitutional systems that create a system of liberty; they embody the citizen's ability to participate in collective decisionmaking; and they establish a bulwark against unjustified coercion by the state by conferring significant power on the people and their associations and organizations.

There is a deeper way in which democracy facilitates freedom, beyond the formation of collective decisions. Individuals define themselves through their choices, and they articulate and develop their underlying values through political engagement with others. So there is a value in democracy that something that of recognizing the individual liberties and freedoms of each citizen; more profoundly, individuals constitute themselves through the discourse and engagement that they achieve within the polity. Debate has partly to do with the question of what is to be done in a particular situation. But it has also to do with the questions of identity—Who am I, and what am I becoming? This avenue of thought found expression in the writings of Rousseau in the eighteenth century and Habermas in the twentieth century (see Rousseau 1983 and Habermas 1975). For Rousseau, we might say that democracy permits a group to arrive at a shared understanding of the common good (the general will) in a way that goes beyond simply summing up the individual goods. And for Habermas, democracy has to do with the establishment of a "communicative group" in which individuals share and refine their values and points of view through civil discourse and disagreement. The process of debate by itself improves the quality of our reasoning and our values and deepens the bonds of civility that unite us into a polity.

Democracy also serves as a morally justified avenue through which disagreements among citizens can be resolved. It establishes a framework of collective decisionmaking that all can recognize as legitimate, so that those on the losing side of an issue can have the confidence that their interests and preferences were given full weight. And it secures the basis for a process of debate and deliberation that may permit divergent parties to come to a more accepting perspective on the other's point of view—or even to see that there are valid elements in the other's position that they themselves might adopt. Democracy facilitates civil and nonviolent negotiation, discussion, and resolution. This is the heart of John Rawls's conception of political liberalism: "Political liberalism looks for a political conception of justice that we hope can gain the support of an overlapping consensus of reasonable religious, philosophical, and moral doctrines in a society regulated by it" (Rawls 1993b: 10).

These points have emphasized the relation between freedom, public and private, and the institutions of democracy. Another important value is served by democracy as well—the value of creating institutions that give citizens and groups the ability to effectively defend their most fundamental interests. The power of the twentieth-century state and of its successors in the twenty-first century is potentially overwhelming. And the power of the state has been used frequently to further the priorities of the state (or the ruler) without regard for the interests, values, and preferences of individual citizens. When political institutions exist that give significant power to citizens, organizations, and associations, we can have the greatest confidence that the state will not brutalize its population; we can be confident that the policies of the state will be aligned with the interests and preferences of the population. In other words, a distinctive value of democracy is the fact that it creates the likelihood of a "virtuous feedback" between the state and the people. When the state's policies are deeply offensive to the people, the mechanisms of democratic politics will exert pressure on the state to change its policies; when those policies are well aligned with the interests of the majority of citizens, the state will be rewarded through electoral success. (This is not to suggest that democracy guarantees good policies by the state but only that it gives the citizenry real power in attempting to change bad policies.)

Institutional Issues

To this point, I have focused on the normative theory of democracy. However, it is crucial to recognize that democracies are complexes of *institutions*—they have real empirical and causal properties, and they function within the context of constraints that give them real empirical properties that may be at odds with the ideal theory. So let me turn now to some of the empirical questions that surround the issue of democracy within the context of developing societies. How do the typical institutions of electoral democracy affect the process, character, and rate of economic development? And is it possible that democratic institutions have built-in biases—for example, temporal (present over future) or class (rich over poor)? Do the institutions of electoral democracy have the potential of inducing more egalitarian economic development? Do such institutions serve to emphasize the interests of the poor? Can broader political participation improve the situation of the poor?

The Theoretical Case

Analysis of political institutions and their workings leads us to expect causal connections flowing in both directions. The institutional arrangements of electoral democracies, with the dynamics created for majoritarian governments by the political calculus of voting blocs, can be predicted to give rise to the likelihood that some development choices will be more difficult than others. That is, the institutions of democracy are likely to impose a characteristic dynamic on the process of economic development. But likewise, features of the economic development experience, both short-run and long-run, may have significant effects on the stability and character of political institutions. For example, the structural adjustment crises of Latin America in the 1980s posed serious challenges to the stability of democratic institutions in a variety of countries. John Peeler (1998) describes the experience of Mexico, Venezuela, Peru, and Bolivia from the point of view of this direction of the causal arrow. Peeler takes the view that there is a generally positive causal relationship between the presence of democratic institutions to effective economic development.

Do the institutions of electoral democracy facilitate or impede development? Samuel Huntington (1987) characterizes the debate over this issue in terms of "conflict" and "compatibility" theorists. Conflict theorists argue that democracy interferes with effective development policies, whereas compatibility theorists hold that democracy is favorable to efficient and equitable economic development. Some of the arguments for the position that democracy is not conducive to economic development incorporate the following ideas: Development requires decisive policy choice and effective policy implementation, and authoritarian regimes are more decisive and more effective in implementing policy. Authoritarian governments are also more able to effectively defer consumption in favor of savings. Democratic regimes are under a political imperative to increase social welfare spending, which reduces the rate of accumulation. In contrast, compatibility theorists maintain ideas along these lines: Progressive development requires policy choices that produce a wide distribution of the benefits of growth, and democratic regimes are more effective at producing wide distribution of benefits (because of the strong tendency of authoritarian regimes to structure economic activity toward rent-seeking activities, enrichment of the ruling circle, and widespread corruption). Democratic regimes are less prone to corruption and rent-seeking; they are less "predatory." And democratic regimes give real political influence to the poor and the dispossessed—thereby lending support to policies that favor the long-term interests of these groups in the developing society.

There has been an extended debate about democracy and development and the relations between democratization and economic growth. Some have maintained that democratic regimes are in general less capable of managing effecting economic development than authoritarian regimes. The central premise of this reasoning stems from the observations that development requires change and that change affects some voters adversely. So governments dependent on electoral support in the next election will typically tend to avoid choices that impose hardship on significant numbers of voters. (Adam Przeworski's arguments in *Democracy and the Market* [1991] represent a thoughtful argument to this effect.) Others have argued that democratic regimes are positively associated with economic development and especially with more egalitarian modes of development. Finally, there is a body of thought that holds that democracy is neither positive nor negative with respect to economic development.

What institutional features of democratic government have the potential to affect the character and pace of economic development? What institutional factors might influence the distributive designs of the policies that are chosen? Several structural features of democracies are particularly important when it comes to economic development—the role and influence of elites in democratic processes, the logic of electoral competition and vote gaining, the role of parties, and the potential influence of grassroots organizations on policy choices and priorities.

It is a familiar fact in the democracies of the developing world that economic elites often manage to retain disproportionate influence within a democratic electoral system. The reasons for this privileging of elite interests are not hard to identify. Elites have privileged access to the instruments of political influence—education, literacy, campaign finance. Elites are able to oppose political strategies through the threat of capital strike (removal of capital and money from the national economy). And elites are compact groups, so that their collective action problems are more easily handled than those of more numerous groups.[6] These considerations suggest that elites are well positioned to defend their economic interests within an electoral competition—with the result that they will be able to preserve the benefits of preexisting antipoor biases in economic policies. This fact suggests that government policies and priorities within democracies will tend to be biased toward elite interests. Policies that are specifically aimed at interests of nonelite groups—land reform, propoor tax reform benefiting the poor, the establishment of social welfare programs that must be financed through business and income taxes—are difficult to achieve, even when they are favorable to a majority of the electorate, because of the concentrated political influence of the elites whose interests would be harmed by these policy choices (Herring 1999, 1983).

Moreover, to the extent that nonelite groups emerge as politically significant, it is possible, perhaps likely, that the groups that stand to gain the most political influence through democratization are not the poor but the near-poor: urban workers and consumers, better-off farmers, and the like. And the interests of these groups are not identical with those of the poor. Consider one example of a pattern that is almost ubiquitous in the developing world: the political influence of urban workers, urban consumers, and civil servants. These groups have an interest in securing food price policies that guarantee lower food costs; they have an interest in development strategies that enhance urban amenities (transportation, sanitation); and they have an interest in wage policies that favor them. Further, these groups are well positioned to back up their demands with effective political action: mobilization around political parties, personal and political relationships with government officials, and the threat of urban unrest. So it is common to find that developing country policies reflect an urban bias, as expressed, for instance, in food price policies, the provision of infrastructure, and wage policies that favor urban workers and civil servants. These politically created benefits improve the material welfare of these groups—but at the expense of the rural poor. The result of these policies is to depress the market-determined incomes of farmers, to reduce the level and quality of amenities flowing to the rural sector, and to further exacerbate the wage differentials between rural and urban sectors. A consequence of this line of analysis, then, is to raise the possibility that more democracy may in fact *reduce* the amount of attention that the poor (and particularly the rural poor) receive within the politics of development policy.[7]

A third form of bias within democratic institutions arises from the relative autonomy of leaders, officials, and agents of government. In theory, democracy gives citizens the ability to remove officials whose choices do not satisfy them. But in practice, officials and leaders have many levers of power and influence that permit them to take actions that serve their private or party interests in preference to the public good. Democratic institutions are vulnerable to the corrupt use of power and influence by officials and leaders. These forms of corruption can range from theft of public resources for private gain to granting of purchasing contracts to family, friends, and allies to the obscure biasing of policies in the direction of private or party interest.[8] Most abstractly, the problem of corruption represents a "principal-agent" problem—the problem of ensuring that the agent is carrying out the will of the principal in executing a policy or procedure. In the case of governmental corruption, the principal is the public and the agent is the government, and it is notoriously difficult for the public to assure that government and its agents are acting in behalf of the public interest. This is not to say that democracies are more prone to corrupt practices than authoritarian regimes; in fact, the historical experience appears to be the contrary. The most egregious examples of corrupt theft of national resources in recent years have occurred in authoritarian and military regimes. But corruption and misalignment between government action and the public good remain recurring possibilities in democracies, and this is so, in large part, because of the relative autonomy of officials and leaders.

These considerations identify a set of antidemocratic tendencies that emerge within democratic regimes—processes that lead to bias in favor of private interests over the public interest. Let us turn now to a different set of factors within democracy that also have the potential for turning government policies away from the goals of progressive economic development. These factors derive from the logic of electoral competition: the strategies that parties take to achieve electoral majorities for candidates and party platforms. Particularly important are issues having to do with "hard choices"—choices that involve sacrifices in the medium term to bring about good results in the more distant future—and the "politics of identity"—electoral strategies that depend on building electoral support on the basis of ethnic or religious identities.

A persistent question about the role of democracy within development has to do with the issue of hard measures—steps that impose short-term hardship for the sake of longer-term gain. The reform of the economies of Eastern Europe represents an important case in point (see Kornai 1990 and Przeworski 1991). Economic reform required a significant restructuring of important economic institutions—the introduction of markets and the hardening of the budget constraint in state enterprises, for example. These processes imposed economic costs on a large percentage of the population for an extended period of time. Electoral democracies are reasonably effective in mobilizing groups in defense of their economic interests, and the results bear the mark of this process. So within an electoral democracy, it is difficult to implement policies that impose economic hardship on politically effective groups. But development (and economic reform more generally) unavoidably involves hardship for various social groups. So the question arises: Does the fact of democracy and the effective political demands that an electoral democracy creates have the effect of paralyzing development?

The answer to this question depends a great deal on institutional variables that lie below the current level of discussion: the political competence of existing parties, the ideology and commitments of the governing party, the quality and effectiveness of leadership, the level of confidence the electorate has in a regime's intentions and competence, the character and goals of existing subparty organizations, and the details of parliamentary institutions.[9] The strongest conclusion that can be drawn on the basis of the recent experience of Poland, for instance, is that it is possible to implement an aggressive program of reform through democratic means but that the political pressures build substantially as the reform program begins to impose hardships on the populace. Moreover, there are instances elsewhere in Eastern Europe (in Hungary, for example) in which governing parties have not succeeded in putting together strong electoral support for a unified program of reform; in these cases, gridlock appears to be a very possible outcome.[10]

The theoretical conclusion that we can draw is a clear one: There is a tendency within electoral democracy toward myopic policy choice, in that the electorate can be readily mobilized to reject policies that have short-term costs and long-term benefits. This systemic myopia can be avoided through good leadership and effective party organization; it is possible to persuade citizens to accept sacrifice for the sake of future gains. But it is also possible for competing parties to make effective use of this conflict of interest across time to build a successful antireform coalition. Effective economic reform requires political leadership that is successful in building confidence in the electorate about the direction of change and the likelihood of success. And it requires the presence of effective political organizations that are capable of communicating with constituents effectively and mobilizing public support for the program of reform. What is best, all things considered, may be unattainable through a step-by-step process of voting for candidates and programs over time.

This feature of democratic policy formation has a strong resemblance to another common deficiency of democratic regimes—the "not in my back yard" (NIMBY) phenomenon. In this case, the conflict of interest is locational rather than temporal. Many choices that a government must inevitably face involve imposing a limited harm, risk, or disadvantage on some in order to secure the public good. Where should the government locate an incinerator, a prison, or a nuclear waste storage facility? Electoral politics give a significant advantage to local and regional groups in their efforts to block decisions that might adversely affect their interests—and yet collectively, all citizens have an interest in such decisions being made on a rational basis.

Both these examples suggest that democracies may face significant obstacles in implementing economic or environmental strategies that serve the public interest, all things considered over time and space. Instead, sectional, regional, or temporal interests may create electoral coalitions that make it impossible to implement policies that are in the common interest of citizens as a whole.

The logic of electoral competition creates a third undesirable possibility for developing countries—the feasibility of a political strategy based on mobilization of ethnic or religious identities. India's political experience since independence offers clear examples of this possibility, through the political success of Hindu nationalism since the 1980s.[11] The concept of "political entrepreneurship" is helpful in this context. Within a democracy, the goal of a leader and a party is to gather a committed and numerous following. The degree of commitment will influence the ability of the organization to do its work (establish field offices, lobby the public, canvass voters); further, the size of the following will influence the electoral success of the leader and party. So the challenge for the leader is to select a set of issues around which he can build a following. The concept of the political entrepreneur postulates that the leader will make calculating and self-interested choices about the choice of issues. This theory implies that the leader is not motivated to identify issues and policies that are best designed to further the public good; instead, his goal is the self-interested purpose of mobilizing an electoral majority. In many countries, the strategy of ethnic or religious mobilization has been calculated to be an effective one. But political activism organized around ethnic and religious identities has all too often led to ethnic and religious conflict and violence (Tambiah 1991; Horowitz 1985; Brass 1985). And even if these strategies do not lead to interethnic violence, they are likely to reduce the level of citizen trust that is needed to achieve consensus around strategies and priorities that serve the common good. So political entrepreneurship appears to create a potential obstacle to the formation of progressive and unifying development policies.

Political parties and organizations represent another significant institutional effect that is created by electoral competition. Parties emerge as potent forces, for good or ill, within developing democracies. The politician has an interest in creating an organization that will help mobilize constituents and voters; so he has an interest in enhancing the power of the political party. But once mobilized, a party is a potent force that can be used for either progressive or regressive purposes. Consider the Institutional Revolutionary Party (PRI), the party that dominated Mexican politics for six decades. Through a combination of violence, intimidation, and local corruption, the PRI succeeded in maintaining electoral majorities for its candidates over many years. Though the PRI represented itself as the party of the dispossessed, its behavior (and the behavior of its elected officials) showed little evidence of progressive commitments for public policy. By contrast, the example of Communist Party, Marxist (CPM) in West Bengal (which will be discussed) provides an instance of a party that is motivated by a progressive reform agenda and that demonstrates in its behavior a long-standing commitment to improving the well-being of the dispossessed.

So far, we have considered a set of institutional factors that hamper the ability of democracies to pursue progressive policies for economic development. Are there factors that enhance the capacity of a democracy to act in support of the long-term interests of its citizens? Indeed, there are many, but three deserve special attention.

First, the simple fact of electoral representation gives voice to the interests of the poor and dispossessed. The electoral process makes it possible for the dispossessed to achieve some degree of representation and political power, and it creates some level of political incentive for leaders to pay attention to the interests of the poor and dispossessed.

Second, certain organizational forms can significantly enhance the political effectiveness of the poor and dispossessed within democracies. In particular, grassroots organizations and associations can have substantial influence within electoral democracies, and their influence can offset the power of elites, the indifference of officials, or the biases of institutions. Examples of effective grassroots organizations are found throughout the world—in democracies and in authoritarian regimes as well. Peasants' organizations in Mexico, labor unions in Indonesia, women's organizations in India, and environmental action groups in Brazil have all found means for expressing an effective voice in the formation of policies and legislation in their countries. Grassroots organizations give the poor and dispossessed an important set of tools for pursuing their political interests. They can collect and disseminate information—for example, information about local pollution, resource depletion, or conditions of labor. They can form alliances with other organizations and movements—which amplifies the influence of each of the partners. They can create forums through which citizens can learn about issues, formulate ideas and positions, and create policy agendas that will be advocated within the broader political process. And they can mobilize votes—which gains political influence with elected officials. So grassroots organizations and associations are a potentially potent force in support of progressive development choices (Cohen and Rogers 1995; Fox 1991).

Third, electoral democracies give significant influence to news media and the press. When there is a free press within a developing society, reporters have the freedom to investigate the workings of government and the conditions of life for the population. This ability to investigate and publish leads to a significantly greater transparency in political life, and it creates new and powerful incentives for officials to pay attention to the public good. Political corruption is a common target of news organizations. By revealing corrupt practices in various parts of government, the press gives the public the information it needs to take effective political action to eliminate these practices. But equally, it gives government a powerful incentive to create its own institutional safeguards against corruption. By revealing the conditions of labor that exist in sweatshops in China, an emerging group of investigative journalists has created a nascent ability in China to compel government to respond to abuses (Chan 2001). And by noting and publicizing the early signs of famine in India, the Indian press compelled government to take effective steps to avoid full-scale famine (Drèze and Sen 1989; A. Sen 1981). A free press within the context of electoral institutions provides a valuable tool for assuring good and responsive government, and this is a positive influence on development policies as well.

This analysis suggests that democratic institutions embody tendencies in both directions: toward the entrenchment of established interests, on the one hand, and toward the creation of progressive economic policies that improve the life prospects of the poor and dispossessed, on the other hand. Structural features challenge the ability of democracies to adopt policies that serve the common good over an extended time; other features lead to some optimism about the ability of democracies to create such policies. In other words, the theoretical case is mixed. Are there empirical grounds for assessing the relative effectiveness of democratic institutions in furthering the goals of progressive economic development? It is to this question that we now turn.

The Empirical Experience of Democracy and Development

Issues of democracy and development have an empirical manifestation; since World War II, over 100 nations have undergone a variety of processes of political and economic development, so it should be possible to examine this 50-year and 100-nation experience for statistical and causal associations among the variables of interest. Is there a demonstrable correlation between the attributes of democracy and the attributes of effective economic development? A large number of empirical studies have been undertaken since 1970s to investigate this question.[12] However, the empirical case is suggestive but inconclusive. The data support some optimism in terms of the compatibility theory: that democratic institutions have a net positive effect on economic development. However, the association is empirically weak, and there are a number of counterexamples in both directions: authoritarian regimes that have a good development record and democratic regimes that have weak development records. (Sirowy and Inkeles 1990 provides a careful review of this issue and the empirical data that pertain to assessment of the various hypotheses. A generally favorable review of the effects of democracy in development is presented in Kohli 1986.)

The issue of the dynamic causal relations between democratic political institutions and the pace and character of economic development can be probed in several ways. First, we can approach the problem theoretically or deductively: Given what we know about the character and institutional dynamics of democratic institutions and given what we know about the character and needs of economic development, what causal connections does underlying theory lead us to expect? Second, we can approach the problem through multicase studies in which we operationalize the concepts of democracy and of the rate and character of development, then check to see whether there are meaningful statistical associations among the resulting variables. Both approaches have been pursued in the literature of the political economy of development, with deeply mixed results.

In their major review of available cross-country studies of democracy and development, Larry Sirowy and Alex Inkeles (1990) conclude that (1) there is little support for a strong positive causal relation between democracy and development, and (2) there is little empirical basis for choosing between the conflict hypothesis and the null hypothesis. Overall, these authors conclude that there are few robust conclusions that can be supported on the basis of existing empirical multicase studies of these factors. Sirowy and Inkeles believe that methodological flaws in the studies are an important part of the problem—leading to the possibility that more refined studies may shed greater light. Adam Przeworski and Fernando Limongi arrive at a similar conclusion. They examine eighteen cross-country studies and determine that these studies do not provide a clear basis for a conclusion about the causal properties of democratic institutions with regard to development (Przeworski and Limongi 1993: 60). Both of these review essays point to the methodological difficulties that stand in the way of an effective statistical test of these causal hypotheses. Jakob de Haan and Clemens Siermann (1996: 193) offer a similar assessment: "Our main conclusion is that the relationship between democracy and economic growth is not robust."

These studies suggest that the empirical record does not support the thesis that democracies experience more rapid economic growth than nondemocratic regimes. However, the reverse is true as well: The empirical record does not suggest that democracies have a worse track record for economic growth than nondemocratic regimes. This suggests that it is reasonable to work on the assumption that democratic institutions are compatible with effective and progressive economic development. And two factors loom large from discussion earlier in this chapter: first, that democracies are preferable because they support human freedom, and second, that democracies are preferable because they create the possibility that the dispossessed will be able to exert political influence on development choices, leading to more equitable development policies.

Important examples in the developing world offer positive instances of democracy and economic reform. Atul Kohli's *The State and Poverty in India* (1987) provides a basis for understanding the political conditions in which democratization is likely to result in poverty alleviation. On the basis of a comparative study of three Indian states (West Bengal, Karnataka, and Uttar Pradesh), Kohli argues that poverty alleviation requires positive policy efforts on the part of the state; the normal workings of a market system do not inevitably or commonly lead to improvement of the condition of the poor. However, some states in India have done better than others in poverty alleviation. What are the social and political factors that influence the welfare of the poor in the process of Third World economic development? Kohli finds that the critical variable is the type of regime in power during the process of economic development: Regimes formed by strong, competent political parties of the Left succeed in tilting the process of development toward poverty alleviation, whereas weak regimes and regimes dominated by the propertied classes have a poor record of performance in poverty reform. Poverty reform requires a political regime that has both the will and the means to implement it, and a regime that is relatively autonomous from the political reach of economic elites. The CPM in West Bengal succeeded in bringing tangible benefits to the poor through poverty reforms including tenancy reform, rural credit programs, and rural employment schemes. CPM is a leftist party with a coherent redistributivist ideology, competent party organization extending down to the village level, and effective leadership. The Urs regime in Karnataka also possessed a redistributivist ideology, but it lacked effective political organization and had a fragmented leadership; its efforts at poverty reform were not successful. And the Janata Party in Uttar Pradesh was dominated by the rural landowning class and lacked the will to implement poverty reforms. Kohli explains the presence or absence of poverty alleviation in a state, then, as the result of the presence or absence of a regime that has both the will and the means to implement poverty reform.

This line of thought suggests that effective state policies aimed at poverty alleviation are most likely to come into place within a context of effective electoral democracy, in the presence of an administratively competent party of the poor.

Democracy and the Poor

How does the presence of democratic institutions affect the viability of progressive economic development strategies? Recall that "progressive" economic development is defined as development designed to result in wide distribution of the benefits of growth, significant and sustained improvement in the quality of life of the population, and significant and sustained improvement in the incomes and assets of the poor and near-poor. Does democracy really increase the likelihood that a country will pursue policies with these characteristics?

The promise of democracy from the point of view of progressive economic development follows from a very simple argument. The poor are numerous. As parties compete for electoral support, they have an interest in adopting policies that favor the interests of the poor. It is, in principle, possible for a political party representing the interests of the disadvantaged to acquire substantial political influence in a Third World democracy, through its electoral significance. And in countries in which there is such a political party, we should expect that government policy will be accordingly tilted back in the direction of the poor. Therefore, we should expect a tendency for state policies to accommodate the economic interests of the poor and to begin to redress the antipoor tilt that is characteristic of authoritarian politics.

As I noted earlier, grassroots organizations are a critically important element in democratic politics in the developing world. These organizations give the numerous poor some of the political capacities that they need in order to significantly influence the priorities and policies of the state.

These considerations suggest that progressive development strategies and Third World democratization movements need to flow hand in hand: Regimes whose political base depends on support from the poor and the near-poor will be the most motivated to pursue a poverty-first program and the most capable of implementing such a program, whereas the existence of such a program within a developing democracy provides a plausible basis for mobilizing further mass support for the progressive development party.

There is a realistic core to this argument, but it is overly optimistic. More extensive democracy *can* be a central means of furthering poverty-first economic development. But it is also clear, both empirically and theoretically, that broad-based electoral democracy does not inevitably result in conferring political influence on the poor. There are constraints on the political capacity of such a party. There are numerous channels through which elite interests can subvert the political goals of a party of the poor. And there are structural constraints on the policies that such a party can advocate, let alone implement, without creating an economic crisis that worsens the condition of the poor.

These arguments are not intended to undermine the significance of democratic institutions in furthering a poverty-first economic strategy. Indeed, it is unlikely that such a strategy will emerge *except* through an effective, politically competent demand for such a strategy by the rural poor, supported by an effective and administratively competent party strongly committed to its interests. But democratization is not the only ingredient of a successful poverty-first policy, and the arguments in preceding paragraphs are designed merely to show that it is quite possible for democratic electoral mechanisms to lead to outcomes that neglect the poor or are positively biased against them.

This line of thought indicates, then, that effective political action in support of progressive economic development policies is most likely to come into place within a context of effective electoral democracy, in the presence of an administratively competent party of the poor.[13]

Notes

1. See Nozick 1974 for a libertarian statement of this position.

2. Perhaps the "no constitution" side is complicated by the fact that it is possible for custom or common law to act as an implicit constitution that constrains the right of legislators to enact certain kinds of legislation. For a deep exploration of issues of constitutionality, see Ronald Dworkin's reasoning on this subject (Dworkin 1977).

3. It should be noted that the principle of majoritarian decisionmaking encounters significant formal challenges. Kenneth Arrow proved that there is no logically consistent and

fully general voting system that maps individual preference orderings onto a single consistent social preference ordering. See Mackay 1980 for a lucid exploration of the Arrow result, and see A. Sen 1970 for a formal discussion of the issues.

4. Michael Walzer's discussion of the different "spheres of justice" is important in this context (Waltzer 1983).

5. See essays in Hunnius, Garson, and Case 1973 for examples of these experiments. See also Jon Elster's treatment of several institutional alternatives to industrial hierarchical command in Elster and Moene 1989 and Elster 1989a.

6. See Miliband 1969 and 1982 and Cohen and Rogers 1983 for a developed analysis of these points.

7. See Michael Lipton's *Why Poor People Stay Poor* (1976) for extensive analysis of some of these mechanisms.

8. Robert Klitgaard (1988) offers a highly valuable institutional analysis of corruption.

9. These issues have been most actively discussed in recent years in the context of the reform processes currently under way in Eastern Europe: Poland, Hungary, and Czechoslovakia. See Przeworski 1991, Kornai 1990, Cohen 1989, and Nove 1983.

10. Adam Przeworski (1991) analyzes the process of economic reform in Poland along these lines.

11. Atul Kohli (1988, 1990) has studied this aspect of Indian politics with great clarity. See also Varshney 2000 and 2002 for a sustained analysis of the relationship between ethnic politics and democracy in India. Similar issues arise in other countries, including Indonesia and Nigeria.

12. See essays in Przeworski et al. 1995 for a variety of important recent perspectives on the role of democracy in just development. Essays in Cohen and Rogers 1995 focus on the intermediary institutions through which democratic values can be secured.

13. Consider the detailed analysis offered by Atul Kohli (1987) of the politics of development in three Indian states.

9

Conclusion: Toward a Global Civil Society

I HAVE NOW EXAMINED MANY of the dynamics that are at work in global economic development today. I have observed the processes that continue to produce deep poverty and material inequality in the modern world. I have looked at some of the processes of globalization that have so greatly increased interdependence among the citizens of the world. And I have taken note of the most fundamental values that ought to guide our thinking about the future and our relations with each other—human rights, the value of democracy, and the value of human equality, to name a few.

In writing about these issues in 2002, it is impossible not to take heed of the violence and terror that characterize our world today. Surely this violence, this hatred, and this disregard of innocent humanity have much to do with the issues we have confronted. So we must ask a profound and deeply important question: What principles, commitments, and institutions can lead us toward a better and more just world—a global civil society? Is it possible that the pursuit of justice and human equality throughout the world is itself a crucial component of a peaceful and humane future for world society? The answer is apparent. International justice and poverty alleviation are issues that will affect global peace and security as well as global ethics. If the world does not make progress in alleviating poverty, in improving the life circumstances of the world's disadvantaged people, and in enhancing human equality, then it appears unavoidable that conflict and violence will continue.

The processes of economic, political, and communications integration of the world that we have discussed here—the processes of globalization—are surely irreversible. The extension of markets and international trade, the increased mobility of capital, the expansion of foreign direct investment, and the extension of the reach of global media are all processes that are likely only to intensify in the coming years. The world of tomorrow will unavoidably be one of increasing global interconnectedness and interdependency. The question is, Will this global interconnectedness be able to lay the ground for a just and peaceful future for humanity, or will it lay the seeds for continuing deprivation, injustice, and conflict? Many of the global economic processes that we have examined are blind and undirected, but we have seen that there are avenues of influence through which we can intervene. The extension of democracy is one such avenue. The creation of effective and farsighted international institutions is a second—an effort that will require the active engagement of citizens of many countries. And the cultivation of a culture of ethical consuming for citizens of the wealthy nations is a third avenue.

The hazards of globalization are already clear. Multinational companies operating within the context of impersonal global market economies have no inherent concern for the human and environmental consequences of their actions. The logic of competition and profit is no less powerful in the twenty-first century than it was in the nineteenth century. So if we do not invent effective national and international institutions that protect the global public good, then we can expect that pervasive harms will accumulate—harms to the environment, harms to the conditions of life and labor, and persistent inattention to the poor and powerless (Kapstein 1999; Stiglitz 2002). Unconstrained globalization has the potential for deepening North-South inequalities, worsening the proliferation of exploitative and harmful conditions of work, and extending the proliferation of environmental degradation—if we allow these outcomes to emerge.

How, then, are we to steer our world toward a future that is humane, just, and supportive of full human development? Throughout this book, I have examined many of the issues and principles that are relevant to answering this question. But it is also important to have a vision of the world in which we wish to live—a concept of a practical utopia, a vision of the world that is both desirable and feasible. Such a concept is critical because it can help guide us in the choices that we make as citizens, as members of human communities, and as cosmopolitans.[1] In this concluding chapter, then, I will reflect briefly on one such concept—the ideal of a *global civil society*—and will consider how some of the issues and principles we have considered in this book are pertinent to attaining this practical utopia. In this conception, I consider a world that is diverse in all the ways that global humanity presents itself. It is a world in which we have succeeded in establishing the economic and political institutions that are necessary to provide a high minimum standard of living for all persons. It is a world in which democratic institutions effectively embody protections for the human rights of all persons. And it is a world in which citizens can have a reasonable confidence in the fairness of the basic institutions that govern their lives.

In attempting to envision a humane future for globalization, I can begin by considering the values associated with a "civil society." This vision emphasizes two aspects of the word *civil*. The first is the value of civility—the value within a community that is placed on mutual respect, tolerance of difference, and a commitment to the legal resolution of conflict (Gutmann and Thompson 1996; Taylor and Gutmann 1992). People embody the value of civility in their actions and their values when they are committed to maintaining a structure of relationship with one another that continually renews the basis of cooperation, respect, and nonviolence. The value of civility rests on the value assigned to respecting the moral importance of the individual human being. But civility is also a social value. It expresses the importance of the ideal of a community of equals in which individuals honor the worth of each others' life plans and purposes. This shared value in turn provides each citizen with the assurance that he or she needs to assume the sacrifices for the public good that citizenship requires. The broad availability of the value of civility gives citizens the confidence they need that their interests will be fairly treated. The value of civility represents a view of social life that stands in sharp contrast to the state of nature that Thomas Hobbes (1996) describes as a war of all against all.

The second aspect of civil life that I want to emphasize here is the notion of civil society—the idea of a society in which members have a variety of crosscutting activities and associations and where the state is not the sole source of social power. On this conception, a civil society is characterized by multiple associations, free activities and choices by individuals, and a framework of law that assures rights and liberties for all citizens. It is a society with multiple forms of power and influence, minimizing the potential for exploitation and domination by powerful elites or the state. And it is a society in which citizens have developed a sense of mutual respect and consideration for each other. Civil association serves to enhance the strength of collective identities among citizens, by building new loyalties and affiliations. Citizenship and unity are built through association with other citizens and the knowledge that they can pursue their interests and values through their associations (Putnam, Leonardi, and Nanetti 1993; Putnam 2000). But I can emphasize as well the importance of civil associations as a counterweight to the power of the state. Citizens have greater security when they are confident that the state cannot act against their interests with impunity.

What is involved in sustaining a civil society? What are the conditions that enhance civility within a community? Several factors are particularly important in this regard. There is solidarity—some degree of shared identity among the individuals who make up the society as groups with interests in common. There is a sense of justice—confidence that the basic institutions are fair to all. There is confidence in the future and a conviction that one's children will have reasonable (and improved) life prospects. There is a sense of dignity—of being treated with human dignity, of being assigned equal human worth. And there is a need for stable, fair, and predictable institutions that give citizens the confidence that they can pursue activities, form associations, and engage in civil discourse without fear. When these conditions are satisfied, we can have the greatest confidence in the stability and flourishing of a civil society.

Several of these features fall within the concept of what John Rawls calls a *well-ordered society*. Rawls introduced the concept of a well-ordered society in *A Theory of Justice* (1971). It is the conception of society "as a fair system of cooperation over time from one generation to the next, where those engaged in cooperation are viewed as free and equal citizens and normal cooperating members of society over a complete life" (Rawls 2001: 4). Citizens within a well-ordered society respect one another, they have confidence that their most basic interests are fairly treated, and they are confident that the basic institutions of society permit them fair access and allow them to pursue their conceptions of the good. A well-ordered society is thus a powerful and pervasive foundation for a stable society, and justice is an important causal factor in sustaining and reproducing such a society.[2] The underlying hypothesis is that shared moral values, including particularly the values that determine the terms of social interaction, create the underpinnings of stability in a society.

And profound disagreement about these values fosters the possibility of serious conflict.

These ideas find their most common application in the context of local or national communities. How does the concept of a civil society pertain to the idea of a world society? Is there any meaning we can assign to the notion of a global civil society? Or does this concept apply only to connected populations engaged in face-to-face interactions with each other? The practical utopia that I advance here depends on the assumption that a global civil society is feasible. This society is a world in which all persons recognize and respect the human reality and worth of all others—near and far. It is a world in which people are tied together through crosscutting civil associations—local, national, and international. These may include labor organizations, women's organizations, environmental organizations, or religious groups. It is a world in which persons share a sense of justice—a basic agreement on the essential fairness of the institutions that govern their lives. And it is a world in which all people have grounds for hope for the future—the conviction that there are opportunities for them to improve their lives, that they will have fair access to these opportunities, and that their children will have better lives than they themselves have had. Such a world has every prospect of sustaining stable, peaceful, and civil social life—both local and international. And this is an ideal worth striving for.

How do the issues we have discussed in the preceding chapters relate to this vision? The connections are profound. I have emphasized the importance of an urgent commitment to ending poverty throughout the world. I have emphasized the importance of democracy and human rights—and the effective legal institutions that can secure both. I have emphasized the deep importance of the values of fairness and human equality, as well as the importance of reshaping international institutions with these values in mind. And these are precisely the values that are needed to establish the basis of peaceful civil society. If these values are genuinely and deeply embedded in our planning for the future—and if the people of the developing world become convinced that these are real, guiding priorities for the people and governments of the wealthy world—then the potential bonds of international civility will be established. And in each country, the positive institutions of law, democracy, and economic opportunity will ceaselessly reinforce the values of civility and mutual respect.

So the values given central place in this book are arguably critical to a decent future for humanity. A world order that is not grounded in a permanent commitment to human dignity and justice is disfigured not only from the perspective of morality. It is also likely to be an increasingly unstable and violent arena for deep and desperate conflict. So for our own sakes and for the sake of future generations, we must commit ourselves in practical and enduring ways to the establishment of global justice, an end to poverty, and the extension of effective democratic and human rights to all persons in all countries.

Three specific points are particularly central. First, poverty is not simply a problem for the poor or for poor countries. Rather, it is a problem for the world and one that we must confront with determination and resources. This means that we need to develop plans for alleviating poverty that have a likelihood of success, we must work toward the political consensus that will be needed in order to carry out these plans, and we need to exercise our democratic rights and voices in order to bring about the large commitment of resources that will be required.

Second, the equal worth of all persons is an essential moral fact. All persons are equally deserving of attention. And much follows from this fact. The extreme inequalities of life prospects between citizens of the North and the South are inconsistent with this principle. The persistence of antidemocratic and authoritarian regimes throughout the developing world is inconsistent with the equal rights and worth of the citizens who suffer under those regimes. And the inequalities of voice that exist in current international institutions represent an affront to the moral equality of all persons who are affected by those institutions.

Third, democracy and human rights are critical. It is only through effective democratic institutions for government and decisionmaking that the interests and concerns of citizens will be aggregated into just policies and progressive social institutions. Democratic institutions permit all citizens to influence the policies that affect the terms of their lives, and they represent a meaningful obstacle to the emergence of exploitation and domination of the powerless by elites.

Are there examples of international settings that embody some of the features of a global civil society? The European Union and the pan-European institutions and identities that the EU is in the process of forging offer a promising example of a system that can bring about a just international order. Here, we find fledgling experiments in the creation of solidarities that transcend language, religion, nation, or place. And we find an emerging discourse of solidarity that may provide the political basis that will be needed to bring about global justice (and the international transfer of resources and knowledge that this will require).[3] There is a measure of "global thinking" among European citizens that offers a basis for optimism about the feasibility of an engaged world citizenry. OECD institutions have already gone a long way toward giving meaningful priority to the needs of developing countries. The OECD and the Development Assistance Committee represent effective and broadly supported institutional agents of change within the processes of economic development. And surveys of European public opinion suggest an emerging and strengthening public support for global justice (European Commission 1996, 1997a, 1997b).

What does the concept of a global civil society imply for the durability of national or cultural identities? Can the Brazilian, Sikh, or Muslim man or woman at the same time be a member of a global civil society? This question can be posed at virtually every level of scale—village, region, nation, or global system. And the answer is everywhere the same. One can be both a cosmopolitan and a Muslim, both a Brazilian Catholic and a citizen of the world (Nussbaum and Cohen 1996; C. Taylor 1992). In other words, my conception of a just global civil society does not presuppose a process of homogenization of world cultures. Instead, it presumes the development of a cross-cultural consensus about the importance of civility as a necessary context for the many cultural, religious, or national differences that will persist and that constitute one of the positive engines of creativity available to the world's people.

What specific conclusions can we draw from our previous discussions? We have seen that progressive economic development involves several characteristics:

- Growth in the productive capacity of society: growth in productivity of labor, agriculture, and capital (leading to growth in per capita incomes and per capita assets)
- Development that leads to significant and continuing improvement in the quality of life for the poor and the near-poor (that is, the majority of the population in most developing societies)
- Development that serves to broaden the distribution of economic assets and incomes

- Development that leads to improvement in conditions of health and safety in the workplace
- Development that leads to improvement in quality of life dimensions for all citizens: improved access to health care, clean water, education
- Development that leads to improvement in gender equity over time
- Development that leads to sustainable environmental change and resource use
- Development that enhances the pervasiveness and effectiveness of democratic institutions
- Development that embodies respect for human rights

These characteristics embody a combination of moral and empirical beliefs. They depend centrally on the moral importance of the free and fully developed human being. They emphasize the importance of the moral equality of all persons. They postulate the moral and institutional importance of democracy. And they recognize the empirical necessity of designing development strategies that enhance productivity and output (growth) while at the same time creating social and economic institutions that enhance human equality and equality of opportunity (equity).

This enumeration identifies some of the most important elements that would be needed to create the foundations of a global civil society. It emphasizes the importance of human development and full opportunities. It stresses the centrality of fairness in the basic institutions of the world order and the domestic economies of the world. It insists on the importance of gender equality. And it gives central importance to the role of democratic institutions and effective guarantees of human rights. From one point of view, then, we can regard the central arguments of this book as an assessment of what global civility requires.

The ideal of a global civil society represents a liberal ideal for the future. It celebrates diversity, mutual respect, and just legal, political, and economic institutions; at the same time, it emphasizes a global commitment to improving the conditions of humanity. It represents, in short, a democratic vision of the future that gives expression to the value of full and free human development for the world's people.

Finally, let me ask again the question with which I began: Why is it important for us to think deeply and well about the ethics of development? These are issues where clear thinking about values and principles can make a material difference in the quality of our thinking, planning, and outcomes. We need to navigate well into the world of the twenty-first century, and thinking about the social, political, and ethical values that surround poverty and inequality is a crucial part of our navigation. Only with a clear understanding of the values and principles that we respect will we be able to design the institutions and policies that will guide us to a future that honors all human beings as free and equal persons. And only through such debate, deliberation, and action will we succeed as a global civilization in creating a just and stable world.

Notes

1. The "Real Utopias" project, directed by Erik Olin Wright at the A. E. Havens Center at the University of Wisconsin, represents a substantial effort to offer rigorous and innovative thinking in support of significant social change. The project "is founded on the belief that what is pragmatically possible is not fixed independently of our imaginations, but is itself shaped by our visions" (Wright 1999). The project has published volumes on associative democracy, market socialism, and new visions of egalitarianism.

2. This conception bears an important similarity to Kant's (1999) concept of the state as a realm of ends, in which the laws of the state embody equality of respect for the autonomy of all citizens.

3. See Jürgen Habermas's discussion of the role of constitutional debate in the emerging European Union (Habermas 2001).

References

Adelman, Irma. 1978. *Redistribution Before Growth—A Strategy for Developing Countries.* The Hague: Martinus Nijhof.

_____. 1986. "A Poverty-Focused Approach to Development Policy." In *Development Strategies Reconsidered,* edited by John P. Lewis and Valeriana Kallab. New Brunswick, N. J.: Transaction Books.

Adelman, Irma, and Cynthia Taft Morris. 1973. *Economic Growth and Social Equity in Developing Countries.* Stanford, Calif.: Stanford University Press.

Agarwal, Anil, and Sunita Narain. 1989. *Towards Green Villages.* New Delhi: Centre for Science and Environment.

Agarwal, Bina. 1994. *A Field of One's Own: Gender and Land Rights in South Asia.* Cambridge South Asian Studies. Cambridge and New York: Cambridge University Press.

American Anthropological Association. 1947. "Statement on Human Rights." *American Anthropologist* 49 (4):539–543.

Anderson, Elizabeth. 2000. "Beyond Homo Economicus." *Philosophy & Public Affairs* 29 (2):170–200.

Anderson, Perry. 1996. *Passages from Antiquity to Feudalism.* London: Verso.

Aristotle. 1987. *The Nicomachean Ethics.* Buffalo, N.Y.: Prometheus Books.

Baden, John, and Douglas S. Noonan, eds. 1998. *Managing the Commons.* 2nd ed. Bloomington: Indiana University Press.

Baker, Dean, Gerald A. Epstein, and Robert Pollin, eds. 1999. *Globalization and Progressive Economic Policy.* Cambridge and New York: Cambridge University Press.

Bardhan, Pranab. 2001. "Some Up, Some Down." *Boston Review* 26 (1):11–12.

Barker, Randolph, Robert W. Herdt, and Beth Rose. 1985. *The Rice Economy of Asia.* Washington, D.C.: Resources for the Future.

Basu, Alaka Malwade. 1989. "Is Discrimination in Food Really Necessary for Explaining Sex Differentials in Childhood Mortality?" *Population Studies* 43 (2):193–210.

Bates, Robert H., ed. 1988. *Toward a Political Economy of Development: A Rational Choice Perspective,* California Series on Social Choice and Political Economy, 14. Berkeley: University of California Press.

Beer, Linda, and Terry Boswell. 2001. *The Effects of Globalization on Inequality: A Cross-National Analysis.* Atlanta, Ga.: Emory University, Claus M. Halle Institute for Global Learning.

Behrman, Jere R. 1988. "Intrahousehold Allocation of Nutrients in Rural India: Are Boys Favored? Do Parents Exhibit Inequality Aversion?" *Oxford Economic Papers*, n.s., 40 (1):32–54.

———. 1992. "Intra-Household Allocation of Nutrients and Gender Effects: A Survey of Structural and Reduced-Form Estimates." In *Nutrition and Poverty: Studies in Development Economics*, edited by Siddiqur Rahman Osmani. Oxford and New York: Clarendon Press.

Berlin, Isaiah. 1969. *Four Essays on Liberty.* London and New York: Oxford University Press.

Blackstone, William T., ed. 1974. *Philosophy & Environmental Crisis.* Athens: University of Georgia Press.

Blyn, George. 1983. "The Green Revolution Revisited." *Economic Development and Cultural Change* 31 (4):705–725.

Bonner, John. 1986. *Introduction to the Theory of Social Choice.* Baltimore: Johns Hopkins University Press.

Brams, Steven J., and Alan D. Taylor. 1996. *Fair Division: From Cake-Cutting to Dispute Resolution.* Cambridge: Cambridge University Press.

Brass, Paul, ed. 1985. *Ethnic Groups and the State.* London: Croom Helm.

Braverman, Harry. 1975. *Labor and Monopoly Capital: The Degradation of Work in the Twentieth Century.* New York: Monthly Review Press.

Braybrooke, David. 1987. *Meeting Needs.* Princeton: Princeton University Press.

Brennan, Andrew A. 1995. "Ecological Theory and Value in Nature." In *Environmental Ethics*, edited by Robert Elliot. Oxford and New York: Oxford University Press.

Brinton, Mary C., and Victor Nee, eds. 1998. *New Institutionalism in Sociology.* New York: Russell Sage Foundation.

Brown, Lester R. 1985. "Reducing Hunger." In *State of the World, 1985*, edited by Lester A. Brown. New York: W. W. Norton.

Brundtland, G. H. 1987. *Our Common Future: The U.N. World Commission on Environment and Development.* Oxford: Oxford University Press.

Buchanan, Allen E. 1985. *Ethics, Efficiency, and the Market.* Rowman & Allanheld Texts in Philosophy. Totowa, N.J.: Rowman & Allanheld.

Burnside, Craig, and David Dollar. 1997. "Aid Spurs Growth—in a Sound Policy Environment." *Finance & Development* 34 (4):4–7.

Byres, Terry J. 1972. "The Dialectic of India's Green Revolution." *South Asian Review* 5 (2):99–116.

Byres, Terry J., and Ben Crow. 1983. *The Green Revolution in India.* Buckingham, United Kingdom: The Open University Press.

Chan, Anita. 2001. *China's Workers Under Assault: The Exploitation of Labor in a Globalizing Economy.* Armonk, N.Y.: M. E. Sharpe.

Chapple, Christopher, and Mary Evelyn Tucker, eds. 2000. *Hinduism and Ecology: The Intersection of Earth, Sky, and Water.* Religions of the World and Ecology. Cambridge,

Mass.: Distributed by Harvard University Press for the Center for the Study of World Religions, Harvard Divinity School.

Chenery, Hollis, and T. N. Srinivasan, eds. 1988. *The Handbook of Development Economics.* Vol. 1. Amsterdam: North-Holland Press.

Chenery, Hollis, Montek S. Ahluwalia, C.L.G. Bell, John H. Duloy, and Richard Jolly. 1974. *Redistribution with Growth.* Oxford: Oxford University Press.

Coale, Ansley J. 1991. "Excess Female Mortality and the Balance of the Sexes: An Estimate of the Number of 'Missing Females.'" *Population and Development Review* 17 (3):517–523.

Cohen, Joshua, and Joel Rogers. 1983. *On Democracy: Toward a Transformation of American Society.* New York: Penguin Books.

_____. 1995. *Associations and Democracy.* London and New York: Verso.

Cohen, Ronald. 1989. "Human Rights and Cultural Relativism: The Need for a New Approach." *American Anthropologist* 91:1014ff.

Colletti, Lucio. 1972. *From Rousseau to Lenin: Studies in Ideology and Society.* New York: Monthly Review Press.

Cooper, Richard N., and P. R. G. Layard, eds. 2002. *What the Future Holds: Insights from Social Science.* Cambridge, Mass.: MIT Press.

Crafts, N.F.R. 1980. "National Income Estimates and the British Standard of Living Debate: A Reappraisal of 1801–1831." *Explorations in Economic History* 17:176–188.

Cronon, William. 1991. *Nature's Metropolis: Chicago and the Great West.* New York: W. W. Norton.

Daly, H. E. 1991. *Steady State Economics.* 2nd ed. Washington, D.C.: Island Press.

Daniels, Norman. 1988. *Am I My Parents' Keeper? An Essay on Justice Between the Young and the Old.* Oxford: Oxford University Press.

Dasgupta, Partha. 1993. *An Inquiry into Well-Being and Destitution.* Oxford: Oxford University Press.

de Haan, Jakob, and Clemens L. J. Siermann. 1996. "New Evidence on the Relationship Between Democracy and Economic Growth." *Public Choice* 86 (1-2):175–198.

Delman, Jorgen, Clemens Stubbe Ostergaard, and Flemming Christiansen, eds. 1990. *Remaking Peasant China: Problems of Rural Development and Institutions at the Start of the 1990s.* Aarhus, Denmark: Aarhus University Press.

Desai, A. R., ed. 1979. *Peasant Struggles in India.* Delhi: Oxford University Press.

Desai, Meghnad, Susanne Hoeber Rudolph, and Ashok Rudra, eds. 1984. *Agrarian Power and Agricultural Productivity in South Asia.* Berkeley: University of California Press.

Deutsch, Eliot, and Gerald Larson, eds. 1987. *Interpreting Across Boundaries.* Princeton: Princeton University Press.

Development Assistance Committee. 1992. *Development Cooperation 1992 Report.* Paris: OECD.

_____. 2001. *Development Cooperation 2001 Report.* Paris: OECD.

Donaldson, Graham. 1984. "Food Security and the Role of the Grain Trade." *American Journal of Agricultural Economics* 66:188–193.

Donnelly, Jack. 1998. *International Human Rights.* 2nd ed. Dilemmas in World Politics. Boulder: Westview.

Drèze, Jean. 1990. *Widows in Rural India: DEP Paper No. 26, Development Economics Research Programme.* London: London School of Economics.

Drèze, Jean, and Amartya Kumar Sen. 1989. *Hunger and Public Action.* Oxford: Clarendon Press.

———. 1995. *India, Economic Development and Social Opportunity.* Delhi and Oxford: Oxford University Press.

Drèze, Jean, and Amartya Kumar Sen, eds. 1991. *The Political Economy of Hunger.* WIDER Studies in Development Economics. Oxford: Clarendon Press; New York: Oxford University Press.

Dworkin, Ronald M. 1977. *Taking Rights Seriously.* Cambridge, Mass.: Harvard University Press.

Elliot, Robert, ed. 1995. *Environmental Ethics.* Oxford Readings in Philosophy. Oxford and New York: Oxford University Press.

Elster, Jon. 1979. *Ulysses and the Sirens: Studies in Rationality and Irrationality.* Cambridge and New York: Cambridge University Press.

———. 1983. *Sour Grapes: Studies in the Subversion of Rationality.* Cambridge: Cambridge University Press.

———. 1988. "Is There (or Should There Be) a Right to Work?" In *Democracy and the Welfare State,* edited by A. Gutmann. Princeton: Princeton University Press.

———. 1989a. "From Here to There; or, If Cooperative Ownership Is So Desirable, Why Are There So Few Cooperatives?" *Social Philosophy & Policy* 6:93–111.

———. 1989b. *Solomonic Judgements: Studies in the Limitations of Rationality.* Cambridge: Cambridge University Press.

———. 1992. *Local Justice.* New York: Russell Sage Foundation.

Elster, Jon, and Karl Ove Moene, eds. 1989. *Alternatives to Capitalism.* Studies in Marxism and Social Theory. Cambridge and New York: Cambridge University Press; Paris: Editions de la Maison des Sciences de l'Homme.

Elster, Jon, and John E. Roemer, eds. 1991. *Interpersonal Comparisons of Well-Being.* Studies in Rationality and Social Change. Cambridge and New York: Cambridge University Press.

Esping-Andersen, Gosta. 1985. *Politics Against Markets: The Social Democratic Road to Power.* Princeton: Princeton University Press.

———. 1990. *The Three Worlds of Welfare Capitalism.* Princeton: Princeton University Press.

European Commission. 1996. "Eurobarometer 44.1: The Way Europeans Perceive Developing Countries in 1995." European Commission Directorate General Development. Available: http://europa.eu.int/comm/public_opinion/archives/special.htm.

———. 1997a. "Eurobarometer 46.0: Development Aid—Building for the Future with Public Support." European Commission Directorate General Development. Available: http://europa.eu.int/comm/public_opinion/archives/special.htm.

———. 1997b. "Eurobarometer 47.0: Attitudes of EU Consumers to Fair Trade Bananas." European Commission Directorate General Development. Available: http://europa.eu.int/comm/public_opinion/archives/special.htm.

Feinberg, Joel. 1974. "The Rights of Animals and Unborn Generations." In *Philosophy & Environmental Crisis,* edited by William T. Blackstone. Athens: University of Georgia Press.

Feinstein, Charles H. 1998. "Pessimism Perpetuated: Real Wages and the Standard of Living in Britain During and After the Industrial Revolution." *Journal of Economic History* 58 (3):625–658.

Feng, Jicai. 1991. *Voices from the Whirlwind: An Oral History of the Cultural Revolution.* New York: Pantheon Books.

Fields, Gary S. 1980. *Poverty, Inequality, and Development.* Cambridge: Cambridge University Press.

Fishlow, Albert, and Karen Parker, eds. 1999. *Growing Apart: The Causes and Consequences of Global Wage Inequality.* New York: Council on Foreign Relations Press.

Floud, Roderick, and Deirdre N. McCloskey, eds. 1994. *The Economic History of Britain Since 1700.* 2nd ed. Cambridge and New York: Cambridge University Press.

Fox, Jonathan A. 1991. "Popular Participation and Access to Food: Mexico's Community Food Councils, 1979–1986." In *Harvest of Want: Hunger and Food Security in Central America and Mexico,* edited by Scott Whiteford and Anne Ferguson. Boulder: Westview Press.

Fox, Jonathan A., and L. David Brown, eds. 1998. *The Struggle for Accountability: The World Bank, NGOs, and Grassroots Movements.* Cambridge, Mass.: MIT Press.

Fung, Archon, Dara O'Rourke, and Charles Sabel. 2001. "Realizing Labor Standards: How Transparency, Competition, and Sanctions Could Improve Working Conditions Worldwide." *Boston Review* 26 (1):4–10.

Gilbert, Neil. 1983. *Capitalism and the Welfare State: Dilemmas of Social Benevolence.* New Haven: Yale University Press.

Gillis, Malcolm. 1987. *Economics of Development.* 2nd ed. New York: Norton.

Gould, Carol C. 1988. *Rethinking Democracy: Freedom and Social Cooperation in Politics, Economy, and Society.* Cambridge: Cambridge University Press.

Greenstein, Fred I., and Nelson W. Polsby, eds. 1975. *Handbook of Political Science.* Vol. 8, *International Politics.* Reading, Mass.: Addison-Wesley.

Griffin, James. 1986. *Well-Being: Its Meaning, Measurement and Moral Importance.* Oxford: Oxford University Press.

Griffin, Keith. 1974. *The Political Economy of Agrarian Change: An Essay on the Green Revolution.* Cambridge, Mass.: Harvard University Press.

_____. 1976. *Land Concentration and Rural Poverty.* New York: Holmes & Meier.

_____. 1988. *Alternative Strategies for Economic Development: A Report to the OECD Development Centre.* Basingstoke, United Kingdom: Macmillan.

Grossman, Gene M., and Alan B. Krueger. 1995. "Economic Growth and the Environment." *Quarterly Journal of Economics* 110 (2):353–377.

Gutmann, Amy, ed. 1988. *Democracy and the Welfare State.* Studies from the Project on the Federal Social Role. Princeton: Princeton University Press.

Gutmann, Amy, and Dennis F. Thompson, eds. 1996. *Democracy and Disagreement.* Cambridge, Mass.: Belknap Press.

Habermas, Jürgen. 1975. *Legitimation Crisis.* Boston: Beacon Press.

_____. 1979. *Communication and the Evolution of Society.* Boston: Beacon Press.

_____. 2001. "Why Europe Needs a Constitution." *New Left Review* 11:5–26.

Haddad, Lawrence, Ravi Kanbur, and Howarth Bouis. 1995. "Intrahousehold Inequality at Different Welfare Levels: Energy Intake and Energy Expenditure Data from the Philippines." *Oxford Bulletin of Economics & Statistics* 57 (3):389–409.

Hadden, Kenneth, and Bruce London. 1996. "Educating Girls in the Third World: The Demographic, Basic Needs, and Economic Benefits." *International Journal of Comparative Sociology* 37 (1-2):31–46.

Haq, Mahbub ul, Inge Kaul, and Isabelle Grunberg, eds. 1996. *The Tobin Tax: Coping with Financial Volatility.* Oxford: Oxford University Press.

Hardgrave, Robert L., Jr., and Stanley A. Kochanek. 1986. *India: Government and Politics in a Developing Nation.* 4th ed. San Diego: Harcourt Brace Jovanovich.

Hardin, Garrett. 1968. "The Tragedy of the Commons." *Science* 162:1243–1248.

Harrigan, Jane, and Paul Mosley. 1991. "Evaluating the Impact of World Bank Structural Adjustment Lending: 1980–87." *Journal of Development Studies* 27 (3):63–94.

Harsanyi, John C. 1977. *Rational Behavior and Bargaining Equilibrium in Games and Social Situations.* Cambridge: Cambridge University Press.

_____. 1982. "Morality and the Theory of Rational Behavior." In *Utilitarianism and Beyond,* edited by A. Sen and B. Williams. Cambridge: Cambridge University Press.

Hart, Gillian Patricia, Andrew Turton, and Benjamin White, eds. 1989. *Agrarian Transformations: Local Processes and the State in Southeast Asia.* Berkeley: University of California Press.

Hausman, Daniel M., and Michael S. McPherson. 1996. *Economic Analysis and Moral Philosophy.* Cambridge Surveys of Economic Literature. Cambridge and New York: Cambridge University Press.

Hayami, Jujiro, and Vernon Ruttan, eds. 1985. *Agricultural Development: An International Perspective.* Baltimore: Johns Hopkins University Press.

Herdt, Robert W. 1987. "A Retrospective View of Technological and Other Changes in Philippine Rice Farming, 1965–1982." *Economic Development and Cultural Change* 35 (2):329–349.

Herring, Ronald. 1983. *Land to the Tiller: The Political Economy of Agrarian Reform in South Asia.* New Haven: Yale University Press.

_____. 1984. "Economic Consequences of Local Power Configurations in Rural South Asia." In *Agrarian Power and Agricultural Productivity in South Asia,* edited by Meghnad Desai, Susanne Hoeser Rudolph, and Ashok Rudra. Berkeley: University of California Press.

_____. 1991. "From Structural Conflict to Agrarian Stalemate: Agrarian Reforms in South India." *Journal of Asian and African Studies* 26 (3-4):169–188.

_____. 1999. "Political Conditions for Agrarian Reform and Poverty Alleviation." Paper presented at the World Bank DFID Conference on the 2001 World Development Report on Poverty, August 16–17, 1999. Birmingham, United Kingdom.

Hirschman, Albert O. 1970. *Exit, Voice, and Loyalty: Responses to Decline in Firms, Organizations, and States.* Cambridge, Mass.: Harvard University Press.

Hobbes, Thomas. 1996. *Leviathan.* Oxford and New York: Oxford University Press.

Hollis, Martin, and Edward J. Nell. 1975. *Rational Economic Man: A Philosophical Critique of Neo-Classical Economics*. London: Cambridge University Press.

Hollist, W. Ladd, and F. Lamond Tullis, eds. 1987. *Pursuing Food Security: Strategies and Obstacles in Africa, Asia, Latin America, and the Middle East*. Boulder: Lynne Rienner.

Horowitz, Donald L. 1985. *Ethnic Groups in Conflict*. Berkeley: University of California Press.

Hunnius, Gerry, G. David Garson, and John Case, eds. 1973. *Workers' Control: A Reader on Labor and Social Change*. 1st ed. New York: Random House.

Huntington, Samuel P. 1987. *Political Order in Changing Societies*. New Haven: Yale University Press.

Hyden, Goran, and Shlomo Reutlinger. 1992. "Foreign Aid in a Period of Democratization: The Case of Politically Autonomous Food Funds." *World Development* 20 (9):1253–1260.

International Labour Organization. 2000. "International Labour Standards and Human Rights" [cited 2002]. Available: www.ilo.org/public/english/standards/norm/.

————. 2002. "Multinational Corporations" [cited 2002]. Available: http://www.itcilo.it/english/actrav/telearn/global/ilo/multinat/multinat.htm.

Ireson, W. Randall. 1987. "Landholding, Agricultural Modernization, and Income Concentration: A Mexican Example." *Economic Development and Cultural Change* 35 (2):351–366.

Kant, Immanuel. 1990. *Foundations of the Metaphysics of Morals and, What Is Enlightenment*. 2nd rev. ed. The Library of Liberal Arts. New York: Macmillan.

————. 1999. *Metaphysical Elements of Justice: Part 1 of The Metaphysics of Morals*. 2nd ed. Indianapolis: Hackett.

Kant, Immanuel, and Herbert James Paton. 1964. *Groundwork of the Metaphysics of Morals*. 1st Harper Torchbook ed., vol. TB 1159. New York: Harper & Row.

Kapstein, Ethan B. 1999. *Sharing the Wealth: Workers and the World Economy*. 1st ed. New York: W. W. Norton.

Keyfitz, Nathan. 1993. "Population and Sustainable Development: Distinguishing Fact and Preference Concerning the Future Human Population and Environment." *Population and Environment* 14 (5):441–461.

Klitgaard, Robert E. 1988. *Controlling Corruption*. Berkeley: University of California Press.

Koestler, Arthur. 1941. *Darkness at Noon*. The Modern Library of the World's Best Books. New York: Modern Library.

Kohli, Atul. 1986. "Democracy and Development." In *Development Strategies Reconsidered*, edited by John P. Lewis and Valeriana Kallab. New Brunswick, N.J.: Transaction Books.

————. 1987. *The State and Poverty in India: The Politics of Reform*. Cambridge: Cambridge University Press.

————. 1990. *Democracy and Discontent: India's Growing Crisis of Governability*. Cambridge: Cambridge University Press.

Kohli, Atul, ed. 1988. *India's Democracy: An Analysis of Changing State-Society Relations*. Princeton: Princeton University Press.

Kornai, Janos. 1990. *The Road to a Free Economy: Shifting from a Socialist System—The Example of Hungary*. New York: Norton.

Krueger, Anne. 1991. *Economic Policy Reforms in Developing Countries*. Oxford: Blackwell.

Kuznets, Simon. 1966. *Modern Economic Growth*. New Haven: Yale University Press.

Lardy, Nicholas R. 1989. "Dilemmas in the Pattern of Resource Allocation in China, 1978–1985." In *Remaking the Economic Institutions of Socialism: China and Eastern Europe*, edited by Victor Nee and David Stark. Stanford: Stanford University Press.

Leopold, Aldo. 1966. "The Land Ethic." In *A Sand County Almanac, with Other Essays on Conservation from Round River*, edited by Aldo Leopold and Charles Walsh Schwartz. New York: Oxford University Press.

Leopold, Aldo, and Charles Walsh Schwartz. 1966. *A Sand County Almanac, with Other Essays on Conservation from Round River*. Enl. ed. New York: Oxford University Press.

Lewis, John P., and Valeriana Kallab, eds. 1986. *Development Strategies Reconsidered*. New Brunswick, N.J.: Transaction Books.

Lindblom, Charles Edward. 1977. *Politics and Markets: The World's Political Economic Systems*. New York: Basic Books.

Lindenberg, Marc, and Shantayanan Devarajan. 1993. "Prescribing Strong Economic Medicine: Revisiting the Myths About Structural Adjustment, Democracy and Economic Performance in Developing Countries." *Comparative Politics* 25 (2):169–183.

Lindert, Peter H. 1994. "Unequal Living Standards." In *The Economic History of Britain Since 1700*, vol. 1, *1770–1860*, edited by Roderick Floud and Deirdre N. McCloskey. Cambridge and New York: Cambridge University Press.

Lipton, Michael. 1976. *Why Poor People Stay Poor: Urban Bias in World Development*. Cambridge, Mass.: Harvard University Press.

————. 1983. *Poverty, Undernutrition, and Hunger*. Washington, D.C.: World Bank.

Locke, John. 1952. *The Second Treatise of Government*. The Library of Liberal Arts, no. 31, Political Science. New York: Liberal Arts Press.

Lyons, Thomas P. 1991. "Interprovincial Disparities in China: Output and Consumption, 1952–1987." *Economic Development and Cultural Change* 39 (3):471–506.

Mackay, Alfred F. 1980. *Arrow's Theorem: The Paradox of Social Choice—A Case Study in the Philosophy of Economics*. New Haven: Yale University Press.

Mackie, J. L. 1977. *Ethics: Inventing Right and Wrong*. Harmondsworth, England: Penguin.

Magnarella, P. J. 1994. "Anthropology, Human Rights and Justice." *International Journal of Anthropology* 9 (1):3–7.

Mak, Grace C. L., and Lawrence H. Summers. 1996. "Investing in All the People: Educating Women in Developing Countries." *Comparative Education Review* 40 (1):83.

Mamdani, Mahmood. 1973. *The Myth of Population Control: Family, Caste, and Class in an Indian Village*. New York: Monthly Review Press.

Marx, Karl, Friedrich Engels, and Dirk Jan Struik. 1964. *Economic and Philosophic Manuscripts of 1844*. New York: International Publishers.

Meier, Gerald M., ed. 1989. *Leading Issues in Economic Development*. 5th ed. New York: Oxford University Press.

Melden, A. I. 1977. *Rights and Persons*. Berkeley: University of California Press.

Melden, A. I., ed. 1970. *Human Rights*. Belmont, Calif.: Wadsworth.

Mellor, John Williams. 1976. *The New Economics of Growth: A Strategy for India and the Developing World*. Ithaca: Cornell University Press.

Messer, Ellen. 1993. "Anthropology and Human Rights." *Annual Review of Anthropology* 22:221–249.

Miliband, Ralph. 1969. *The State in Capitalist Society.* New York: Basic.

_____. 1982. *Capitalist Democracy in Britain.* Oxford: Oxford University Press.

Mill, John Stuart. 1989. *On Liberty, with The Subjection of Women and Chapters on Socialism.* Cambridge Texts in the History of Political Thought. Cambridge and New York: Cambridge University Press.

Mill, John Stuart, Jeremy Bentham, John Austin, and Mary Warnock. 1974. *Utilitarianism: On Liberty: Essay on Bentham.* New York: New American Library.

Moon, Bruce E. 1991. *The Political Economy of Basic Human Needs.* Ithaca: Cornell University Press.

Morris, Morris David. 1979. *Measuring the Condition of the World's Poor: The Physical Quality of Life Index.* Pergamon Policy Studies. New York: Published for the Overseas Development Council by Pergamon Press.

Morsink, Johannes. 1999. *The Universal Declaration of Human Rights: Origins, Drafting, and Intent.* Pennsylvania Studies in Human Rights. Philadelphia: University of Pennsylvania Press.

Mueller, Dennis C. 1976. "Public Choice: A Survey." *Journal of Economic Literature* 14 (2):395–433.

Mueller, Dennis C., ed. 1989. *Public Choice II.* Cambridge and New York: Cambridge University Press.

Nagel, Thomas. 1970. *The Possibility of Altruism.* Oxford: Oxford University Press.

Nee, Victor, and David Stark, eds. 1989. *Remaking the Economic Institutions of Socialism: China and Eastern Europe.* Stanford: Stanford University Press.

North, Douglass C. 1990. *Institutions, Institutional Change and Economic Performance.* Cambridge: Cambridge University Press.

Nove, Alec. 1983. *The Economics of Feasible Socialism.* London: George Allen & Unwin.

Nozick, Robert. 1974. *Anarchy, State, and Utopia.* New York: Basic Books.

Nussbaum, Martha Craven. 2000. *Women and Human Development: The Capabilities Approach.* The John Robert Seeley Lectures. Cambridge and New York: Cambridge University Press.

Nussbaum, Martha Craven, and Joshua Cohen, eds. 1996. *For Love of Country: Debating the Limits of Patriotism.* Boston: Beacon Press.

Nussbaum, Martha Craven, and Jonathan Glover, eds. 1995. *Women, Culture, and Development: A Study of Human Capabilities.* WIDER Studies in Development Economics. Oxford: Clarendon Press; New York: Oxford University Press.

Nussbaum, Martha Craven, and Amartya Kumar Sen, eds. 1993. *The Quality of Life.* Oxford and New York: Clarendon Press.

Ocampo, José Antonio. 2001. "Rethinking the Development Agenda." Paper presented at the Annual Meeting of the American Economic Association, January 5–7, 2001, New Orleans, La.

Ocampo, José Antonio, and Rolando Franco. 2000. "The Equity Gap: A Second Assessment." Paper presented at the Second Regional Conference in Follow-up to the World Summit for Social Development, May 15–17, 2000, Santiago, Chile.

O'Donnell, Guillermo. 1979. *Modernization and Bureaucratic-Authoritarianism: Studies in South American Politics.* Berkeley: University of California Press.

Opeskin, Brian R. 1996. "The Moral Foundations of Foreign Aid." *World Development* 24 (1):21-44.

Organisation for Economic Cooperation and Development. 2001. *2001 Development Co-Operation Report.* Paris and Washington, D.C.: Organisation for Economic Cooperation and Development, OECD Publications and Information Center.

Osmani, Siddiqur Rahman. 1982. *Economic Inequality and Group Welfare: A Theory of Comparison with Application to Bangladesh.* Oxford: Clarendon Press; New York: Oxford University Press.

Osmani, Siddiqur Rahman, ed. 1992. *Nutrition and Poverty.* Studies in Development Economics. Oxford and New York: Clarendon Press.

Ostrom, Elinor. 1990. *Governing the Commons: The Evolution of Institutions for Collective Action.* Cambridge and New York: Cambridge University Press.

Otsuka, Keijiro, Violeta Cordova, and Cristina C. David. 1992. "Green Revolution, Land Reform, and Household Income Distribution in the Philippines." *Economic Development and Cultural Change* 40 (4):719–741.

Overseas Development Institute. 1995. "NGOs and Official Donors." Overseas Development Institute Briefing Paper 1995 (4) [cited 2002]. Available: http://www.odi.org.uk/briefing/odingos.html.

————. 1997. "Foreign Direct Investment Flows to Low-Income Countries: A Review of the Evidence." Overseas Development Institute Briefing Paper 1997 (3) [cited 2002]. Available: http://www.odi.org.uk/briefing/3_97.html.

————. 1999. "What Can We Do with a Rights-Based Approach to Development?" Overseas Development Institute Briefing Paper 1999 (3) [cited 2002]. Available: http://www.odi.org.uk/briefing/399.html.

Oxfam International. 2001. "Towards Global Equity: Strategic Plan Summary 2001–2004" [cited 2002]. Available: http://www.oxfam.org/strategic_plan/equity.htm.

Parfit, Derek. 1984. *Reasons and Persons.* Oxford: Oxford University Press.

Pearse, Andrew Chernocke. 1980. *Seeds of Plenty, Seeds of Want: Social and Economic Implications of the Green Revolution.* Oxford: Clarendon Press.

Pearson, Scott R. 1991. *Rice Policy in Indonesia.* Ithaca: Cornell University Press.

Peeler, John A. 1998. *Building Democracy in Latin America.* Boulder: Lynne Rienner.

Perkins, Dwight, and Shahid Yusuf. 1984. *Rural Development in China.* Baltimore: Johns Hopkins University Press.

Perry, Elizabeth J., and Christine Wong, eds. 1985. *The Political Economy of Reform in Post-Mao China.* Cambridge: Council on East-Asian Studies.

Pinstrup-Andersen, Per, ed. 1988. *Food Subsidies in Developing Countries: Costs, Benefits, and Policy Options.* Baltimore: Published for the International Food Policy Research Institute by Johns Hopkins University Press.

Popkin, Samuel L. 1981. "Public Choice and Rural Development—Free Riders, Lemons, and Institutional Design." In *Toward a Political Economy of Development: A Rational Choice Perspective,* edited by Robert H. Bates. Berkeley: University of California Press.

Przeworski, Adam. 1985. *Capitalism and Social Democracy.* Cambridge: Cambridge University Press.

_____. 1991. *Democracy and the Market: Political and Economic Reforms in Eastern Europe and Latin America.* Studies in Rationality and Social Change. Cambridge: Cambridge University Press.

_____. 1992. "The Neoliberal Fallacy." *Journal of Democracy* 3 (3):45–59.

_____. 1995. *Sustainable Democracy.* Cambridge: Cambridge University Press.

Przeworski, Adam, and Fernando Limongi. 1993. "Political Regimes and Economic Growth." *Journal of Economic Perspectives* 7 (3):51–70.

Putnam, Robert D. 2000. *Bowling Alone: The Collapse and Revival of American Community.* New York: Simon & Schuster.

Putnam, Robert D., Robert Leonardi, and Raffaella Nanetti. 1993. *Making Democracy Work: Civic Traditions in Modern Italy.* Princeton: Princeton University Press.

Putterman, Louis. 1985. "The Restoration of the Peasant Household as Farm Production Unit in China: Some Incentive Theoretic Analysis." In *The Political Economy of Reform in Post-Mao China,* edited by Elizabeth J. Perry and Christine Wong. Cambridge: Council on East-Asian Studies.

Ramachandran, V. K. 1990. *Wage Labour and Unfreedom in Agriculture: An Indian Case Study.* Oxford: Oxford University Press.

Ramachandran, V. K., and Madhura Swaminathan, eds. 2002. *Agrarian Studies: Essays on Agrarian Relations in Less-Developed Countries.* New Delhi: Tulika Books.

Rawls, John. 1971. *A Theory of Justice.* Cambridge, Mass.: Belknap Press of Harvard University Press.

_____. 1985. "Justice as Fairness: Political Not Metaphysical." *Philosophy & Public Affairs* 14:223–251.

_____. 1993a. "The Law of Peoples." In *On Human Rights,* edited by S. Shute and S. Hurley. New York: Basic Books.

_____. 1993b. *Political Liberalism.* Cambridge, Mass.: Harvard University Press.

_____. 1999a. *Collected Papers.* Edited by S. Freeman. Cambridge, Mass.: Harvard University Press.

_____. 1999b. "Social Unity and Primary Goods." In *Collected Papers,* edited by S. Freeman. Cambridge, Mass.: Harvard University Press.

_____. 2001. *Justice as Fairness: A Restatement.* Cambridge, Mass.: Harvard University Press.

Renteln, Alison Dundes. 1990. *International Human Rights: Universalism Versus Relativism.* Frontiers of Anthropology. Newbury Park: Sage Publications.

Reutlinger, Shlomo, and Marcelo Selowsky. 1976. *Malnutrition and Poverty: Magnitude and Policy Options.* Baltimore: Johns Hopkins University Press.

Robertson, Geoffrey. 1999. *Crimes Against Humanity: The Struggle for Global Justice.* London: Allen Lane.

Rodrik, Dani. 1997. *Has Globalization Gone Too Far?* Washington, D.C.: Institute of International Economics.

Roemer, John. 1982. *A General Theory of Exploitation and Class.* Cambridge, Mass.: Harvard University Press.

_____. 1988. *Free to Lose: An Introduction to Marxist Economic Philosophy.* Cambridge, Mass.: Harvard University Press.

_____. 1998. *Equality of Opportunity.* Cambridge, Mass.: Harvard University Press.

Rousseau, Jean-Jacques. 1983. *On the Social Contract; Discourse on the Origin of Inequality; Discourse on Political Economy.* Indianapolis, Ind.: Hackett.

Sabel, Charles F. 1982. *Work and Politics: The Division of Labor in Industry.* Cambridge Studies in Modern Political Economies. Cambridge and New York: Cambridge University Press.

Sabel, Charles F. and Jonathan Zeitlin. 1985. "Historical Alternatives to Mass Production: Politics, Markets and Technology in Nineteenth Century Industrialization." *Past and Present* 108:133–176.

Sandel, Michael J. 1982. *Liberalism and the Limits of Justice.* Cambridge and New York: Cambridge University Press.

Sanford, Jonathan E. 1989. "The World Bank and Poverty: A Review of the Evidence on Whether the Agency Has Diminished Emphasis on Aid to the Poor." *American Journal of Economics and Sociology* 48 (2):151–164.

Scanlon, Timothy M. 1975. "Preference and Urgency." *Journal of Philosophy* 72 (19):655–669.

Schacht, Richard. 1970. *Alienation.* Garden City, N.Y.: Doubleday.

Scheffler, Samuel. 1982. *The Rejection of Consequentialism: A Philosophical Investigation of the Considerations Underlying Rival Moral Conceptions.* Oxford: Oxford University Press.

Schrecker, Ellen. 1986. *No Ivory Tower: McCarthyism and the Universities.* New York: Oxford University Press.

Scott, James C. 1985. *Weapons of the Weak: Everyday Forms of Peasant Resistance.* New Haven: Yale University Press.

_____. 1990. *Domination and the Arts of Resistance: Hidden Transcripts.* New Haven: Yale University Press.

Seligson, Mitchell A., and John T. Passé-Smith, eds. 1993. *Development and Underdevelopment: The Political Economy of Inequality.* Boulder: Lynne Rienner.

Sen, Amartya Kumar. 1970. *Collective Choice and Social Welfare.* San Francisco: Holden-Day.

_____. 1977. "Rational Fools: A Critique of the Behavioural Foundations of Economic Theory." *Philosophy & Public Affairs* 6 (4):317–344.

_____. 1980. *Levels of Poverty: Policy and Change—A Background Study for World Development Report, 1980.* Washington, D.C.: World Bank.

_____. 1981. *Poverty and Famines: An Essay on Entitlements and Deprivation.* Oxford: Oxford University Press.

_____. 1983. *Poor, Relatively Speaking.* Dublin, Ireland: Economic and Social Research Institute.

_____. 1984. "Well-Being, Agency and Freedom: The Dewey Lectures 1984." *Journal of Philosophy* 82 (4):169–221.

_____. 1987. *On Ethics and Economics.* New York: Basil Blackwell.

_____. 1993. "Capability and Well-Being." In *The Quality of Life,* edited by Martha Craven Nussbaum and Amartya Kumar Sen. Oxford: Oxford University Press.

————. 1999. *Development as Freedom*. New York: Knopf.

Sen, Amartya Kumar, and Geoffrey Hawthorn. 1987. *The Standard of Living*. The Tanner Lectures. Cambridge and New York: Cambridge University Press.

Sen, Amartya Kumar, and Bernard Williams, eds. 1982. *Utilitarianism and Beyond*. Cambridge: Cambridge University Press.

Sen, Bandhudas. 1974. *The Green Revolution in India: A Perspective*. New York: Wiley.

Shue, Henry. 1980. *Basic Rights: Subsistence, Affluence, and U.S. Foreign Policy*. Princeton: Princeton University Press.

Sicular, Terry, ed. 1989. *Food Price Policy in Asia: A Comparative Study*. Ithaca: Cornell University Press.

Singer, Peter. 1972. "Famine, Affluence and Morality." *Philosophy & Public Affairs* 1 (3):229–243.

Sirowy, Larry, and Alex Inkeles. 1990. "The Effects of Democracy on Economic Growth and Inequality: A Review." *Comparative International Development* 25 (1):126–157.

Smart, J.J.C., and Bernard Arthur Owen Williams. 1973. *Utilitarianism: For and Against*. Cambridge: Cambridge University Press.

Sober, Elliott. 1995. "Philosophical Problems for Environmentalism." In *Environmental Ethics*, edited by Robert Elliot. Oxford and New York: Oxford University Press.

Solzhenitsyn, Aleksandr Isaevich. 1974. *The Gulag Archipelago, 1918–1956: An Experiment in Literary Investigation*. 1st ed. New York: Harper & Row.

Starr, Chauncey. 1996. "Sustaining the Human Environment: The Next Two Hundred Years." *Daedalus* 125 (3):235–253.

Stiglitz, Joseph E. 2002. *Globalization and Its Discontents*. 1st ed. New York: W. W. Norton.

Streeten, Paul. 1987. *What Price Food? Agricultural Price Policies in Developing Countries*. Ithaca: Cornell University Press.

Streeten, Paul, Shahid Javed Burki, Mahbub ul Haq, Norman Hicks, and Frances Stewart. 1981. *First Things First: Meeting Basic Human Needs in Developing Countries*. New York: Oxford University Press.

Tambiah, Stanley J. 1991. *Sri Lanka: Ethnic Fratricide and the Dismantling of Democracy*. Chicago: University of Chicago Press.

Taylor, Charles. 1989. *Sources of the Self: The Making of the Modern Identity*. Cambridge, Mass.: Harvard University Press.

————. 1992. *The Ethics of Authenticity*. Cambridge, Mass., and London: Harvard University Press.

Taylor, Charles, and Amy Gutmann. 1992. *Multiculturalism and the Politics of Recognition: An Essay*. Princeton: Princeton University Press.

Taylor, Lance. 1983. *Structuralist Macroeconomics: Applicable Models for the Third World*. New York: Basic Books.

————. 1990. *Socially Relevant Policy Analysis: Structuralist Computable General Equilibrium Models for the Developing World*. Cambridge, Mass.: MIT Press.

Timmer, C. Peter. 1986. *Getting Prices Right: The Scope and Limits of Agricultural Price Policy*. Ithaca: Cornell University Press.

Timmer, C. Peter, Walter P. Falcon, and Scott R. Pearson. 1983. *Food Policy Analysis*. Baltimore: Published for the World Bank by Johns Hopkins University Press.

Todaro, Michael P. 1994. *Economic Development.* 5th ed. New York: Longman.

Tucker, Mary Evelyn, and John H. Berthrong, eds. 1998. *Confucianism and Ecology: The Interrelation of Heaven, Earth, and Humans.* Religions of the World and Ecology. Cambridge, Mass.: Harvard University Center for the Study of World Religions, distributed by Harvard University Press.

Tucker, Mary Evelyn, and John Grim, eds. 1994. *Worldviews and Ecology: Religion, Philosophy, and the Environment.* Maryknoll, N.Y.: Orbis Books.

Tucker, Mary Evelyn, and Duncan Ryuken Williams, eds. 1997. *Buddhism and Ecology: The Interconnection of Dharma and Deeds.* Religions of the World and Ecology. Cambridge, Mass.: Harvard University Center for the Study of World Religions, distributed by Harvard University Press.

Twomey, Michael J. 2000. *A Century of Foreign Investment in the Third World.* Routledge Studies in International Business and the World Economy, 20. London and New York: Routledge.

United Nations. 2000. *The World's Women 2000: Trends and Statistics.* New York: United Nations.

United Nations Development Programme. 1990. *Human Development Report.* Vol. 1990. New York: Oxford University Press.

_____. 1999. *Human Development Report 1999.* Oxford: Oxford University Press.

_____. 2000. *Human Development Report 2000.* Oxford: Oxford University Press.

United Nations Environment Programme. 2002. *Global Environmental Outlook 3.* Nairobi, Kenya: United Nations Environment Programme.

Valdés, Margarita M. 1995. "Inequality in Mexico." In *Women, Culture, and Development: A Study of Human Capabilities,* edited by Martha Craven Nussbaum and Jonathan Glover. New York: Oxford University Press.

van den Bergh, Jeroen, and Jan C.J.M. van der Straaten, eds. 1997. *Economy and Ecosystems in Change: Analytical and Historical Approaches.* Cheltenham, United Kingdom: Elgar.

Varshney, Ashutosh. 1995. *Democracy, Development, and the Countryside: Urban-Rural Struggles in India.* Cambridge Studies in Comparative Politics. Cambridge and New York: Cambridge University Press.

_____. 2000. "Is India Becoming More Democratic?" *Journal of Asian Studies* 59 (1):3–25.

_____. 2002. *Ethnic Conflict and Civic Life: Hindus and Muslims in India.* New Haven: Yale University Press.

Walzer, Michael. 1983. *Spheres of Justice: A Defense of Pluralism and Equality.* New York: Basic Books.

Whiteford, Scott, and Anne Ferguson, eds. 1991. *Harvest of Want: Hunger and Food Security in Central America and Mexico.* Conflict and Social Change Series. Boulder: Westview Press.

Williams, Bernard Arthur Owen. 1985. *Ethics and the Limits of Philosophy.* Cambridge, Mass.: Harvard University Press.

Williamson, John. 1993. "Democracy and the 'Washington Consensus.'" *World Development* 21:1329–1336.

Womack, James P., Daniel T. Jones, Daniel Roos, and Massachusetts Institute of Technology. 1990. *The Machine That Changed the World: Based on the Massachusetts*

Institute of Technology 5-Million Dollar 5-Year Study on the Future of the Automobile. New York: Rawson Associates.

World Bank. 1978. *World Development Report.* Vol. 1978- . Washington, D.C.: World Bank.

_____. 1986. *Poverty and Hunger: Issues and Options for Food Security in Developing Countries.* Washington, D.C.: World Bank.

_____. 1989. *World Development Report 1989.*

_____. 1990. *World Development Report 1990: Poverty.* Oxford: Oxford University Press.

_____. 1995. *The World Bank's Strategy for Reducing Poverty and Hunger: A Report to the Development Community.* Washington, D.C.: World Bank.

_____. 1998. *Assessing Aid: What Works, What Doesn't, and Why.* Oxford: Oxford University Press.

_____. 2001a. *World Development Indicators 2001 on CD-ROM.* Washington, D.C.: World Bank.

_____. 2001b. *World Development Report 2000/2001: Attacking Poverty.* Oxford: Oxford University Press.

Wright, Erik Olin. 1999. "The Real Utopias Project: A General Overview" [cited 2002]. Available: http://www.ssc.wisc.edu/~wright/OVERVIEW.html.

Index